THE

EPIDEMIC

THAT

REVOLUTIONIZED

MEDICINE

AND

AMERICAN

POLITICS

THE
FEVER
OF
1721

STEPHEN COSS

SIMON & SCHUSTER
NEW YORK LONDON TORONTO SYDNEY NEW DELHI

Simon & Schuster
1230 Avenue of the Americas
New York, NY 10020

Copyright © 2016 by Stephen Coss

First Simon & Schuster hardcover edition March 2016

SIMON & SCHUSTER and colophon are
registered trademarks of Simon & Schuster, Inc.

For information about special discounts for bulk purchases,
please contact Simon & Schuster Special Sales
at 1-866-506-1949 or business@simonandschuster.com.

The Simon & Schuster Speakers Bureau can bring authors to your live event. For
more information or to book an event, contact the Simon & Schuster Speakers
Bureau at 1-866-248-3049 or visit our website at www.simonspeakers.com.

Interior design by Ruth Lee-Mui

Manufactured in the United States of America

1   3   5   7   9   10   8   6   4   2

Library of Congress Cataloging-in-Publication Data

Coss, Stephen, author.
The fever of 1721: the epidemic that revolutionized medicine and American politics /
Stephen Coss.
First Simon & Schuster hardcover edition. | New York : Simon & Schuster, 2016. |
Includes bibliographical references and index.
LCCN 2015027337 | ISBN 9781476783086 (hardback) | ISBN 9781476783123
(ebook) | ISBN 9781476783116 (trade paper)
LCSH: Smallpox—Vaccination—History. | Smallpox—Vaccination—United States—
History—18th century. | Medicine—United States—History. | BISAC: HISTORY
/ United States / Colonial Period (1600–1775). | POLITICAL SCIENCE / Political
Freedom & Security / General. | HISTORY / United States / State & Local / New
England (CT, MA, ME, NH, RI, VT).
Classification: LCC RC183.1 .C67 2016 | DDC 616.9/1200973—
dc23 LC record available at http://lccn.loc.gov/2015027337

ISBN 978-1-4767-8308-6
ISBN 978-1-4767-8312-3 (ebook)

For Judy,
and for my sons:
Dylan, Kevin, Brett, and Stephen

CONTENTS

CONTENTS

PART THREE
AMERICAN MONSTERS

INTRODUCTION

Seventeen twenty-one might be the most important anonymous year in the evolution of both modern medicine and American liberty.

During the worst smallpox epidemic in Boston's history, a lone physician conducted an experiment that saved hundreds of lives, launched a new medical discipline, and helped pave the way for the eradication of the world's most devastating disease. The procedure he employed, known as variolation or inoculation, would, over time, be modified and extended to the fight against other fatal diseases, preventing the deaths of untold millions of persons. In 1721, though, it was considered primitive, barbaric, and tantamount to attempted murder. Town officials, the medical establishment, and many rank-and-file Bostonians opposed it. Some of those opponents seemed willing to do anything to stop it.

But the smallpox epidemic wasn't the only fever gripping Boston that year. By 1721 the members of the elected Massachusetts assembly were in the midst of an unprecedented political rebellion against the Crown-appointed governor. Many officials in London were convinced that the

Americans were in revolt and determined to wrest their independence from England.

The convergence of the inoculation controversy and the political uprising yielded a remarkable byproduct: America's first independent newspaper. Never before had a successful paper dared publish without pledging its allegiance to the government. The *New-England Courant* not only refused to solicit an official blessing; it went out of its way to discomfit the political and religious establishments. Nominally (and opportunistically) founded to oppose inoculation, it quickly expanded its scope to include a spirited public discussion of political liberty and corruption. Caught up in the political excitement of the day, its publisher argued for political self-determination, a society that valued individual merit over noble birth, and freedom of the press. Even after he was jailed for casting aspersions on the competency and integrity of the most powerful men in Massachusetts—the royal governor included—he pressed ahead, challenging and scandalizing authority and insisting upon the radical notion that the press operated outside the control of the government.

IN APRIL 1721 smallpox came to Boston for the first time in nearly two decades. It arrived aboard the HMS *Seahorse*, a British warship. By the time the epidemic had burned itself out a year later, approximately half the town's eleven thousand inhabitants had been infected. Among those who had escaped death were nearly three hundred men, women, and children who had undergone inoculation.

The procedure began with an incision in the skin of a healthy person. The incision was then implanted with viscous fluid from the vesicles or pustules of someone broken out in smallpox. The idea was to produce an extremely mild and easily tolerated case of the disease and confer immunity to future infection. Prior to 1721, inoculation was virtually unknown in America and had never been attempted. The proposal to try it in Boston came from an improbable source: the Puritan minister Cotton

Mather. Mather, a theological conservative and master of the fire-and-brimstone jeremiad, was already one of the most controversial figures in Boston, chiefly as a consequence of his involvement in the Salem witch hysteria nearly three decades earlier. Generally regarded as a man prone to superstitions and "infatuations," he had become, in the years since Salem, an adherent of Enlightenment science and an enthusiastic monitor of the latest and most exotic medical developments in Europe and beyond.

The town's most esteemed physicians dismissed Mather's proposal out of hand. But one doctor, Zabdiel Boylston, accepted his challenge. In 1721 Boylston was forty-two years old and successful both as a physician and an apothecary shop owner. He had achieved a measure of fame for his uncommonly good track record with surgeries but was relegated to the second tier of medical practitioners because he lacked the educational and social pedigrees of many of his colleagues.

Without Boylston's daring, James Franklin would never have launched the *New-England Courant*. For nearly four years, the struggling Boston printer had been looking for an opportunity to start a newspaper modeled on the best London publications—a weekly that would be witty, literate, provocative, and ambitious, the antithesis of the two generally dull and perfunctory Boston newspapers already in circulation. In 1721 he leveraged the public's hunger for information and opinions about inoculation to put his plan into action. If his *Courant* had done nothing more than reprint excerpts of Lockean essays on liberty by John Trenchard and Thomas Gordon, along with the topical *Spectator* commentaries of Joseph Addison and Richard Steele, it would have made a noteworthy contribution to the evolution of both American journalism and American independence. But it went further. Side by side with the essays of the great political and social thinkers of the European Enlightenment, James published distinctively American essays and letters penned by himself and his friends. They presumed to criticize and satirize the religious and political establishments of colonial Massachusetts with a boldness that scandalized their fathers' generation. The *Courant* was the *Onion, Daily Show,* and *Colbert Report* of its day. Indeed, an argument can be made that American social and political satire began with James Franklin's newspaper, and that everything that followed, from Mark Twain to Will Rogers to Matt Stone's and Trey Parker's *South Park*, is descended from it.

At the same time he was inventing American social and political commentary, James Franklin was also helping invent the man generally regarded as the first American. Two years after being pulled from school, twelve-year-old Benjamin Franklin had been indentured as his older brother's apprentice. For the better part of the next three years, as he learned the trade that would make him wealthy, Ben had embarked upon his storied self-education. His inspiration, and many of his texts, came from his brother's printing house, which contained a large and diverse library of books and periodicals and served as a meeting place for James Franklin's clever and loquacious friends. Their conversations about books and pamphlets, and debates about politics, religion, and the social issues of the day, fired young Benjamin's mind and imagination, and he began to see his destiny unfold before him. Then, in 1721, the fifteen-year-old was given a front-row seat to the inoculation controversy. What he learned from that debate, and from his involvement in the newspaper that grew out of it, changed his life and helped define him as an author, a publisher, a political philosopher, an experimenter, and a diplomat. In a sense, everything Benjamin Franklin ever really needed to know he learned in 1721. By early 1722 he was ready to take the public stage, disguised as a country widow named Silence Dogood.

It's fitting that the political movement that would one day make Benjamin Franklin famous as an American patriot was coming of age at the same time he was. The man behind that first organized push toward American independence was a doctor-turned-businessman-turned-politician named Elisha Cooke Jr. The son of one of the colony's wealthiest men and most beloved politicians, Cooke "the younger" had inherited his father's fortune, talent for politics, and bitter and abiding resentment toward England for its 1684 cancellation of the original Massachusetts charter, which had given the colony a remarkable degree of political autonomy. Shortly after being elected to the Massachusetts House of Representatives for the first time in 1716, he had put all three of those inheritances to work opposing and obstructing the royal government. Before three years had elapsed, the pugnacious, hard-drinking Cooke had built America's first political machine. He had also become the bane of English officials, one of whom accused him of poisoning the minds of his countrymen "with his republican notions, in order to assert the independency of New England."

In 1721 a smallpox epidemic sparked a profound leap forward in medical science. It also served as a catalyst for the invention of American journalism, the coming of age of Benjamin Franklin, and the beginning of American independence itself. This book is about that epidemic and the political rebellion that accompanied it. It is the story of five remarkable men and how their courage, daring, vision, and desperation in a time of crisis defined their destinies and ours.

PROLOGUE

On December 11, 1719, a strange light appeared in the Boston night sky. Red waves radiated from the northeast horizon upward into the heavens like the glow of an ethereal fire. Then the light "spread itself thro' the Heavens from *East to West*" and "streamed with white Flashes or Streams of Light down to the Horizon . . . very bright and very strong."[1] It weakened and disappeared after an hour, only to reappear several hours later in a new and "somewhat dreadful" form, flamelike at one moment and "blood red" the next.[2] One observer, Harvard College's scientific tutor Thomas Robie, admitted to being reminded of descriptions of Judgment Day but hastened to add that he attached no apocalyptic "Prognostications" to what he had witnessed. "I don't mean that this Sight was not suprizing to me . . ." he later wrote, "but I only mean that no Man should fright himself by supposing that dreadful things will follow, such as Famine, Sword or Sickness."[3]

Although Robie himself had no use for the traditional Puritan interpretation of an unusual celestial phenomenon (which in this case he correctly identified as the aurora borealis), he understood that many of his fellow Bostonians still did. Only thirty-nine years had passed since a bright comet had caused a Boston minister to preach a famous apocalyptic jeremiad titled "Heavens Alarm to the World. Or A Sermon Wherein Is Shewed, That fearful Sights and Signs in Heaven are the Presages of great Calamities at hand."[4] The belief that certain events in the skies and on the earth were signs of God's displeasure with the wickedness of the people and a warning that Heaven's vengeance was imminent continued to have currency. So did the idea that when bad things happened they were manifestations of that vengeance. Nine years earlier, when a huge fire had destroyed half of Boston, the Reverend Increase Mather—the same minister who had delivered the earlier comet jeremiad—had preached "Burnings Bewailed, In A Sermon . . . In which the Sins which Provoke the Lord to Kindle Fires, are Enquired into."[5] Now there were so many potential catastrophes looming over the town that one did not need to be particularly inclined toward what Robie called "Ignorance and Fancy" to suspect that that divine vengeance was imminent.[6] On the frontiers of Massachusetts and New Hampshire the Indians were becoming increasingly provocative and warlike. In the Atlantic and the Caribbean, pirates were running amok, threatening the oceangoing commerce integral to the harbor town's economic survival. And it had become clear that even if Massachusetts never lost another silver coin to a pirate, a commercial system rigged to favor the Crown at the expense of the colony might still cause it to run out of money. A pamphlet published soon after the appearance of the strange celestial lights claimed that Massachusetts had lost nearly a million pounds of silver and gold since the beginning of the new century. Soon, it warned, there wouldn't be enough currency left to pay debts or taxes or even to buy food.[7] Arguing that the silver shortage disproportionately harmed the poor and the middle class, a group of up-and-coming businessmen and members of the Massachusetts House of Representatives continually pushed the royal governor to approve large emissions of paper currency. The governor and his wealthy friends, many of whom traded directly with

England and so had plenty of silver at their disposal, pushed back. The cure for the shortage of silver, they insisted, was not to give people more money but to force them to live with less. Equilibrium would be restored if the poor and middle class stopped living beyond their means and above their station—meaning that they stopped shipping off their silver to England for luxury goods they had no business buying.

The friction over the currency question was only one point of contention between the Crown-appointed governor and the popularly elected provincial assembly. Indeed, by late 1719 that relationship had become adversarial on so many fronts that many Bostonians believed England would smite Massachusetts before God did. From the very beginning—or at least since the 1650s, when it had begun ignoring and defying the Navigation Acts—the colony had been a thorn in the paw of the mother country, frequently uncooperative and sometimes unruly and defiant. But now three years of unprecedented bickering and fighting had "brought the governor and the people of Massachusetts into an attitude of obstinate antagonism to one another."[8] The dispute was approaching a flash point. Soon, many feared, England would cancel the "new" Massachusetts charter (granted in 1691), depriving the colony of any vestige of self-governance and instituting martial law in its place.

A little over a month after the appearance of the northern lights, another glow appeared on the horizon. This time it was anything but ethereal. The Boston Harbor lighthouse was on fire. The blaze had been ignited by hot oil dripping from one of the lamps at the summit of the fifty-plus-foot structure. While the people watched helplessly, the fire consumed the lighthouse interior. It might have been worse; no one had been killed or hurt and the fire had burned itself out before compromising the structural integrity of the exterior. Thanks to a determined effort by the town, Boston Light was repaired and back in operation by late the following month. Still, the temptation to interpret the conflagration as something more than an accident was powerful. The question was whether it was the punishment foretold by the lights in the sky—a manifestation, perhaps, of

God's anger over the rampant and sinful materialism and lust for luxury imports that the town's burgeoning ocean trade had fostered—or a more emphatic and dramatic omen, either of the collapse of Boston's teetering, trade-based economy or of some other and even more terrible conflagration still to come.

ON OCTOBER 28, 1720, a merchant brigantine commanded by a thirty-eight-year-old Bostonian named John Gore entered the outer reaches of Boston Harbor and made its way to the Nantasket Roads, the southern of two deepwater channels that served as nautical highways into and out of the harbor. Gore's ship passed Little Brewster Island, whose lighthouse had been gutted by fire eight months earlier, and continued inward, gliding past Georges Island and Rainsford Island and then rounding the southern tip of the knife-shaped Long Island before bending to the north. This amounted to the "clubhouse turn" for returning vessels. Just ahead, the Nantasket Roads joined up with the southward bending President Roads to begin the final two-mile stretch to the harbor wharves.

Gore was just over four miles from completing his nearly two-month, 3,280-mile voyage from England when he veered off course, tacking sharply north in the direction of a forty-nine-acre island whose odd configuration consisted of two low, rounded hills connected by a thin spit of land. From the vantage point of passing ships, the island looked like a pair of pince-nez laid flat on the surface of the water.[9] Indeed, passing "Spectacle Island" was all that most ships ever did. Clear-cut for firewood during the early years of the town, the ungainly island had sat deserted for decades. Then in 1717 the Massachusetts assembly had designated it as the site for a public quarantine hospital. The resulting facility, bare bones in every respect and lacking in medical personnel, was better described by its informal name, "the pest house." It was a repository for persons suffering from contagious and deadly distempers, especially smallpox, measles, yellow fever, and, should it ever make the jump from Europe, the plague. In February 1718

4

the General Court (the name for the Massachusetts legislature) had passed a law requiring ships carrying infectious diseases to anchor near Spectacle Island and to transfer infected persons to the pest house until they died or recovered completely. The water bailiff had authority to order a diseased merchant ship to quarantine there. But inspections were cursory, more concerned with contraband than disease. More often than not it fell to the captain to self-quarantine. The unpopularity of that decision with ship owners, who paid captains to complete their voyages with all deliberate speed, and with healthy crew members and passengers, who having spent weeks or months at sea had no appetite for being stopped short within sight of their final destination, made it a challenge for even the most ethical captains. Differentiating between a relatively harmless disease and a deadly one complicated the issue. So did determining whether a contagion that had surfaced early in a long voyage had burned itself out by the time the ship had reached Boston Harbor weeks or months later.

That had been John Gore's dilemma. A few days out of Bridgehampton he had discovered a case of smallpox aboard his ship. Soon a second case emerged, followed rapidly by a third and a forth. By the time Gore's brig had passed the midpoint of its voyage, one man was dead and six more were in various stages of illness. Somehow, despite the inadequacy of the medical care and the hardships of passage on a cold, heaving ocean, all of those men had survived and were nearly or completely recovered by the time the ship entered Boston Harbor. Happily, no new cases had broken out. But Gore knew that there was still at least one person aboard who remained vulnerable to infection. If that man developed the disease a day or two after the ship's arrival he might trigger another epidemic like the one that had killed hundreds of Bostonians and sickened thousands more in 1702 and 1703. That person was Gore himself.

He might have begun to suspect that something was wrong by the time his ship initiated its final approach to the wharf. Sometimes at its onset smallpox produced an odd malaise—the sense that one's body was out of gear and working improperly. Not certain that he was sick, but unsure that he was well, Gore had erred on the side of caution, setting a trajectory for Spectacle Island. By late that day, a Friday, he had begun to experience the disease's early symptoms: a quickened pulse and steady climb in body temperature. By the middle of the next day he had intense pain in his head, stomach, and groin. Then came vomiting and chills. When he woke up the following morning feverless and feeling well save for a slightly sore throat, he must have tried to reassure himself that he had shaken off whatever had brought him low. Within a few hours, though, a mild red rash began to form on his cheeks and forehead. Then his voice went hoarse and his throat broke out in sores that stung like paper cuts. As his throat swelled, swallowing went from excruciating to nearly impossible. Now the fever was back and climbing and the rash was growing redder and thicker and spreading to his arms, chest, and back. By Monday, October 31, his fever was raging and the rash had metamorphosed into hundreds of discrete, angry pustules. Seven days later he was dead. He was buried on Spectacle Island on the evening of November 8 without formal ceremony or the presence of his wife of seven years, who had not been informed that her husband lay mortally ill a few miles offshore.

For the rest of November and nearly all of December the government concealed the fact that a case of smallpox had come as close to Boston as Spectacle Island. Public panic over the possibility that an epidemic was imminent was one concern. A bigger fear, though, was that rumors of smallpox in Boston might be enough to cause trading partners to embargo the port, devastating the town's anemic economy. Both of Boston's news-papers conspired in the cover-up. When on December 12 the *Boston News-Letter* ran a story about a town threatened by an epidemic, it was Marseilles, not Boston; and the epidemic was bubonic plague, not smallpox.[10]

Government officials continued holding their breaths, waiting for a second case of smallpox to appear on the mainland, until December 26, nearly two months after Gore's vessel had arrived at Spectacle Island. On that day, at the bottom of the left-hand column of the *News-Letter*'s back page, a notice datelined "Boston" began:

The Danger of the Small-Pox being over at present thro' the Mercy of GOD; we may now venture to inform the Publick of the deplorable and general loss we have lately sustained, in the death of Capt. JOHN GORE of this Town.[11]

It went on to eulogize Gore for his legacy of honorable service, which had culminated in a final act of heroic selflessness. But many readers fixed on the opening sentence, which confirmed that after more than eighteen years without an outbreak of smallpox Boston had come perilously close to being visited by its most dread disease.

Probably by this point few Bostonians were shocked by the news. Six weeks was a very long time to keep a secret in a peninsular town whose approximately eleven thousand inhabitants were concentrated in an area of less than four square miles. What the newspapers didn't disseminate, tavern gossip generally did, albeit with all the exaggerations and inaccuracies that accompanied that form of communication. Nor was it difficult to corroborate the rumor that a ship was anchored at Spectacle Island. All it took was climbing to the summit of Beacon Hill, the tallest of Boston's three peaks, from which it was possible to "overlook all the islands which lie within the bay, and descry such ships as are on the sea-coast."[12]

But it was one thing to suspect smallpox was close by and another to have the government confirm it. How Bostonians reacted to that admission depended on whether they had experienced the previous smallpox epidemic. For those too young to remember it, there was a thrill not unlike the one they felt while viewing the African lion—the first ever in America—on display at the Boston home of Mrs. Martha Adams. Smallpox, too, was a beast—snarling, fierce, deadly, and exotic. Seeing it up close and safely caged was titillating. But for those who had survived the last epidemic, losing loved ones or nearly their own lives, the announcement produced only an uneasy relief. Historically, a new smallpox epidemic arrived approximately every twelve years. Boston was now six years overdue for its next visitation. When it finally came, that epidemic might prove as catastrophic and all-encompassing as the ones that had nearly exterminated the Abenaki, the Massachusett, the Wampanoag, and the Pawtucket during the seventeenth century. What they knew for certain was that no cage could hold smallpox indefinitely. Sooner or later the beast would escape and devour the town.

PART ONE

TROUBLE
NEAR

The common people of this Province are so perverse, that when I remove any person from the Council, for not behaving himself with duty towards H.M. or His orders, or for treating me H.M. Govr. ill, that he becomes their favourite, and is chose a Representative.

—Samuel Shute, royal governor of Massachusetts, letter to the
Council of Trade and Plantations, London, June 1, 1720

A *Devil* was once an *Angel*, but Sin has brought him to be a *Fallen* Angel; an Angel full of Enmity to God and man.

—Cotton Mather, "A Discourse on the Power
and Malice of the Devils," in *Memorable Providences
Relating to Witchcrafts and Possessions* (1689)

I

IDOL OF THE MOB

For a few hours on a sunny, crisp morning in October 1716, royal governor Samuel Shute's administration looked quite promising, at least from the outside. Salutes fired from the cannon of the town's batteries and the guns of two British warships in the harbor alerted Boston of Shute's imminent arrival and brought thousands of people to the waterfront for a glimpse of the first new governor in fourteen years. By the time the *Lusitania* docked at the end of Long Wharf a line of spectators extended the full third-of-a-mile length of the wharf and another quarter mile up King Street to the Boston Town House, where the formal welcome and swearing in would be conducted.

The man who appeared on deck, waving to his new constituents and acknowledging their cheers, had small, wide-set eyes, a puggish nose, full cheeks, and a capacious double chin that billowed like a sail over the top of his neck cloth. He was plumper and older than the war hero people had heard about, the man who had fought valiantly under Marlborough and been wounded on the battlefield in Flanders. Aside from his military credentials, all average Bostonians knew about the fifty-four-year-old re-tired colonel was that he had been raised a Puritan. Shute had converted to the Church of England, presumably in the interest of career advancement. But the knowledge that he shared the religious heritage of a majority of Bostonians was a comfort to those who remembered the hostility of an earlier, Puritan-hating Anglican governor who had commandeered their meetinghouses for Church of England services and had made an ostenta-tious show of his celebration of Christmas, a holiday Puritans not only refused to recognize but considered sacrilegious. More than anything, though, what excited the people of Boston about Samuel Shute was that he was not Joseph Dudley, his predecessor. With a new chief executive came new hope for solutions to the colony's challenges, better coopera-tion between the executive and legislative branches of the colonial govern-ment, and more equitable relations with the mother country.

But many political insiders were skeptical that Samuel Shute consti-tuted a new start, a change from the status quo. Although they, too, knew little about the man, they had discovered that his appointment had been finagled by friends of Joseph Dudley, who had first bribed the man origi-nally appointed to replace Dudley into relinquishing the position. The mere possibility that Shute was in the pocket of Dudley and his son Paul, the colony's attorney general, was enough to earn him enemies among his new constituents. Many persons had never forgiven Dudley for his be-trayal of Massachusetts nearly three decades earlier, when he had served as henchman to the most despotic governor in the colony's history, Edmund Andros. In 1689, the people had risen up and deposed Andros, jailing and eventually deporting him to England along with Dudley and another man, Edward Randolph. Thirteen years later the Crown had sent Dudley back to Massachusetts as its governor. Fears that he would revenge himself on his jailers with draconian assaults on individuals and group liberties had proven largely unfounded. But his administration had been both arbitrary enough and corrupt enough to spur two unsuccessful attempts to have him recalled. Having survived those, he might have remained governor for the rest of his life had Queen Anne not died prematurely at age forty-nine and her successor, George Louis, not decided to do as most new monarchs did and replace his predecessor's appointments with men who would be in his debt. On his way out of office, Dudley had given his political opponents two final reasons to despise him, tacitly approving the scheme to rig the selection of his replacement, and double-crossing supporters of a plan to alleviate the worsening silver currency shortage by creating a private bank that would emit paper currency. After making those men believe that he would endorse the venture, he had worked secretly behind the scenes to assure its defeat.

The bank's supporters were still smarting from that act of duplicity as the carriage carrying the man Dudley's friends had picked to replace him made its way up King Street. In the months prior to Shute's departure for America, Dudley's men had thoroughly indoctrinated him in their anti-private-bank philosophy, preparing him to fend off any new attempts to launch the bank or force the government to emit paper currency. But the currency controversy was about to change in ways the new governor was unprepared to handle, evolving from a dry and somewhat tedious argument over monetary policy into a far-reaching debate over class entitlement, freedom of dissent, Americans' liberties as Englishmen, and the colony's right to self-determination, and becoming, as one historian put it, "the secret of political alignment" for a generation of emerging patriots and loyalists.[1]

SHUTE MADE TWO stops along the parade route up King Street. The first was to greet a group of the town's ministers. The second was to meet with Joseph Dudley. That meeting took place in view of a "great Concourse of People" and a sizable group of dignitaries who had gathered at the foot of the Town House for Shute's public welcoming ceremony.[2] Those dignitaries included members of the Massachusetts House of Representatives (who were known as deputies); their colleagues in the upper house, the Governor's Council (who were known as councilors or assistants); the president of Harvard College; and numerous judges and other prominent gentlemen of the province. No one among that group was more put off by the conspicuous show of affection between the old governor and the new than the Boston representative Elisha Cooke, who had been elected to the Massachusetts House for the first time the previous year at the relatively young age of thirty-eight. Cooke came from Massachusetts political royalty: He was the grandson of John Leverett, an early governor of Massachusetts, and the son of Elisha Cooke Sr., the colony's most influential anti-Crown politician. Cooke Sr. had been the most outspoken critic of England's 1684 revocation of the founding Massachusetts charter, the act that had taken the power to choose its own governor away from the colony and given it to England, and one of the leaders of the 1689 uprising against Andros, the tyrant England had installed as royal governor shortly after the charter's cancellation. He had been nearly as critical of the "New Charter" of 1691, which had restored some liberties but left with England both the power to appoint the governor and to disallow objectionable laws. Thereafter, he and members of his "Old Charter Party" had categorically opposed "royal authority over the colony and the governors' attempts to rule by prerogative."[3] Outraged by the traitorous Joseph Dudley's appointment as royal governor, Cooke Sr. had become his "pointed enemy."[4] The historian John Eliot wrote that Cooke Sr. "never missed the opportunity of speaking against his [Dudley's] measures, or declaring his disapprobation of the man."[5] Right up until his death in 1715 he had also criticized Dudley's "Prerogative Party" supporters, men who, he charged, kowtowed to the royal governor and the Crown in order to pad their fortunes or, in the case of some of the once-prominent families from the colony's founding era, to prop up their diminishing status.

Elisha Cooke Sr. and his only son were so closely aligned politically that one detractor would describe Cooke Jr.'s contempt for English authority as a disease he had "caught" from his father.[6] Indeed, he had followed his father's example in nearly every respect. Both father and son had attended Harvard College, trained as physicians, and left the regular practice of medicine for success as businessmen. The younger Cooke's ventures included a salt plant on Boston neck, a stake in Long Wharf (to that point the largest infrastructure project in America), and investments in Boston warehouses and taverns and in thousands of acres of prime Maine timberland. His real passion and talent, though, were for politics. Outmaneuvered by Joseph Dudley in his first foray into political dealings at the provincial level—the attempt to launch a private bank—he had nevertheless proven himself a formidable opponent. Dudley's biographer wrote that the cagey old governor, who had survived two recalls, understood that Cooke Jr. and his bank partners represented "a faction more dangerous than any other combination he had faced."[7]

With wealth, education, social standing, and a talent for public speaking—his oratory was described as "animating, energetic, concise, persuasive, and pure"—Cooke had the credentials and skills necessary to succeed as a conventional eighteenth-century politician.[8] It surprised no one that within months of his election to the House he had already achieved a leadership position. But other, more unconventional talents and tactics would help him rise above conventional politicians and become the most significant and powerful Boston politician in the decades preceding the American Revolution—more hated by England than anyone but Samuel Adams (in whose political education Cooke would pay a formative role).

Shortly after their defeat of the private bank, Dudley's Prerogative Party men had attempted to change the form of Boston's government from the town meeting to an English-style incorporated borough system. Boston was and always had been the locus of political resistance and general incorrigibility. The town meeting, Dudley knew, fed that rebelliousness, since it gave all the people, even those without the vote, the power to speak their minds, required votes on all major issues, and mandated the yearly election of selectmen who managed town affairs. By instituting an incorporated system whereby representation came from aldermen appointed for life and vested with the power to choose a mayor, controlling the town became as simple as either arranging for the "right" men to be chosen alders or using favors and bribes to influence them. Recognizing what Dudley and his friends were up to, Cooke had published two anonymous pamphlets that declared incorporation "an oligarchic plot" by political and economic elites bent on rigging the government, the currency system, and the entire economy for their benefit.[9] The pamphlets reminded rank-and-file Bostonians that each freeholder had the "undoubted right" to "speak his Opinion, and give his Advice, and Vote, too, concerning any Affair to be transacted by the Town," and that to turn over that power to an alderman was to squander this "great Privilege their Ancestors have conveyed to them."[10] In asserting that the people were "Free-born and in bondage to no Man," in claiming inviolable political liberties, and in rejecting the assumption that the wealthy, the powerful, the highborn, and, by extension, the royal, were superior to the average man, Cooke's pamphlets articulated, perhaps for the first time, a distinctly and defiantly American political identity.[11]

The success of those pamphlets—the incorporation plan was dropped before the next opportunity to vote on it—gave credence to Cooke's instinct for a new kind of politics. No one, not even Cooke's father, had thought to cultivate popular support or opposition to leverage a political agenda. Most conventional politicians wouldn't have known how to do it if they had wanted to. Cooke, though, had begun to master the art of speaking the language of the people. His classrooms were the taverns of Boston, where, by lending an ear and buying a round, he earned a reputation as not only "a drinking man without equal" but also a political leader "generous to needy people of all classes."[12] After a few rums the social and economic differences between the hardscrabble tradesmen and the wealthy Harvard man melted away, and the former saw the latter as one of their own. It helped that he looked the part. With a broad, fleshy face, full lips, jutting knob of a chin, and slight broadening at the bridge of his nose, he looked more like a workingman than an aristocrat, and more like a brawler than a fast-talking dandy. As he set about evolving his father's Old

Charter Party into what would come to be known as the Popular Party, he took every opportunity to exploit his workingman image. Eventually he would sit for his only known portrait wearing a brown periwig, the color of a tradesman. A future royal governor would sneer at his willingness to court the favor of the middling and the poor, mocking him as "the idol of the Mob."[13] But it was the support of the "mob" that would make Cooke the Crown's most formidable threat.

HAVING REACHED THE Town House, Samuel Shute was welcomed with a brief proclamation thanking God for his safe arrival. That sentiment was punctuated by musketfire from two companies of militia. When the smoke cleared, the governor was escorted into the Town House and up the stairs to the Council chamber, where his commission was read along with that of the new lieutenant governor—Joseph Dudley's son-in-law, William Dummer. Then both men laid their hands on the Bible and, in the words of one observer, "kiss'd it very industriously," completing the ceremony.[14] At one o'clock Shute was feted at a large, formal dinner whose guest list included his Council and "many" members of the Massachusetts House.[15] After toasts had been drunk and the meal consumed, the speaker of the House turned to Shute, explained that the governor's official residence, the Province House, was not yet ready for him, and offered him lodging in the home of William Tailer, the man who had served as interim governor between the end of Dudley's commission and Shute's arrival. The offer was important symbolically, since Dudley and the pro-bank Tailer had argued acrimoniously over who should occupy the governorship until Shute arrived, with each man accusing the other of trying to steal control of the colony. Tailer's welcoming gesture reassured the people that a smooth, orderly transition of power was under way. Similarly, acceptance of the offer would send the message that although Shute was friendly with Dudley, he planned to work with both of the colony's political factions. But much to the surprise of nearly everyone in attendance, Shute declined the offer, announcing that he had already accepted an invitation to stay with Paul Dudley, whose devotion to England's prerogative rule of the colony eclipsed his father's and who years earlier had infamously asserted that Massachusetts would "never be worth living in for Lawyers and Gentlemen, till the Charter is taken away."[16] In his diary that evening the conservative judge and councilor Samuel Sewall would write: "The Governour's going to Mr. Dudley's makes many fear that he is deliver'd up to a Party. Deus avertat Omen!" [God forbid!].[17] Maybe the only man neither in on the plan nor shocked by it was Elisha Cooke, who expected no better from any man who had won endorsement by both the Crown and the Dudleys. While others had hoped that Shute's arrival would bring a fresh start, Cooke had simply wanted an excuse to attack. And now, on his first day as governor, Shute had given him one.

ALTHOUGH ENGLAND HAD the power to appoint any governor it saw fit, a loophole in the 1691 charter had left the amount and disposition of his compensation entirely to the discretion of the Massachusetts House. The deputies had quickly capitalized on that royal oversight by declining to pay the governor a salary, as England had assumed they would, instead awarding him a biyearly "present" in whatever amount they saw fit.[18] The more amenable the governor, the more money he stood to receive. This, of course, undermined England's absolute authority over the man they placed in the position. The Crown had sent several governors to Boston with strict orders to undo the loophole. All had failed. In April 1717, Samuel Shute made his bid, calling for a fixed salary for himself and his successors. In years past it had been Elisha Cooke Sr., the man who had come up with the discretionary, nonsalary system for paying royal governors, who marshaled the House to hold firm against English pressure. Now it was his son who rounded up the votes to defeat the measure. Future efforts would prove equally futile. "In most of the royal governments," wrote historian Timothy Pitkin, "after much difficulty, these recommendations [for fixed salaries] were finally complied with. The assembly of Massachusetts, however, could never be induced to yield . . . Thus the people of Massachusetts still continued, as in the case of the navigation acts, to claim the right of Englishmen, to grant their money *when* and *how* they pleased."[19] Shute's peevish response to that defeat—after rejecting a House request for a new emission of paper currency (he had approved an earlier one, probably expecting that it would buy him victory in the salary vote), he shut down the General Court with important business still pending—tweaked Cooke's indignation. Soon thereafter he made his first sidelong attack on Shute's administration, accusing royal surveyor Jonathan Bridger of shaking down settlers in Maine (at that point a territory of Massachusetts and therefore Shute's responsibility) for the privilege of harvesting white pines on their own land. Cooke knew that since the Lords of Trade and Plantations viewed the pines, which were ideal for ship masts, as a strategic resource, they would be irate over anything that threatened their uninterrupted supply to the Royal Navy—and that whether they blamed him or Bridger (they blamed him), they would also condemn Shute for his failure to manage the situation.

The governor and his nemesis formally became enemies on May 29, 1718, when Shute got his revenge on Cooke by exercising his right to "negative" (veto) the Popular Party leader's elevation from the House to the Council. The negative effectively expelled Cooke from the General Court. Eight months later, Shute struck again, arranging for Cooke to be stripped of his position as clerk of the superior court. This time Shute was angry because Cooke had called him a "blockhead" while in a heated argument with one of his supporters.[20]

London welcomed the news of Shute's punitive assertiveness. Rumors that he might be recalled for his failures to obtain a fixed salary and stop Cooke from harassing Jonathan Bridger faded. But in Massachusetts, where a House investigation substantiated Cooke's claims against the royal surveyor, the governor's vindictiveness had the opposite effect, ending his honeymoon with the people and solidifying support for Cooke, who in

March 1719 was handily elected a Boston selectman for the first time. Weeks later he was elected one of the town's four deputies to the Massachusetts House, putting him back in the General Court and in a position from which the governor had no authority to remove him. The town's three other seats also went to men from his party. Indeed, throughout Massachusetts, the 1719 elections produced a change "unfavorable to the governor's interest," with the election of a majority of men philosophically aligned with Cooke and his Boston friends.[21]

But the size and scope of the victory were only part of the story. In Boston, Cooke had done what many had believed impossible, convincing a people so worried about vesting too much power in any one person that they almost never allowed the same man to serve as a selectman and House deputy simultaneously, to elect an identical slate of ideologically aligned candidates at both levels of government. Oliver Noyes, William Clark, and Isaiah Tay, Boston's new House members, were all Boston selectmen. They had been elected, one correspondent wrote, "by a considerable majority, notwithstanding all endeavours used to the contrary."[22] It was a shift too seismic to have happened on its own, proof that a force was at work beneath the surface of Boston politics. Evicted from the Council, Cooke had devoted himself to expanding his base by turning Boston's drinking establishments into "political nodes" where propaganda could be disseminated and political support nurtured with free drinks. The success of that effort was apparent in a single statistic: In Boston in 1719, the number of voters was double the average in the years from 1698 to 1717.[23] Both in the town and throughout the colony, Cooke had orchestrated a dominant victory by getting out the vote, something no one before him had thought or bothered to do.

But even a man who loved rum as much as Cooke had not been able to visit every bar, make every speech, and buy every drink. To carry out his strategy, he had formed a "small clique" or "political club" that operated in semi-secrecy and that in years to come would be known as the Boston Caucus Club.[24] Throughout the decades leading up to the American

Revolution, "America's first urban political 'machine'" would grow and spin off new caucuses and related secret societies like the Sons of Liberty, providing the infrastructure and the leadership for the eventual all-out rebellion against Great Britain.[25] No one understood its importance more than the men who headed up that effort. "Our Revolution was effected by caucuses," wrote John Adams, a former caucus member, in 1808.[26]

COOKE'S POWER CAME at the price of growing threats from England. By the time the Boston lighthouse caught fire in January 1720, England had censured the Massachusetts House twice, the first time for "countenancing and encouraging" Cooke's attacks on Bridger and again for imposing duties on imports from England.[27] London reminded the House that it forbade any law that hindered English trade and warned the people of Massachusetts that they would "do well to consider, how far the breaking this condition, and the laying any discouragements on the shipping and manufactures of this Kingdome may endanger their Charter."[28] The growing anti-Massachusetts sentiment at Trade and Plantations was fed by a steady stream of accusatory letters from Surveyor Bridger. The king's rights had never been "called into question," wrote Bridger in one such letter, until the "Incendiary" Cooke had "endeavoured, to poyson the minds of his countreymen, with his republican notions, in order to assert the independency of New England, and claim greater privileges than ever were designed for it *etc.*"[29] When, in May 1720, Cooke finally stood for and was elected speaker of the House, formalizing his control over that body, Bridger penned another letter. "These people," he wrote, "will only be governed by a severe Act of Parliament w[i]th, a good penalty fixed."[30]

All too aware of how Cooke-as-speaker would play in London, Samuel Shute refused to accept the vote. A standoff ensued. No one had questioned Shute's power to negative Cooke's earlier selection as councilor—the governor's authority relative to the upper house was an accepted fact. But the House's right to the speaker of its choice was nearly as sacrosanct, by tradition if not explicitly by law. Only once before had a governor refused to accept a speaker. And even in that case the governor, Joseph Dudley, had relented when two years later the same man was elected again. Now, after three days of deadlock and with no prospect of either side giving in, Shute again shut down the Court, warning in his closing remarks that Massachusetts would "suffer" if its representatives continued to insist on having Cooke as their speaker.[31]

Shute's threats notwithstanding, the new elections that preceded the restart of the General Court sent mostly the same men to the House. Bostonians were particularly defiant. Voting just four days after the Boston newspapers dutifully printed Shute's saber-rattling closing speech, they reelected the Popular Party slate of Cooke, Noyes, and William Clark. The only change in the town's contingent was the addition of Dr. John Clark, a Popular Party member negatived from the Council by Shute at the same time he had disallowed Cooke's speakership.

With a rematch over his selection as speaker in the offing, Cooke went on the offensive, publishing a pamphlet reminiscent of the ones that had helped defeat the attempt to incorporate the Boston government. He characterized Shute's attempt to bar him from the speaker's chair as an effort by England to deprive the people of Massachusetts of their rights. Employing logic and language that might have come from the pen of a Samuel Adams or James Otis a half century later, he wrote:

> The happiness or infelicity of a People, intirely depending upon the enjoyment or deprivation of Libertie; Its therefore highly prudent for them to inform themselves of their just Rights, that from a due sence of their inestimable Value, they may be encouraged to assert them against the Attempts of any in time to come.[32]

Cooke's rhetoric stirred his fellow House deputies. But the knowledge that Shute would again negative Cooke and shut down the session, paralyzing the government and preventing vital and already overdue measures from being enacted, eroded their resolve to insist on his speakership. On July 13, after two votes in which Cooke received a plurality of votes but not enough to again take the speaker's chair, they elected a centrist deputy named Timothy Lindall. It was a significant win for the governor, but it came at the price of the House's resentful belligerence. For the rest of the session the deputies voted down every proposal Shute put forward, refusing to fund the celebration of the king's birthday, approving only a token allocation in support of Shute's efforts to forge a diplomatic solution to the growing and "universally dreaded" Indian threat along the eastern frontier, and reducing the amount of their "grant" to the governor by £100, a cut made even larger by the stipulation that payment be made in drastically depreciated Massachusetts paper currency rather than silver.[33] Shute's reaction was a conspicuous and ominous silence. Ten tumultuous and mostly unproductive days after the session began, the governor ordered the Court closed, this time without even bothering to deliver his traditional closing remarks.

Even those who believed the colony was better off without Cooke as speaker were growing tired of Shute's reflexive shutdowns, which suggested that he cared more about having his way than about the business of the province and the well-being of its people. Indeed, by 1721 it had come to seem that the governor viewed every setback as a personal affront requiring a retaliatory action. The opening of the General Court session that March offered the most combative version of Samuel Shute the colony had yet seen. Still angry over the slight he had received at the end of the final session of the previous year, when the deputies had awarded him the second half of his compensation for the year, again reducing it by £100 and leaving him £200 plus depreciation short of the £1,200 he had received each of the previous three years, he demanded that his salary be increased. He also demanded that the House pass a law giving him pre-publication censorship powers—which were necessary, he asserted, because of an emerging threat to his authority: a series of critical pamphlets that he termed "*Factious* and *Scandalous*" and "tending to disquiet the minds of His Majesties good Subjects."[34]

There was no chance the deputies would supplement Shute's pay. The odds that they would bow to his demand for licensing authority over the colony's printed materials were not much better. Just over a year earlier he had tried to prevent the House from printing a harsh rebuttal to a speech in which he had blamed it for the colony's bad reputation in London. His claim that the Crown had vested him with absolute power over the press had failed to stop the deputies from going ahead with their counterattack. Although now he had framed his request for pre-publication censorship authority as a response to threats from outside the government, the deputies knew that he would turn it against them the first time they took to print to defend their actions or criticize his.

The sudden and untimely death of Oliver Noyes, Cooke's lieutenant and close friend, delayed the House response. The Court adjourned for several days until Noyes, who had suffered a stroke and died the following day, was buried. Perhaps because they were offended that the governor and lieutenant governor had been conspicuously absent from his funeral, the deputies came back to work more intransigent than ever. They turned down not only Shute's demands for money and censorship authority but "directly or virtually, every proposal" he put forth during the next ten days.[35] By March 31, the governor had had enough. He shut down the session with "a very sharp Speech," admonishing the House members to "a Loyal and Peaceable Behavior" during the recess.[36] The implied accusation that the deputies were about to foment some kind of mob violence or armed rebellion was ludicrous. But reading it into the official record meant it was sure to get to London, where the Lords of Trade would take it at face value and decide the Americans were even more nefarious and dangerous than they had formerly believed.

It was ironic, then, that when an act of political violence did take place the very next day it came from the governor's nephew. John Yeamans was drinking at Richard Hall's tavern across the street from the Town House when he got into a heated argument with another patron—his uncle's arch-enemy Elisha Cooke. At some point Yeamans lost control and struck

Cooke. A Cooke supporter named Christopher Taylor lit out after Yeamans, vowing to "have some of his blood"; when he couldn't find him, he settled for insulting the governor, who was passing in a carriage.[37] The authorities fined Yeamans for striking Cooke and Taylor for threatening Yeamans and the governor. With that, the matter was put to rest.

Within days of shutting down the assembly, Samuel Shute was off to his other government in New Hampshire. He left a colony paralyzed by acrimony and gridlock and sinking beneath the weight of its problems and threats. The Abenaki Indians had become actively hostile toward the colony's frontier settlers, making war increasingly likely. On top of a crippling currency shortage and runaway inflation, the recent collapse of the English financial markets resulting from the bursting of the "South Sea Bubble" meant an inevitable evaporation of investments in the colony.[38] And now the charter seemed doomed. It was hard to imagine how things could get worse.

2

JAMES AND
BENJAMIN

I n September 1719, John Campbell was fired as Boston's postmaster, a job he had held for seventeen years. For fifteen of those years he had also put out the *Boston News-Letter*, America's first continuously published newspaper. Campbell had invented the *News-Letter* to monetize one of his more tedious duties: producing a handwritten summary of news gleaned from incoming English newspapers and official documents and from his discussions with ship captains and the couriers who delivered domestic mail. Before delivering the letter to the royal governor he made copies by hand, which he then sold to other government officials and prominent businessmen. When the demand exceeded his ability to hand-copy the letter, he enlisted the printer Bartholomew Green to produce a typeset version. The resulting sheet resembled British newspapers, but its writing was perfunctory and its subject matter was safe and formulaic. "Our paltry News Letter," one subscriber called it.[1] And so it had remained for more than a dozen years. Dull and unpopular—its circulation had increased by just fifty copies in all the years since its inception—it was also, by the summer of 1718, thirteen months late in reporting news from Europe. Its founder's firing seems to have stemmed from a comparable tardiness in his other postmaster duties.

Campbell's replacement, William Brooker, assumed that he would get the *News-Letter* along with the postmaster's office, since Campbell had gone out of his way to justify publishing the newspaper for a profit by arguing that it was a logical and necessary obligation of the postmaster, a claim he would trot out every few years in attempts to get the government to underwrite a venture that proved more burdensome and less profitable than he had hoped. But when Brooker took office, Campbell refused to relinquish the *News-Letter*. He ignored his successor's claim to ownership and went right on publishing it.

Realizing after two months that Campbell was not going to budge and that the government didn't care enough about the *News-Letter* to adjudicate its ownership, Brooker decided to start his own paper. The challenge was to successfully launch a second newspaper in a town that had shown little enthusiasm for the one it already had. Brooker, though, had two advantages over Campbell. One was that, as postmaster, he could distribute his newspaper throughout the colony at government expense. The other was that his newspaper wouldn't have the baggage that went with being the "paltry" *News-Letter*. Since the profit margin was certain to be small, especially at the start, getting his product printed as cheaply as possible was imperative. Of the town's four full-time printers, three were out of the question. Bartholomew Green already printed the *News-Letter* and, as the most established and successful Boston printer, would have been too expensive anyway. Thomas Fleet was also busy enough that he had no need to lower his rate. Although Green's nephew Samuel Kneeland had only been in business a short time, he was already producing nearly as many imprints as Fleet and, with his uncle feeding him work, had no pressing need to strike a deal with the new postmaster. That left James Franklin.

In 1717, twenty-year-old James Franklin had returned to Boston from his printer's apprenticeship in England anxious to set up as the town's third full-time printer. James was the middle of Josiah Franklin's six sons with his second wife, Abiah Folger Franklin. His plan was to work as a journeyman for Bartholomew Green until he had saved enough money to buy a press and type. But once inside Green's printing house he discovered that Samuel Kneeland was nearing the end of his apprenticeship. Most apprentices got a suit of clothes at the conclusion of their indenture; as Green's nephew and a member of the most prominent family in New England printing, Kneeland was almost certain to get his own printing house. Many persons doubted that Boston had enough printing business to support even one more printer. No one believed it could sustain two more. If Kneeland set up first, James knew, he would have a prohibitive advantage, especially given the connections in business and government that came with being a Green. But if James managed to set up first, Green would probably decide to establish his nephew somewhere else, as had happened several years earlier when Green had sent his younger brother Timothy to Connecticut rather than have him vie with Thomas Fleet, who had recently arrived from England and opened up a printing house on Pudding Lane.

Josiah Franklin was skeptical of his son's plan. He wanted James either to bide his time until Green retired or relocate to Newport, Rhode Island, where John Franklin, James's half brother, had established himself in their father's trade, tallow chandler, and where a printer had yet to settle. But James had big ambitions and was convinced that Boston was the only place in America with an intellectual and cultural milieu capable of supporting the kind of printing he wanted to do. It was a literate town where people loved philosophy, politics, argument, and gossip, the fodder for the books, pamphlets, and broadsides that came off a printer's press. So in late 1717 and the first weeks of 1718 he pressed his father hard for a loan to buy his equipment and beat Kneeland into the market.

While Josiah had James in one ear, he had his youngest son in the other. Nearly two years had passed since Benjamin Franklin had taken John's place as his father's apprentice. Now he was eleven. With a hearty constitution and a chest and shoulders already powerful from swimming, he was well suited for the hard, physical work of making candles and soap. But he had no heart for the hot, smelly drudgery of it. Benjamin wanted Josiah to release him from his indenture and allow him to apprentice as a sailor. Josiah, who had already lost one sailor son in a shipwreck, refused to hear of it. He knew, though, that ships routinely signed on boys without checking to see if they were indentured elsewhere. His best hope for keeping his son from stealing away was finding him a more amenable trade on dry land. A daylong father-and-son tour of Boston's trades had proven unfruitful, and a prospective apprenticeship with Josiah's nephew, a cutler, had fallen through. As Benjamin approached his twelfth birthday he was still in his father's tallow shop and still miserable.

In the first weeks of 1718 Josiah relented to the demands of his sons, but with a catch for each of them. He would secure a £100 loan for James to start his business. But since printing was a two-man operation, James would need to bring on Benjamin as his apprentice. James resisted, unhappy at being saddled with his young, willful sibling. Unable to talk his father out of the condition but desperate for the loan, he extracted large, peevish concessions, including two extra years of unpaid labor from his little brother and an up-front placement fee, a demand that had so deeply insulted Josiah when it had come from his nephew, the cutler who had agreed to take Ben as his apprentice, that Josiah had walked away from the deal.

Benjamin was as unhappy as his brother. Even a twelve-year-old could see how unfairly the proposed indenture favored the master. And he had reservations about being tethered to a brother who was virtually a stranger, having been out of the country for most of his young life, and who, since his return, had shown himself to be moody, mercurial, and fond of drink. Josiah had been right to think that a boy who loved reading and books as much as his youngest son would spark to working with type and ink. But to Benjamin, nine years of indenture to someone who had already taken unfair advantage of him appeared an eternity. Unfortunately, his only option was to remain in his father's tallow shop. And that was unacceptable.

In June or July 1718, James Franklin returned from England with a sixty-year-old screw-and-lever "common press" constructed of unseasoned English elm, and a single font of type. By late July the Franklin printing house had opened on the southeast corner of Queen Street and Dorset Alley, about two hundred paces from the Boston Town House and directly across from the "gloomy pile of the town prison."[2] In August, James produced his first major imprint, *A Catalog of Curious and Valuable Books*. Its colophon read: "Boston: Printed by J. Franklin, at his printing-house in Queen Street, over against Mr. Sheaf's school; where all sorts of printing work and engraving on wood, is done at reasonable prizes [*sic*]. 1718"[3] Typographical error aside, the sixteen-page imprint, which contained original woodcuts of putti and flowers, spoke well for James's abilities as a page designer, carver of woodcuts for illustrations, and printer. A second imprint, a sermon by Thomas Prince and Ebenezer Pemberton on the occasion of Prince's ordination as assistant minister of the Old South Church, followed about a month later. Although the assignment came through Samuel Gerrish, Boston's leading bookseller, it's likely that Josiah Franklin, an active member of the Old South, had lobbied the ministers on his son's behalf. At least one additional imprint would follow before the end of the year.

The slow start made it clear that beating out Green and Fleet for the traditional products of the colony's presses—sermons, government proclamations and records, and a smattering of political and scientific tracts— was going to be tougher than James had anticipated. His biggest challenge, though, was Samuel Kneeland, who had not been relocated to some far-away place as James had counted on but, rather, had been set up directly across the alley from the Franklin printing house. It was hard not to see Kneeland's extreme proximity as a message, if not an act of intimidation. The Greens had ruled New England printing since 1649, when Kneeland's great-grandfather Samuel Green Sr. had taken over for the colony's first printer, Stephen Daye. Boston's printing was their birthright, and they would fight the interloper James Franklin for every unclaimed scrap of it.

Faced with the near certainty that he would get too little of the colony's traditional business to survive, James looked for other ways to occupy his press. One presented itself on a blustery Monday morning early in November 1718, when the keeper of the Boston lighthouse drowned along with his wife, their daughter, and three other persons: a servant, a slave, and a family friend. What stunned and surprised people wasn't that the lighthouse keeper and members of his family had been lost to the sea—many people had expected it, given the danger that came with living perched atop a small rocky island only eighteen feet above sea level near the mouth of the harbor, completely exposed to the vicissitudes of the weather and the waves—but that it had happened in conditions far less threatening than the storm that, a year or two earlier, had swept fifty-nine of the family's sheep into the sea. The smallish boat transporting the party from a larger vessel to Little Brewster Island had mysteriously capsized just yards from the island's rocky shore. Along with that irony there was poignancy: The family had been returning to their island home after attending religious services on the mainland. The fact that the body of the servant had not been recovered amplified the horror. Most garishly of all, the entire tragedy had unfolded in full view of another family daughter, who had stayed behind at the lighthouse and had come down to the water with a friend to greet her parents and sister.

While apprenticing in England, James Franklin had become familiar with Grub Street ballads, temporary poems that, like their sixteenth- and seventeenth-century predecessors, were frequently "comical, political, romantic or simply lewd," and that "placed an emphasis on current events," including "recent disasters."[4] "Ripped from the headlines" is how we would describe them today. The bizarre tragedy that had befallen the lighthouse keeper, James knew, was perfect for such a ballad, which might turn a good profit if some "hack" poet capable of writing serviceable verse for little or no money could be found.

As it happened, he had just such a poet in his employment. Benjamin Franklin had been dabbling with verse since 1715, when his father's brother, a self-proclaimed poet also named Benjamin, had arrived from England and moved in with the family. After a straightforward account of the drownings appeared in the *Boston News-Letter*, James put his indentured bard to work.[5] Satisfied with the result, he printed it, loaded Benjamin down with copies, and shoved him out the door to peddle them on the street, probably by declaiming his own verses for dramatic effect.

As Franklin remembered in his *Autobiography*, the ballad "sold wonderfully, the Event being recent, having made a great noise." No verified copy survives; but for all its presumed flaws—Franklin later declared it "wretched stuff"—it was competent enough that people accepted the verse of a twelve-year-old as the handiwork of an adult.[6]

Three months later, when news reached Boston that the infamous pirate Blackbeard (a.k.a. Edward Teach) had been captured and killed along the coast of North Carolina, the brothers published another ballad. It appeared in March 1719 and recounted the drama in detail. Trapped in a cove by naval forces, a drunken Teach had stood at the bow of his ship and spewed curses at his adversaries for hours before unleashing a furious barrage of cannon fire. When the firing had ceased, the pirate, more audacious and heavily armed than his would-be captors, seemed to have prevailed. But when he boarded one of the ships that he assumed had been vanquished, he was ambushed by crew members lying in wait belowdecks. In the ensuing close-range combat, a lieutenant named Maynard shot and wounded Teach. Then another man finished him off, decapitating him so that his head lay "flat on his Shoulder."[7] The victorious sloop had sailed back to Virginia with Blackbeard's head, distinctive for his long, dark beard fastened in clumps with red ribbons, mounted to its bowsprit. "Teach, the Pirate," as the ballad was called, was a more modest success than "The Lighthouse Tragedy." It was profitable enough, though, that James realized he had hit upon a source of revenue to replace the printing of linens, calicoes, and other fabrics for the housewives of Boston—until now his stopgap for making ends meet. Boston was unlikely to go more than a few months without some new drama or tragedy suitable for exploiting— a fire, a murder, a suicide, the loss of one of the colony's ships in a storm or a run-in with Indians or more pirates. When it struck, James could put his brother to work sensationalizing it for profit.

But Josiah Franklin had had it with his sons' ballads, which were as scandalous to the better sort of Bostonian as they were popular with everyone else. "The Lighthouse Tragedy" and "Teach" had stepped on the toes of the ministers, whose job it had always been to contextualize tragedy and triumph. Related from the pulpit, drownings and executions were object lessons in God's will. (The title of the Reverend Cotton Mather's self-described "pungent and useful" funeral sermon for the lighthouse keeper and his wife and daughter had begun with the words "Providence Asserted and Adored.")[8] Sensational and amoral, the brothers' ballads not only embarrassed their pious father but also posed a threat to his campaign to be elected as a church deacon. Soon after "Teach" hit the streets, Josiah summoned his now thirteen-year-old son, "ridiculing" his effort at poetic composition and warning that he would go to ruin if he continued writing verse.[9] He was exercising his clout as his older son's silent partner by effectively shutting down the juggernaut at its source. Benjamin would write no further ballads.

James had no choice but to go back to printing fabrics. When even that failed to generate enough revenue to sustain him, he began jobbing out custom woodcuts to his fellow printers. Two years earlier he had returned to Boston cocky about his ability and determined to show the Greens what *real* printers did for a living. Now he was practically working for them. As his frustration and worry increased, so did the tension between the brothers. It was challenging enough for James and Benjamin to work side by side, day after day, in cramped quarters. Having too little work to keep the type clacking and the press groaning was worse. With no words to set, forms to ink, or pages to cut and hang for drying, James might have spent more time than usual at the tavern, returning to the shop after several hours agitated by the political talk and the drink. On those occasions Benjamin probably found it impossible to look busy enough or tread lightly enough to suit his master. The stresses of this fallow, anxious period might have precipitated James Franklin's first acts of physical violence against his brother, what Benjamin later described as "the blows his passion too often urged him to bestow upon me."[10] Both brothers were desperate for something to change when William Brooker came calling, looking for a printer and a bargain.

THE *BOSTON GAZETTE*, America's second newspaper, debuted on December 21, 1719. Like Campbell's *News-Letter*, Brooker's paper was a weekly published on Monday, usually as a single sheet with two columns of news on each side. For years, Campbell had featured the words "Published by Authority" in his masthead. Now they were prominently displayed at the top of Brooker's newspaper. In both cases the claim to a government imprimatur was a stretch. Neither publisher had received the official endorsement of the authorities; each had proactively assumed it, reasoning that since his paper was tied to the postmaster's office, and the postmaster's office was part of the royal government, the newspaper was, by extension, the official one of the government. The notion, in part, was to glean prestige and circulation from the perception that it was the mouthpiece of the governor and his administration. But it was also intended to assure that government that it would print only what it found acceptable—in short, that it would not be another *Publick Occurrences both Forreign and Domestick*, which in 1690 had so offended the Massachusetts government that it had been censored out of existence after its first issue, with its publisher, Benjamin Harris, thrown in jail for good measure. At that point newspapers were still a fairly recent innovation—the first London paper had started up only twenty-five years earlier—and governments on both sides of the ocean regarded the press as an enemy of the established order, "a font of sedition and rebellion."[11] Three decades later the government's fear of the press—or at least its hostility toward it—had eased enough that newspapers were beginning to flourish. But it still behooved a newspaper publisher who wanted to remain a newspaper publisher to soothe the apprehensions of the powerful. John Campbell, wrote William Sloan and Julie Williams, had positioned himself "not as an energetic editor, but as an official conduit of information" whose product was "a formal, chronological record of news items."[12] For the most part, Brooker took the same approach. When he did venture an opinion, he was careful to align with the interests of the governor and the Council. Indeed, the biggest difference between his paper and Campbell's was that his looked better. James Franklin had given it a cleaner, less cluttered design and a handsome woodcut illustration on each side of the masthead.

The *Gazette* was well received, and, for the first time since starting his printing house, James Franklin had a steady source of revenue. Relieved and vindicated by his new status, his natural cockiness returned. "The Printer hereof prints Linens, Calicoes, Silks &c. in good Figures, very lively and durable Colors," he wrote in an advertisement in April 1720, "and without the offensive Smell which commonly attends the Linens Printed here."[13] Once again he was ready to show Boston what real printing was all about. But he remained judicious in accepting additional work, mindful that as printer for the postmaster it was incumbent upon him to avoid imprints that might anger the royal government. His few partisan tracts hewed to the Prerogative Party line. If privately he disagreed with some of the opinions he was publishing, he knew better than to say so.

Three months into the *Gazette*'s run, William Brooker was abruptly dismissed as postmaster, collateral damage, it appears, of a political turf war in London. His replacement, an Englishman named Philip Musgrave, took over both that job and the *Gazette* in May 1720. James continued as the printer through June and July. But by August 22 he was out. The new colophon in that Monday's issue read: "BOSTON: Printed by S. KNEELAND, and may be had at the Post-Office, where Advertisements are taken in."[14]

It was the second time in just over a year that a member of the Green family had shouldered a Franklin out of a prized opportunity. In April 1719 Josiah Franklin had stood for deacon of the Old South Church, a move he had been planning and working toward for years, if not decades, by cultivating the respect and friendship of what Benjamin Franklin called the "leading people" in Boston.[15] Realizing that he needed the most powerful sponsor possible to overcome the bias against him for his menial occupation and rudimentary formal education, he had focused on Samuel Sewall, who besides being one of the colony's most powerful political figures was also the Old South's most influential layman. Josiah had managed to gain membership in Sewall's exclusive prayer group; but, given the chance to offer the tallow chandler a full-throated endorsement, the judge had demurred. In a three-way race for two deacon spots, Bartholomew Green had come in first and Josiah had come in a distant third.

Like his father, James Franklin had courted the establishment. With one minor transgression—his broadside ballads—he had toed the line, staying out of trouble with the censors. But despite those efforts, he, too, had failed. There might have been friction with Musgrave, who was said to have a "crabbed, surly, snappish Temper."[16] But the new postmaster's main motivation for replacing James with Kneeland appears to have been personal ambition: He wanted to rise socially and economically as fast as possible in his new town. A partnership with Kneeland, a son of the Green family, gave him "a more credible link to the Boston establishment" than James did.[17]

Confronted by the harsh truth that even in America, where society was less stratified than in England, wealth and social status trumped personal merit, Josiah Franklin faded quietly into the background, never to strive again. But his son couldn't afford to give up. He had a printing press, a shop, and large loans to repay. Two months before Musgrave switched printers, Josiah had signed bonds for loans totaling nearly £250, most or all of which, his biographer Nian-Sheng Huang believes, went to James.[18]

Perhaps enough of the money remained now to sustain him and Benjamin for a time. Eventually, though, James would need to find some new way to generate printing income or close his business and spend the rest of his life working for one of his competitors and trying to pay off his large debts on a journeyman's salary.

THE TALK OF Boston in late February 1721 was a pamphlet titled "A Letter to an Eminent Clergyman." It declared class war on the wealthy opponents of paper currency, who were "commonly, tho falsly, call'd Great" even though their "sordid, narrow, selfish, Spirit" was to blame for the economic troubles of the middling and the poor. It went on to decry the "multiplying of Nobility . . . in an Over-proportion to the Common People" and "an Overgrown Clergy," whose members, it charged, "bring nothing to the Stock." The anonymous author entreated voters to reject corrupt politicians tied to moneyed interests and elect "Good, Honest and Trusty Men."[19]

The day after "A Letter" went on sale in Benjamin Gray's bookshop the censors ordered Gray to the Council chamber. Under interrogation, he admitted having "caused" the pamphlet's printing but refused to divulge either its author or printer.[20] Miffed at his intransigence, the councilors called for him to be charged with seditious libel, along with anyone else whose involvement could be established.

About two weeks later, Gray reprinted "News from the Moon," a Daniel Defoe essay scolding public officials for imagining every public criticism was a libel against them.[21] But it was the ad announcing its availability—specifically a line that suggested Gray's shop would go on selling "A Letter" in defiance of the cease-and-desist order—that infuriated the government anew and made the governor and his Council more determined than ever to see him punished.[22]

It was no coincidence that when Samuel Shute made his session-opening speech to the General Court a few days later, he demanded pre-publication censorship authority.[23] The House's rejection of that demand was heartening to the publisher, author, and printer of "A Letter to an Eminent Clergyman," who saw it as a victory for press freedom over oppression and a good omen for the dismissal of their charges. But it wasn't until May 2, when a grand jury discharged Gray from his recognizance, that the three men behind the scandalous pamphlet could relax. One of those men, the author, was fated to remain a mystery. But press historians feel certain that James Franklin had been its printer. Indeed, James seems to have also printed "News from the Moon" and several other pro-paper-currency, anti-prerogative pamphlets during the first months of 1721.

He had begun the year reeling from the previous twelve months, during which he had produced about half as many pamphlets as his next closest competitor, Fleet, and a sixth as many as the town's most successful printer, Bartholomew Green.[24] His desperate straits had made it easy to accept the risk of printing Gray's pamphlets. So far, taking that risk had paid off. He and Benjamin had turned out two more imprints in the first quarter of 1721 than during the entirety of 1720. And the reward was more than monetary. For the first time he had the satisfaction of printing political sentiments that aligned with his own.

Now the one major threat to this success, the specter of a fine or jail if his involvement with "A Letter" was uncovered, was gone. Coming on the heels of the previous year's dismissal of charges against John Colman for his pamphlet predicting economic disaster and societal chaos, Gray's victory seemed to promise that James could go on printing more or less whatever he wanted with impunity. But it wasn't that simple. There was a chance that the next ship from England might bring the news the governor had been hoping for—confirmation of his absolute power over the press. In the meantime, the Council, miffed at the impudence of the press, seemed more inclined to exercise its powers than it had for more than a decade. In recent years the censors had accused John Colman, Benjamin Gray, and even Thomas Fleet of libel. Those men had evaded prosecution only by offering a pro forma apology for what they had "done amiss."[25] It seemed increasingly doubftful now that a self-abasing apology would be enough to spare the next man brought before them. And there was no telling what might become of an offender who refused to grovel.

3

THE FALLEN ANGEL

Cotton Mather began 1721 worried about his mounting debts, anxious over the future of his children, his ministry, and his colony, bitter over the miserable state of his marriage, and stinging from the published attacks of his political enemies. He was delivering his Sunday sermon from the pulpit of the North Church on February 12, his fifty-eighth birthday, when he began stuttering. Within seconds he found himself completely debilitated, too ill, he later wrote, to continue. Four days later he was still too incapacitated to honor his obligation to deliver the town's Thursday lecture.[1] It was as though the frustration and resentment that had been building in him for more than a decade had finally overwhelmed him, reducing him to a sputtering, incoherent rage.

After about two weeks he was able to resume his normal duties and activities. But he was far from whole. He was conducting a baptism on the afternoon of April 23 when he broke into tears. In his diary he took what was, for him, the unprecedented step of positing that his troubles might be deserved, punishment for unspecified "Crimes," and that he should "patiently bear the Indignation of the Lord." But he still felt victimized by "the malignant and venomous Disposition of a great part of the Town and Countrey," including members of his own congregation, who were threatening to defect to a new church, the largest and most *"Beautifull House"* in Massachusetts.[2] It was scheduled to be dedicated the following month, and would be called the "New Brick Church." But now it seemed poised to earn its other, unofficial name, the "Revenge Church."

ALL BY ITSELF, Cotton Mather's name probably made it inevitable that he would tend toward the messianic. It had been bestowed upon him in honor of his grandfathers, arguably the two most illustrious religious figures in New England Congregationalism. John Cotton had preached the farewell sermon for John Winthrop and the first wave of Puritan settlers when they sailed for America in 1630. Richard Mather had been one of the inventors of Puritan church government, the New England Way. Even as a young child their grandson had believed he was destined to carry forward their legacies and serve some special purpose in God's plan. Driven by a demanding and emotionally distant father and his own sense of dynastic mission, he was, by age eight, reading fifteen chapters of the Bible every day and taking his playmates to task for their "wicked words and ways."[3] At fifteen he became the youngest Harvard College graduate of the century. When less than a year after his 1685 ordination he convinced a condemned murderer to make a moving gallows conversion, people began saying that he was, indeed, something special, particularly in regards to his ability to banish the most malevolent kinds of wickedness. It was only natural, then, that when the children of John Goodwin were afflicted with "Strange fits" allegedly because a spell had been cast upon them by the family's laundry-woman, a witch, Mather was consulted.[4] After more than a month in his home, thirteen-year-old Martha Goodwin's "fits" were cured, and the triumphant minister vowed to "confute the Sadducism" of his "debauched age" and show no patience for those who doubted the reality of the Devil and witches.[5] The book he began writing shortly thereafter, *Memorable Providences, Relating to Witchcrafts and Possessions*, established him as New England's resident expert on demonic possession.

Mather had been a minister for seven years and was widely viewed as a religious prodigy, the golden boy of New England Congregationalism, when two Salem Village girls, nine-year-old Elizabeth Parris and her twelve-year-old cousin Abigail Williams, began suffering fits and contorting their bodies into unnatural shapes. Accusations of witchcraft snowballed, leading to a rash of arrests and the establishment of a special court to try the accused. Mather was tapped as its expert consultant. Neither a judge nor a prosecutor, he had no direct responsibility for the executions that would make the Salem witch trials infamous. But his failure to speak up against the court of oyer and terminer, even after he had come to doubt the validity of the "spectral evidence" it was using to convict and condemn the accused—and even after other ministers, his own father included, had denounced the court's methods—helped brand him one of Salem's villains.[6] Even then he might have outlived this tragic lapse of judgment and character had he not compounded it by refusing to apologize. It was his unwavering insistence on his blamelessness that gave critical mass to the attacks of his nemesis Robert Calef, the cloth merchant who, in the words of Mather biographer David Levin, managed to tie to Mather "a tin can that rattled through nearly three centuries."[7] In a sense, Mather's biggest Salem crime was his failure to learn and change, to control his tendencies to speak and act precipitously, to overstate, exaggerate, show off, and cling unalterably to certain convictions. His inability to correct those flaws and rein in those excesses would shape his life and warp his legacy.

But the blowback from Salem was not immediate. Indeed, by all outward appearances, Mather continued to flourish. Over the course of the subsequent decade his books continued to sell and his flock continued to grow. By 1700 his North Church had fifteen hundred members—nearly 25 percent of the total population of Boston.[8] His personal life, though, was characterized by unremitting tragedy. Three children died in as many

years, all from violent seizures. Two of his young daughters were criti-
cally burned and permanently disfigured in separate accidents involving
fires. Early in 1702 his wife, Abigail, became ill with cancer or tuberculosis and was dead by year's end. One of the persons who began to question whether God was punishing Mather and other perpetrators of Salem
was Calef, who in a 1695 note to the minister Samuel Willard wrote that
the surprising number of strange, gruesome, or untimely deaths among
men responsible for the witchcraft scandal and members of their families
ought to be viewed as "remarkable providences intended for their moral
instruction"—a play on the title of the Mather book that had helped fuel
the Salem hysteria.[9] The appearance in 1700 of Calef's *More Wonders of the
Invisible World*, his answer to Mather's post-Salem attempt to exculpate
himself and the witch judges, marked the beginning of a change in the
public's attitude toward Mather—or at least in its willingness to express
those feelings. From time to time now, the minister was the victim of
anonymous taunts. Intoxicated college boys sometimes gathered beneath
his bedroom window late at night and sang rude songs. In 1703 someone
drew a picture of a hanged man, wrote Mather's name on it, and tossed it
over the gate of the minister's house. As time went on, Mather more frequently found himself singled out for abuse, "the butt of scurrilous letters,
defamatory broadsides, derisive gossip and even physical threats"—like a
1712 murder attempt in which a drunk sea captain approached Mather's
house brandishing a cutlass and ranting at the top of his lungs that he
would be "content to lie a year in Hell" for the satisfaction of killing him.[10]

The erosion of Mather's official influence post-Calef was gradual but
inexorable. By 1710 he had lost his high standing in Boston's three seats
of power—the government, the church, and Harvard College. His few
years as an advisor to the first governor under the New Charter, William
Phips, were a dim memory. Angry that Mather and his father, Increase,
had been instrumental in his earlier arrest and deportation, Joseph Dudley
had locked him out of any influence. Dudley and several others had similarly forced Increase Mather out of the Harvard presidency, sabotaging

his plan to anoint his son as his successor. Arguably, Mather himself had done the most to hurt his religious standing, undermining his unofficial role as leader of the ministers by getting caught in a petty and inept scheme to prevent the formation of the Brattle Street Church, the first liberal-leaning Congregational church in Boston.

Blocked from every traditional path to distinction, but still convinced of his destiny as the natural leader of his community, Mather had set about redefining public service and leadership in his own image. In 1710, in a short book titled *Bonifacius, An Essay Upon the Good,* he declared that the true measure of a man was not political power, wealth, or even traditional notions of sectarian religious piety but, rather, his willingness to "Do Good." The book enumerated ways in which schoolmasters, magistrates, rich men, officials, lawyers, ministers, and physicians could display a "practical piety," with an emphasis on expanding the clergy's involvement in medicine, one of Mather's lifelong interests and the career path he had nearly taken years earlier when his first and most prolonged stuttering attack appeared to have ended his dream of becoming a minister.[11] Indeed, "doing good" as defined by *Bonifacius* included enlightening the community in every area of science (or "natural philosophy," as it was referred to at the time), from medicine to astronomy to botany—all subjects Mather had been studying since boyhood.[12]

By December 1712 he had sent thirteen letters to the Royal Society in London. The Society, whose president was the great Isaac Newton and whose members included the astronomer Edmond Halley, was the world's most prestigious scientific organization. Publication in its journal, the *Philosophical Transactions,* was an accomplishment second only to full membership. Mather was looking for both publication and membership. In addition to his scientific letters, which concerned a wide range of topics from earthquakes to advanced mathematics and included several medical topics, he had also sent personal letters to the organization's secretary, Richard Waller, and one of its members, the physician and geologist John Woodward, offering a "Modest Intimation" that he would welcome a nomination for membership.[13] Becoming the first American-born "Fellow of the Royal Society" would set him apart and, he hoped, earn him the admiration of all New England. Just as important, the addition of "F.R.S." to the title pages of his books would identify him unquestionably as a man of reason and not, as Calef had claimed, superstition.

In October 1713 he received a letter informing him that it was the "*Desire and Purpose*" of the Society to accept him into its ranks. The letter seemed to imply that a forthcoming vote on his membership was a mere formality. "*I shall be made, A FELLOW OF THE ROYAL SOCIETY,*" he exulted in his diary. He called it a "marvellous Favour of Heaven" that would put him "above the Contempt on [of] envious Men."[14] But elation was replaced with terror and despair when, the very next month, a measles epidemic killed his second wife and three of his children— the seventh, eighth, and ninth of his offspring to die. Reeling from the loss, he found some solace and meaning in "doing good" by writing and publishing a pamphlet instructing laypersons about the progression of measles and how best to treat the disease. The result was so competent, accurate, and original that medical historian Ernest Caulfield rated it as "one of the very few classics of early American medicine."[15] He then began work on a hugely ambitious scientific book, a compendium or "catalogue" of scientific knowledge that he completed and sent to England for printing in 1715.[16]

Four years elapsed between the time Mather began sending his scientific letters to London and his first opportunity to see any of them in print. When he thumbed through a copy of the *Philosophical Transactions* in the summer of 1716 he was disappointed to discover that the editors had taken more than one hundred pages of his observations and ruminations and abridged them to just nine pages. But he resisted the impulse to vent his umbrage in a letter. His relationship with the Society still offered his best prospect for winning the respect of the people, and he would do nothing to jeopardize it. And he reasoned that now that he was member of the organization—which he assumed must be the case, even though he had yet to hear the results of the vote—his contributions would receive the complete and respectful treatment they deserved.

Samuel Shute arrived in Boston three months later. Years earlier Mather had written off his hopes for political influence. Now, though, he reflexively put aside his nearly six-year commitment to doing good through science and medicine and began a campaign to ingratiate himself with the new governor, praising him extravagantly in a May 1717 sermon that proclaimed Shute a war hero and the best thing the new king had done for the colonies.[17] Shute, who by this point was beginning to feel besieged by Cooke and his faction, welcomed the fawning and granted Mather the access he craved.

Elisha Cooke observed the workings of this mutual admiration society warily. As long as Mather confined himself to cheerleading for Shute, he was content to wave it off. That was not the case, though, when he discovered that the minister had hosted a secret summit for "About nineteen or twenty principal Members of the House" in an attempt to win them away from their support for him.[18] Confronted by Cooke's colleague, Oliver Noyes, Mather argued pragmatically that it was wise "to do everything that may have a tendency to make his [Shute's] government an easy station to him," because a more punitive and less Puritan-friendly governor might be in the offing.[19] The argument had merit; but Cooke and almost everyone else in Boston believed that Mather's motivation was more selfish: that he and his father, the two "uncrowned heads of the New England Congregational church," would do nearly anything for political influence.[20]

Mather's failed attempt at political action on Shute's behalf ought to have warned him off becoming too deeply enmeshed in the growing hostility between the governor and Elisha Cooke. But as the Popular Party leader grew more powerful and Shute more frustrated and hostile toward the Massachusetts charter, the minister found it more difficult to limit his involvement to defending the governor and soothing his frequent temper tantrums. Finally, in March 1719, Mather lost control. The sermon he preached to the General Court that month was a political diatribe dressed in the vestments of a religious address. It damned the House for its "Monstrous *Ingratitude*" toward the governor and warned of apocalyptic political ramifications. Mather claimed that he had received a "Grievous Vision" from Heaven that the "Criminal Mutinies" of the governor's enemies would condemn Massachusetts to "a Parliamentary Cognizance."[21] The only way to prevent this prophecy from coming to pass was for the elected government to acquiesce completely to Shute. It was a classic fire-and-brimstone jeremiad, with England standing in for God as the vengeful deity. Both the House and the Council declined to appropriate money for its printing, fearful, as Samuel Sewall wrote in his diary, that Mather had spoken "so much of his visions of Convulsion and Mutiny" that the sermon alone might serve as "an Invitation to the Parliament, to take away our Charter."[22] But Shute ordered it printed anyway at government expense and with the addition of a page that read: "Published by Order of his Excellency the GOVERNOUR."

A few months later, Judge Sewall was at home when a messenger delivered an issue of the *London Flying Post* containing a transcript of a November 1718 letter from Cotton Mather to Parliament member John Shute Barrington, Samuel Shute's brother. The letter lavished extravagant praise on the governor and portrayed him as hugely popular, a ludicrous claim even then. Although the newspaper had arrived without a note of explanation, Sewall knew that it had been sent by Elisha Cooke and was a warning that the Popular Party leader would no longer abide Mather's meddling.[23]

SAMUEL SEWALL RECEIVED another strange delivery on the evening of April 13, 1720. This time it was a letter claiming that his friend Mather was in desperate straits. The unsigned letter warned that if Sewall declined to help the minister rid himself of a certain legal and financial obligation, the result might be "the Death, or some thing worse than that soon coming on that distressed tho' worthy Gentleman."[24]

Four years earlier Mather had volunteered to administer the estate of a man named Nathan Howell. It was a favor to Howell's widow, Katherine, who was the daughter of Mather's third wife, Lydia, by her previous marriage. Flummoxed by legal complexities and ill suited to badger debtors, the minister had failed to free up any of the estate's considerable assets, obliging him to take Katherine and her two sons into his home with disharmonious results. Now, a few years later, the estate was still no closer to being settled, Katherine had remarried, and she and her new husband, Sewall's nephew, were threatening to have Mather arrested for "maladministration." Moreover, a sheriff had served Lydia Mather a summons directing her and her husband to answer a large claim against both the Howell estate and that of Howell's business partner, Lydia's late husband. The letter to Sewall informed him that Mather lacked the money to pay the claim and that his "Tirrible" wife, who had received a large inheritance from her first husband, refused to make him a loan.[25] The anonymous letter writer wanted the judge to stop his nephew's threats and use his legal influence to have the estate removed entirely from Mather's hands.

Sewall must have suspected that the letter had come from Mather himself. And he knew that the desperation it revealed had to do with more than his money troubles. As its unflattering reference to Mrs. Mather revealed, the minister's five-year-old marriage was foundering. Lydia was exasperated with her husband's financial incompetence and his quirks and insecurities and at odds with his children, especially his daughters. He insisted that her "paroxysms" against him and the girls were caused by insanity.[26] But if Lydia was mentally unstable, her husband's insecurities did nothing to help. Unable to lavish her with the material goods her wealthy first husband had provided, he had declared her enjoyment of material and temporal pleasures sins and his own impecuniousness pious. Increasingly convinced that he was disparaging her and pitying himself in his diaries, she had confiscated several of them, refusing his demands for their return.

Mather feared that the mercurial Lydia would embarrass him in public. But his eldest son posed a greater threat. Twenty-one years earlier, an angel had promised Mather that the boy about to be born would grow up to "glorify Jesus Christ on earth."[27] Instead, Increase Mather Jr.—also called "Cresy" or "Creasy" by his father—had become an incorrigible wastrel who had impregnated a prostitute in 1716. His father lived in daily apprehension over what abomination he might commit next.

Meanwhile, Mather seemed headed toward certain embarrassment and worse as a consequence of having pushed a country minister named Peter Thacher on his sister congregation in the North End, the "New North." A few months earlier, New North members opposed to Thacher as their second minister had rioted during his installation ceremony, storming the balcony and disrupting the proceedings by shouting and pouring alcohol on the heads of the people below. Shortly thereafter they had made good on their threat to break away and start another North End congregation. Now fund-raising was under way and a rumor had begun to spread that a sizable portion of Mather's North Church congregation, outraged over his meddling, was resolved to join them.

Well aware of Mather's propensity to overstate his problems and confident that the minister's despair did not rise to the level of the suicide at which he seemed to be hinting, Sewall made no immediate response to the letter. But the simple fact that Mather would raise so extreme a solution to his problems spoke to the severity of his psychic strain. It manifested itself the way it usually did, by robbing him of what little discretion he possessed. Just over a month later, following the General Court session that had been cut short by Shute's negative of Cooke as speaker, it was revealed that Mather had urged the governor to negative John Clark from the Council. Universally respected as a doctor and a civic figure, Clark was also Mather's former brother-in-law. Indeed, he had taken in Mather's daughter Elizabeth after her falling out with Lydia and had been providing her food and shelter on the day her father had pushed to have him banned from the government. The public exposure of an act of personal betrayal ought to have mortified Mather and, by reminding him yet again that he lacked "the smallest gift for political intrigue," put an end to his meddling once and for all.[28] But Mather made it his mission to prevent Cooke's reelection as speaker by, among other things, authoring a pamphlet against him. "News from Robinson Cruso's Island" was a takeoff on Daniel Defoe's 1719 novel. In Mather's version, Crusoe finds himself in Boston, an "Island now known by the Name of *Insania*," where a governor "of a kind and generous Temper" is affronted by an "Obnoxious" man whom the people, out of some "strange humour," have made their spokesman. Crusoe (Mather) asks whether there is truly "but one Man in the Country qualified for a Prolocutor," and whether Bostonians "are not in continual danger of coming under a Parliamentary Cognizance" by showing themselves "an Ungovernable People."[29] In the appendix that followed, Mather reminded readers that the Popular Party leader had been censured by the Council for calling Shute a blockhead and had falsely and recklessly claimed Massachusetts's authority over the Maine woods.

It's doubtful that Mather's pamphlet was responsible for Cooke's failure to win the speaker's chair at the reopened General Court. But it gave Cooke and his supporters a focus for their anger. In August 1720, they targeted Mather with "unnamed scurrilities." He dashed off several letters in which he called them "idiots and fuddlecaps" and "American (worse than African) monsters."[30] They retaliated in December with "New News from Robinson Cruso's Island," which portrayed Mather as a comic figure, "the great DON-DAGO, the *Primate-wou'd-be* of our Island."[31] In public the minister kept up a defiant face. But he recognized his enemies were savvier at utilizing the modern devices of rhetorical attack. To his friend John Winthrop he confided, "I own myself not a match for them."[32]

THE SUDDEN DEATH of Oliver Noyes occurred about a month after Mather's debilitating stuttering attack in the pulpit. The minister's shameful assessment of that death as "a wonderful token for good," and his unkind (and inaccurate) description of Noyes as "the greatest Hinderer of good, and Misleader and Enchanter of the People, that there was in the whole House of Representatives," bespeak a mind perverted by the "near shattering anxiety" that had caused his breakdown.[33] That warped perspective was evident again two weeks later when the obstreperousness of the deputies had him praying for more divine retribution—that "two or three wicked Men" in the House would "feel the Hand of GOD upon them."[34]

He must have been beside himself when Shute angrily shut down the General Court and vowed to categorically condemn the House in a letter to London. But that day, March 31, 1721, also brought the happiest of surprises: the arrival of one hundred printed copies of the "catalogue" of scientific discoveries whose manuscript he had sent to London for printing nearly six years earlier. The title page of that book, *The Christian Philosopher*, bore the initials "F.R.S."—Fellow of the Royal Society. Years earlier its research and writing had restored his emotional balance and sense of purpose after the measles deaths of his wife and children. Now its arrival soothed his vengeful mania and reminded him of his better, enlightened self. But Mather's psyche was a seesaw susceptible to the slightest push. In the first week of April, his son Cresy and "some detestable Rakes in the Town" were arrested after "a Night-Riot" of vandalism, which started Mather on a downward trajectory.[35] Shortly thereafter he defaulted on a claim against the Howell and George estates. Special dispensation to sell off a Howell asset spared him from debtors' prison. But there was no guarantee that allowance would be made again.

Members of his congregation began defecting on April 30. "Tis incredible, what Numbers are swarming off into the New Brick Meetinghouse in the Neighborhood," he wrote the next day.[36] Weeks earlier, in an attempt to mollify his congregation's New Brick sympathizers, he had agreed to preach at the church's dedication on May 10. Now doing so would mean bestowing blessings on a meetinghouse populated significantly by persons who had repudiated him.

He was the first guest minister to speak that morning. For twenty or so minutes he preached a generic sermon about the need to exalt God, steering clear of the defections except to disabuse the New Brick founders that they had lured his people away. "There is none brought into our Congregations, but it is our SAVIOUR who brings them in," he declaimed. "There are none taken out of our Congregations, but is our SAVIOUR who takes them out." But after noting that the physical beauty of the New Brick meant nothing "if the Beauties of Holinesss be wanting," he focused on his repudiation. The "very Great Withdraw" of people from his church, he claimed, was not the "Trouble" it appeared but, rather, "a Strong and a Strange *Consolation*" since both he and his father were "done with a world that has nothing in it worth Staying for" and "within a Few Weeks of seeing the Best Hour that ever we saw."[37] What this meant—a literal or metaphorical death and ascension into Heaven, it seemed—no one knew. Few probably cared. It was just one more false and self-serving Mather prophesy.

This time, though, Mather was correct. Although he himself didn't realize it, he was, in fact, within weeks of his finest hour. But it had nothing to do with his death and everything to do with the death that had stolen into Boston aboard a sailing ship. Ever since Salem, he had been searching for redemption. Now he would be given the chance to save the town from its most dread disease. But it would mean staking what was left of his reputation on an obscure medical procedure he had happened upon a few years earlier—one so fantastical that people were certain to accuse him of perpetrating another Salem, sacrificing the lives of the innocent to an egomaniacal delusion.

PART TWO

GRIEVOUS CALAMITY

I in the Burying Place may see
Graves Shorter there than I;
From Death's Arrest no Age is free,
Young Children too may die;
My God, may such an awful Sight,
Awakening be to me!
Oh! That by early Grace I might
For Death prepared be.

—From *The New-England Primer*
(required reading for every Boston
schoolchild in the eighteenth century)

That disease [smallpox] . . . was then the most terrible of all the ministers of death . . . filling the churchyards with corpses, tormenting with constant fears all whom it had not yet stricken, leaving on those whose lives it spared the hideous traces of its power, turning the babe into a changeling at which the mother shuddered, and making the eyes and cheeks of the betrothed maiden objects of horror to the lover.

—Thomas Babington Macaulay, *History of England*,
Chapter 20, "William and Mary," 1859

4

THE MOST
TERRIBLE MINISTER
OF DEATH

T he word *smallpox* came into usage in late fifteenth-century Europe in order to distinguish it from "the great pox," a new and in some ways similar disease, venereal in nature and known today as syphilis. The nickname was ironic: The virus that causes smallpox is anything but small. At about twice the size of the typical influenza virus, it is a giant among viruses. Its size befits the devastation it wreaked. During its millennia-long rampage it surpassed cholera, bubonic plague, and yellow fever in "time span, number of victims, and geographical coverage."[1] Between 1350 B.C., the date of what is believed to be the earliest recorded description of the disease (in Egyptian papyri), and 1702, "nearly one-tenth of all mankind had been killed, crippled or disfigured" by the disease.[2] (It had also caused an estimated third of all cases of blindness.) During the seventeenth century alone it had killed an average of 400,000 Europeans each year.[3] In one horrific year in Ireland it had wiped out a sixth of the population. In North America, Mexico, and South America, "virgin" populations of indigenous peoples often suffered infection rates in excess of 80 percent.[4]

The first known smallpox epidemic in pre-colonial New England, most likely introduced inadvertently by French explorers from Nova Scotia in 1617, is believed to have reduced the Indian population in New England from as many as thirty thousand to about three hundred.[5] The area most severely affected had so many deaths that survivors were unable to bury all the dead. From that time forward the Indians called it Mattapannock, whose loose translation is "a place where evil is spread about." English settlers changed the name to Dorchester in 1630.[6]

Smallpox began taking its toll on the Puritans even before they set foot in America. Several of the ships carrying the men, women, and children who would become the founders of the Massachusetts Bay Colony developed infections en route from England. The hardest hit of the ships lost fourteen people midvoyage. Three years later, smallpox struck again, this time when an epidemic centered in the Connecticut River Valley spread north. Although Boston and the Massachusetts Bay Colony were affected, the Plymouth Colony suffered the brunt of its lethality. The Pilgrim physician Samuel Fuller, who had come over on the *Mayflower*, was one of its victims. Once again, as in 1619, the area's indigenous peoples suffered catastrophic losses. Of the approximately 1,000 Indians who contracted the disease, more than 950 died. Plymouth governor William Bradford described them covered with smallpox and "cleaving" to their sleeping mats, their skin tearing loose when they were turned over. They died, he wrote, "like rotten sheep."[7]

Smallpox would visit Boston six more times before 1721. One of the worst of those epidemics began across the river in Charlestown in 1677 and infected nearly one out of every four persons, killing upward of seven hundred people out of a total population of four thousand. "Never was it such a time in Boston," wrote a teenaged Cotton Mather, who described the burying places filling quickly, "corpses following each other close at their heels."[8]

Every visitation brought its own particular horrors. Writing about the 1689 epidemic in the first and only issue of his ill-fated newspaper,

Benjamin Harris described the gruesome spectacle of newborn children emerging from the wombs of their uninfected mothers "full of the Distemper." An outbreak in the summer of 1702 had grown so deadly by the "black Month of December" that the government, fearful of mass panic, had limited the ringing of church bells at funerals to "a first and second tolling, each bell not to exceed the space of half of one quarter of an hour."[9]

By that point a pattern had emerged: A new epidemic arrived in Boston approximately every twelve years. According to that formula, the epidemic of 1702 and 1703 should have been followed by one in about 1715. But neither that year nor the five that followed had produced the expected outbreak. Some people said that the measles epidemic of 1713 had taken the place of smallpox—that God had decided the measles deaths were punishment enough and had mercifully canceled the smallpox visitation, resetting the clock so that another twelve years would elapse before it returned. Given their abject helplessness in the face of the disease, it was as useful a way as any to look at it. The alternative was to see the entire generation that had come of age in the nearly two decades since the last epidemic as fuel for the inevitable conflagration, a mountain of dry kindling ripe for a spark.

5

HIS MAJESTY'S SHIP
SEAHORSE

The first decades of the eighteenth century were "the golden age of piracy." From 1716 to 1726, approximately 4,000 pirates terrorized trade routes in the West Indies and along the Atlantic coast of North America and the western coast of Africa.[1] By 1721 pirates had succeeded well enough in hampering English trade that the Crown had made their capture and prosecution a priority. That year lay in the middle of a ten-year period during which at least 450 pirates were hanged in England and its colonies and outposts. In Boston, an executed pirate's gibbeted body was attached to a post on tiny Bird Island, about a mile offshore, where it was left to rot in plain view of incoming ships. The message of this "Profitable and Serviceable Spectacle" was plain.[2] The town had a zero tolerance policy toward piracy.

One of the vessels the Crown had commissioned in its ongoing battle against the buccaneers was the HMS *Seahorse*, a "sixth rate ship" or frigate with a single deck, twenty guns capable of firing lead balls weighing about six pounds, and a crew of approximately 120 men. It was considerably smaller than the biggest of the ships of the line that lumbered into position for major naval battles with more than one hundred guns on three decks and crews of up to 800 men. But its speed and maneuverability were essential for chasing pirates, something its captain was obsessed with. Thirty-six-year-old Thomas Durrell, who for years had commanded a fourteen-gun sloop, finally had a ship capable of taking the fight to the enemy. But within a year of receiving its command he had been ordered to Boston, the Crown's third most active seaport (and the busiest outside of England), where, as the town's "station ship," the *Seahorse*'s primary duty would be defensive: providing a protective escort for merchant convoys sailing routes where pirates lurked. Durrell would be permitted to engage the enemy only to stave off an attack on the convoy or when he was between convoys. Even then, his search-and-destroy missions would be limited to the general vicinity of Boston Harbor. For a man as aggressive and single-mindedly focused on military action as Durrell, the posting was a profound disappointment.

Dutifully he set sail from England early in August 1720, arriving in Boston October 11 after a stop in New York to deliver that colony's new royal governor, William Burnet. His dissatisfaction with his new job was evident in the impatient tone of a notice he placed in the *Boston Gazette* six weeks later. It declared that he would sail for Barbados on December 20, taking with him "all such Ships and Vessels as will then be ready and desirous to sail," and seemed to suggest that he would not wait so much as an extra day for stragglers. His peevishness was more conspicuous in a companion notice ordering his crew to "immediately repair on board to their duty, as they will answer to the contrary."[3] No doubt the threatening tone was, in part, a reaction to the rash of desertions that had struck the *Seahorse* following its arrival in Boston. But it also hinted at why the captain had trouble holding on to a crew. Strict and imperious, Durrell had a style of command that was effective in battle—over the course of his career he would score several noteworthy naval victories, including the single-handed capture of the *Princesa*, one of the biggest ships afloat, in

1740. But he was precisely the kind of martinet whose excess of authority helped create the very high seas outlaws he was determined to eliminate. In any case, his stern public threat in the *Gazette* failed to stem the tide of desertions. He continued to lose crew members so that by his declared departure date he found himself down twenty-three men, all but three of whom had deserted.[4]

The announcement of *Seahorse*'s December 20 departure continued to run as late as December 19, when its captain apparently conceded that he didn't have the manpower to sail. The ship remained in port until January 6, 1721, the fifteenth birthday of James Franklin's apprentice. It might have been that young Benjamin, facing the unhappy prospect of six more birthdays shackled to his brother and Boston, watched the man-of-war glide toward the mouth of the harbor with a stab of longing and envy. Little did he or anyone else know that it was embarking upon a voyage that would result in the deaths of at least half a dozen crew members and nearly cost the life of every man aboard.

The trip south was routine—too routine for Captain Durrell. Soon after the ship reached Barbados on January 27, he traded out part of his crew for eighty-six armed soldiers and headed immediately for open water, "heaving hard" in search of pirates reputed to be lurking in the area.[5] Having drawn a bead on an enemy ship, he launched an all-out pursuit, ignoring signs of worsening weather and sailing the *Seahorse* into the teeth of a storm so vicious that it snapped the ship's rigging and nearly toppled its masts. Two deaths recorded in the ship's log in February were probably casualties of the storm and the captain's reckless zeal. For Durrell, though, the real tragedy seems to have been that the pirates had been permitted to escape.

The *Seahorse* limped back to Barbados where, for the better part of the next month, it underwent patchwork repairs to make it seaworthy enough to complete the voyage back to its home port. When it set sail late in March it was ten sailors short of the number it had arrived with. In addition to the two men lost in the storm, eight were unaccounted for. The ship lost another sailor on March 30, shortly after it had gotten under way. As in the case of the sailors who had died in February, no cause of death was listed in the ship's logs.[6]

APRIL 20 WAS the day Governor Shute had designated for the province's traditional New Year's fast. (According to the Julian or Old Style calendar still technically in use at the time, New Year's Day was March 25.) On that Thursday the people of Boston gathered in their churches and prayed for God's mercy in the year to come. Now, with the royal governor off in New Hampshire and the General Court in recess, there was a lull in the havoc of the past few months and it seemed possible, if not entirely likely, that God would answer those prayers. For the moment, at least, the snarling specter of disaster seemed to have turned from them to other peoples in other parts of the world. The newspapers reported that a massive earthquake had "swallowed up" entire towns in China; that pirates were running amok in Bermuda, the West Indies, and Newfoundland; and that the plague, which since the previous year had been ravaging much of Europe, especially Poland and France, was abating in Marseilles, active in Aix, and threatening Lyons.[7]

Bostonians had been following that epidemic closely for months, with the newspapers offering lurid details of its deadly rampage. It was "impossible to express the Desolation of Marseilles," the *Gazette* had reported, "where the Plague rages more and more, and carries off above a hundred People every Day." Other reports described the effects of the disease— "Gangrenous Inflammations in all the lower parts of the Belly, Breast, and Neck"—and its lightning-quick lethality, its ability to render the afflicted "well and dead in twenty-four hours."[8] The exotic nature of the plague contributed to the fascination; it remained one of the few deadly distempers that had yet to touch their town. What little they knew of it came through reports like these and mostly secondhand accounts of the London epidemic of 1665 and 1666, which had claimed nearly one hundred thousand lives. But that fascination was also fed by a real, if unspoken, fear.

Although the Navigation Acts forbade non-British imports, contraband French commodities regularly infiltrated the town. As the horrors of the plague epidemic continued in France, concern was growing that imports from the infected areas, smuggled in under the noses of the British customs officials, would prove a conduit for its eventual delivery to Boston.

Focused on a potential threat from that unfamiliar contagion, the town seems to have underestimated—or perhaps missed entirely—a far more imminent threat from a deadly disease it knew all too well. The first warning came on April 13, when the *Boston News-Letter* reported that an outbreak of smallpox in London had killed Earl Stanhope and seriously stricken Lord Sunderland and Secretary Craggs (the man who had penned some of the most scathing criticisms of Samuel Shute's administrative failures).[9] Considering how regularly cargo and passengers from the English capital arrived in Boston, that information alone ought to have caused customs officials to increase their vigilance. But it was another warning four days later that should have sounded an alarm. A brief dispatch buried on the back page of that day's *Boston News-Letter* announced that a Rhode Island sea captain recently returned from the Caribbean had witnessed a "very Mortal" outbreak of smallpox on Barbados, one that was killing "20 or 30 Persons" every day.[10]

Although by that point the first ships in the convoy Thomas Durrell was escorting back from the infected area had already arrived in Boston Harbor, most or all of them had yet to dock. There was still time for the authorities to order a rigorous inspection of the ships known to have made Barbados their port of call. But even if such an inspection had taken place it probably would not have extended to the *Seahorse*, which, because of its connection to the Royal Navy, was under no obligation to submit to the authority of the water bailiff.

The *Seahorse* was anchored offshore and waiting to dock on April 20 when it lost another crew member, a Boston man named Samuel Gregory.[11] The cause of death was almost certainly smallpox. With the disease active aboard his ship and his arrival at Long Wharf imminent, Captain Durrell was legally obligated to protect the public on the mainland from infection by setting a course for the pest house on Spectacle Island and quarantining his ship there. But when he finally weighed anchor two days later he sailed to Castle Island instead. Located about two miles offshore, the island was dominated by a quadrangular fortress that was built of large, squared stone and served as an unofficial English military base. (In 1689 the Bostonians deposing royal governor Edmund Andros had demanded that he surrender the "Castle" to them.) Officially, Durrell's reason for docking there was his desire to get repairs going on his ship while he waited for room to open up on Long Wharf. But the island also gave him a friendly refuge from excessive scrutiny if not a de facto military immunity. It was the perfect way to hide bad news from Boston officials.

FOR ONE REASON or another, fifteen-year-old Charles Paxton, one of the newer members of the *Seahorse* crew, had asked to remain behind in Boston during the ship's voyage to Barbados. Despite his difficulties assembling and keeping a full crew, Captain Durrell had granted the favor, probably because Charles's father, Wentworth Paxton, was a former naval captain who had once commanded a smaller version of the HMS *Seahorse*. A condition of the leave was that Paxton rejoin the crew as soon as they arrived in Boston. One day after the *Seahorse* docked at Castle Island, Charles and one of his family's African servants loaded his gear into a small boat and headed out to the ship. After transferring Charles's belongings to his quarters and perhaps socializing with other black men aboard, the servant returned to shore. In all likelihood he took a few of his young master's crewmates with him—men who were anxious to enjoy their hard-won shore leave and perhaps just as anxious to escape the sickness festering below the deck of their ship. They were not alone. During the ship's five-day stay at Castle Island, shipmates of Charles Paxton continued to shuttle into Boston, so that by the time the *Seahorse* made the short trip from the island to the end of Long Wharf, arriving late in the afternoon on April 27, upward of two dozen members of its crew were already walking the streets of Boston.

6

PESTILENCE AND POLITICS

When Samuel Shute returned from New Hampshire on April 30, Thomas Durrell was waiting for him. The captain informed the governor that a pirate ship had been spotted near Tarpaulin Cove at the base of Cape Cod and asked for permission to go after it. Since the *Seahorse* was still unfit for battle, he needed to fit out a merchant sloop with guns. Shute granted his request and two days later the improvised warship set sail in pursuit of the renegades. Its crew was comprised of about fifty sailors from the *Seahorse* and that ship's second-in-command, Lieutenant Andrew Hamilton. Why the pirate-obsessed Durrell remained behind, passing up what was for him an all-too-rare opportunity for military glory, is unknown. He might have considered command of the small, makeshift warship beneath his dignity. Or it might have been that the nagging trouble belowdecks on the *Seahorse* had made it necessary for him to take care of matters in Boston.

The lead story in the May 8 *Boston Gazette* was another plague update from France. In the overwhelmed infirmaries of Aix, fifty persons had died nearly every day for a month. It was believed by some, the paper reported, that the "violency of the Distemper" corresponded with the phases of the moon. Others claimed that a cure had been found in the form of "a particular sort of Girdle." Locally, the big news was that a free black man named Joseph had been convicted of "Barbarously Murdering his Wife" and had been sentenced to death.[1]

While Boston newspaper readers discussed the fate of that black man, the town's selectmen were meeting in an emergency, closed-door session to discuss the condition of two others, both of whom, they were informed, had been discovered sick with smallpox. The identity and whereabouts of one man was unclear—he was identified only as "a Certain Negro man" who "came from Tertudos in His Majesties Ship Seahorse." The other was described as a servant of Captain Wentworth Paxton; he was the same black man, it would soon become clear, who had transported Paxton's son to the *Seahorse*. The selectmen ordered him quarantined in the family home and provided with a "sutable" [*sic*] nurse. They also ordered that no person be allowed into the sickroom without their permission. To enforce that order, "two prudent persons" would be commissioned to stand guard at the doors of the house. And then, because it appeared "very likly" [*sic*] that smallpox was present aboard the warship, they voted to ask Dr. John Clark to conduct an inspection "and Report in what State of Health or Sickness the Ships Company are in."[2] No additional measures were deemed necessary. With Paxton's servant quarantined and the other black man presumed to have returned to his ship, the spread of the disease appeared to have been checked. Issuing a public alert or conducting a search for additional victims would only generate panic and unnerve trading partners. Six months earlier the decision to keep the discovery of smallpox aboard a merchant vessel captained by John Gore a secret had spared Bostonians needless fear and probably a false embargo that would have devastated the town's already teetering trade-based economy. Now, as then, the disease had been detected early and the afflicted had been located. There was every reason to believe that once again disaster had been averted.

• • •

THE FIRST PRIORITY of the May 12 Boston town meeting was politics, not public health. After choosing Elisha Cooke moderator, the freeholders elected him, John Clark, and William Clark—all Popular Party men—to the House of Representatives. The final seat, vacated by the death of Oliver Noyes, went to a thirty-eight-year-old newcomer named William Hutchinson. It was remarkable for any man not named Cooke to be elected into provincial politics before age forty; Hutchinson's early elevation to the highest level of public service suggests that he was a political prodigy. His relative, the future Massachusetts royal governor Thomas Hutchinson, who was just a boy at the time of William's election to the House, described his political genius as a natural ability to "moderate the passions of those who were less temperate" rather than "encouraging the same extremities himself."[3] But if Thomas Hutchinson was right that William was a consensus builder—a different kind of politician from the "less temperate" Elisha Cooke—he was wrong in going on to claim that William was wholly independent from the Popular Party leader. By 1721 Cooke had a lock on Boston politics and would not have permitted Noyes's seat to be filled by anyone who was less than fully loyal to his political philosophy. Still, the election of a young man well liked by everyone and inclined to build bridges rather than burn them offered hope that a spirit of cooperation might ultimately return to the government.

The entire morning session passed without any mention of smallpox. When the afternoon session commenced at three o'clock, political business again took precedence. A committee was created to draw up instructions for the town's House members to take into the General Court session scheduled to begin May 31. The town had done something similar on a few previous occasions, instructing its representatives how to vote on questions pertaining specifically to Boston. But this would prove to be something different. When the committee reported back to the town, it would be with instructions that went far beyond the geographical boundaries of Boston, touching upon virtually every major issue facing the province. The idea, explained historian G. B. Warden, was for Cooke to harness the town meeting as "a means of attracting popular support and justifying his political attacks on the Dudleys as a popular mandate."[4] The all-encompassing instructions constituted nothing less than the first modern political platform in Massachusetts history.

With the political questions settled, John Clark was summoned to report on the health situation aboard the *Seahorse*. The news was not good. The master's log and the ship's paybook, he told the officials and townspeople in attendance, contained a number of unexplained deaths—including, most recently, of Able Seaman John Dunn, who had died aboard ship a few days after it had docked at Long Wharf—but no record of smallpox. His search of the ship's quarters, however, had revealed two men in the throes of smallpox and another who appeared to be suffering its onset. What he had subsequently discovered, but seems to have withheld from the public at this juncture, was that "sundry others"—some unspecified number of the approximately forty-three *Seahorse* crew members walking the streets of Boston—were also infected with smallpox.[5]

Now that the *Seahorse* had been shown to be the source of the smallpox cases, quarantine was the logical next step. The selectmen were instructed to ask the governor to "Call a Councell in Order to Advise about the Sea-horse man of war, being Sent down to Spectacle Island."[6]

That meeting took place the same day behind closed doors and off the record. By the time it was over the plan to send the *Seahorse* to Spectacle Island had been replaced by one to withdraw the ship only as far as Bird Island, about a mile offshore. The change was legally significant. An order to withdraw the ship to the quarantine station would have formalized its status as diseased and would have opened its captain to charges of knowingly transporting a pestilence to the town, a crime punishable by a fine of £50 or a jail term of six months. It's possible that Thomas Durrell, conscious of that possibility, had moved to preempt it over the course of the two days following Dr. Clark's inspection of his ship. On

May 10, one day after that inspection, he had discharged three members of his crew as "Unserviceable" without elaborating. They were probably the same three men, noted Jennifer Lee Carrell, that Clark had discovered sick with smallpox.[7] Having effectively erased evidence of infection aboard his ship, Durrell might well have gone to the governor (with whom he would subsequently develop a close friendship) and convinced him to resist any attempt to formally quarantine the *Seahorse*, appealing to him as a fellow Englishman and military man. Certainly Durrell's preemptive appeal to Shute would explain why the governor balked at the town's reasonable and logical request that the ship be moved to the official quarantine station. Pressured by the selectmen—and perhaps by his conscience—he had ultimately gone partway, ordering the ship removed to Bird Island as a means of assuaging the fears of Bostonians while sparing Durrell exposure to legal retribution for his irresponsibility.

Durrell's narrow escape from official culpability left him neither contrite nor even temporarily humbled. Offended at the imputation that his ship had brought smallpox to Boston, adamant that no cases of the disease had ever been present below its deck, and resentful over being importuned with its removal from Long Wharf, he refused to provide a crew for the ship's relocation to Bird Island. It was left to the harbor pilot, Timothy Clark, to round up an ad hoc crew, a task complicated by the need to find men who had already survived smallpox and who therefore could board the infected ship without fear of contracting the disease.

It took Clark two days to put a crew together. By then it was Sunday. Under normal circumstances, the ban on performing work during the Sabbath would have postponed the ship's removal until the next day. But spurred by the death of another *Seahorse* crew member, Gunner's Mate Joseph May, officials made an exception. While most of Boston prayed, Timothy Clark and his crew sailed the *Seahorse* to Bird Island. Shortly after the move, Captain Durrell vented his resentment by hiring a trumpeter for the ship and ordering him to play the instrument at times most likely to disturb or offend the people on shore. This act of defiance and contempt would continue far beyond the three weeks the *Seahorse* spent in unofficial quarantine. Three years after the trumpeter's hiring, Samuel Sewall would finally confront Durrell, inform him that the practice was "offensive," and demand that it be stopped.[8]

The infected ship had been at Bird Island for eight days when the *Boston News-Letter* presented the first public statement by the authorities since smallpox had surfaced two weeks earlier. The paper reported that "a strict search and enquiry of the Inhabitants at their respective Houses" by a team of government officials including selectmen, judges, constables, and overseers of the poor had "found none Sick of that Distemper, but a Negro Man at the House of Capt. Paxton near the South Battery, being the House that was first visited therewith," adding that the servant was "almost recovered" and would be removed to Spectacle Island in a day or two.[9] A town meeting held that day concerned itself almost entirely with the report of the committee tasked with formulating instructions for Boston's provincial representatives. Of the ten instructions approved by the voters that day, the most striking authorized the deputies to "vindicate this People from any unjust aspersions that are or may be cast upon them" and to prevent the passage of any bills that attempted to encroach upon their liberties under the pretense of protecting public safety—a response to Shute's insinuation at the close of the last session that the people of Boston were "inclined to Riots & Tumults." Another instruction, which called for the Boston deputies to "promote some further Law Effectually to enable the Select men of Each Town, to prevent the Spreading of any Infectious Sickness among them," might have been the beginning of an attempt to wrest from the royal governor the authority to send ships into quarantine.[10] Conspicuously absent from the minutes of the meeting was any mention of the "Infectious Sickness" already afflicting the town. It might have been that authorities believed that the notice published earlier that day sufficed. It's at least as likely, though, that they had resolved to steer clear of the topic because they knew the situation was not as secure as that notice claimed. Two days later the selectmen would order that a contingent of free black men and Indians be dispatched to clean "the Streets & Lanes within this Town" in order to "prevent the Smal pox Spreading."[11] (One theory about the disease was that it was caused by a miasma of "invisible particles released into the air from putrefying animal or vegetable matter, or from noxious or poisonous objects," all of which, along with raw sewage, were plentiful in the drains and gutters of the town's thoroughfares.)[12] It's hard to imagine that an undertaking so comprehensive would have been authorized had officials been confident that only one man had been afflicted. Indeed, just one week after the appearance of the newspaper article insisting that the Paxton servant was the only person ill, both newspapers delivered ominous news. The *Gazette* reported:

> There are now Eight Persons sick of the Small Pox in the Town and no more according to the best information; one in Bennets-Street, at the North-End, Three in Treamount-Street, Two in School-Street, one in Battery-March, and one in Winter-Street.[13]

The announcement of eight new cases was shocking. But the worst news was the geographic distribution of those cases. Bennett Street sat just beyond the shadow of Mather's church in the North End. Treamount Street, the location of the highest concentration of the sick, was a little more than half a mile to its south. The southernmost end of that street intersected with School Street, whose two cases brought the pestilence closer to the center of town. Winter Street was about an eighth of a mile south of there. Battery March, which extended west from the town's southern waterfront battery, was nowhere near any of the other streets. The implication was unavoidable: There was no one completely removed from the danger. At least one active case of smallpox was present in every part of the town.

•   •   •

TWENTY OF THE ninety-seven members of the Massachusetts House were absent when the General Court assembled on the final day of May. Fear of smallpox contagion seems to have been responsible for the high number of no-shows. The deputies in attendance wanted out as quickly as possible. Before the first day of the session was over they had appointed a committee to ask the governor to move the proceedings to Cambridge, "by reason of several People in Boston, are visited with the Small Pox."[14] They were not so preoccupied by smallpox or frightened of infection, however, that they refrained from challenging—some might say *provoking*—Shute. One of their first acts was to seat the newly elected speaker, the Popular Party's John Clark, without waiting for the governor's approval. In rapid succession then, they replaced House clerk John White, whom some considered a lackey of Shute and the Dudleys, and then voted to exclude two of the governor's most stalwart allies, Jonathan Belcher and Lieutenant Governor William Dummer, from the Council. Attempting to deny seats on the board to men Shute clearly wanted as advisors was, as Thomas Hutchinson later described it, "a very extraordinary contempt of the governor."[15] Implicit in the governor's authority to exclude men from the Council (a power that no one disputed) was the notion that he had the right to have the Council he desired. Not surprisingly, Shute was apoplectic over this blatant overreach of House authority and declared his intention to shut down the General Court immediately. Once his friends had calmed him down he ordered the House to reinstate Belcher and Dummer in accordance with "the constant method of the General Assembly for Twenty Eight Years last past, and founded on the *Royal Charter*."[16] When they balked, he told them he would refuse to consider their request for a move to a safer venue until they complied. After a short standoff, the deputies capitulated—but only, they told the governor, out of expediency. Considering "the Distemper in the Town, and being desirous the Court should be forthwith Removed to Cambridge," they were "willing to Send up the List after the Usual Form; Saving their Right to Assert their Priviledges at a more convenient time."[17]

With the Council of his liking in place, Shute granted the change of venue and recessed the Court until ten o'clock in the morning on June 6, when business would resume in Cambridge, a neighboring town thus far untouched by smallpox. Despite the irksomeness of the House's nonconcession, he had prevailed. But it had taken his willingness to expose House members to a deadly disease to do it.

AN UNSEASONABLY CHILLY and wet spring had helped tamp down the spread of smallpox by keeping people inside, with their doors and windows shut against the elements. But as May gave way to June the weather warmed. People threw open their windows and emerged from their semi-hibernation to mix more frequently in public. Almost immediately the cases began to multiply. With each passing day another two or three bright red quarantine flags—some bearing the words "God have mercy on this house"—materialized over Boston doorways.[18] With guards stationed outside an increasing number of infected homes, some streets seemed to be under martial law. Five days into the new month the pestilence was near enough to overrunning the Latin School that the selectmen ordered classes moved to the Town House, which was empty due to the General Court recess. For parents who had lived through Boston's last encounter with smallpox, the sense of relief was fleeting. If the distemper continued to spread, the Town House, too, would eventually become infected. There would be no safe harbor in all of Boston.

7

ONESIMUS

In the weeks following the embarrassment of his dedication sermon at the New Brick Church, Cotton Mather sought refuge in his garden, where he took walks and searched for signs of the tardy spring, desiring, he wrote, "to read the Glories of my SAVIOUR in them."[1] The inspiration and rejuvenation he failed to find in the dreary weather and still slumbering garden came to him from a very different and unexpected source. It was "Divine Providence," he wrote, that he was selected to preach the lecture at the hanging of Joseph Hanno, the black man convicted of murdering his wife.[2] Mather had always excelled at the execution sermon; in some respects the high point of his ministerial career remained his very first one, for a murderer named James Morgan, decades earlier. On May 25 both Mather's lecture and Hanno's execution were attended by what the minister described as a "great Assembly."[3] In his diary, he exulted in having made "a good Impression upon the People," especially the "wicked and froward Husbands" and *"Ethiopian Slaves."*[4] (He would later revise "good impression" to "great impression.") The lecture had both "served the cause of Piety" and bolstered his wounded ego.[5]

Mather was conspicuously reenergized when, one day later, he opened his diary, took up his pen, and declared: "The grievous Calamity of the *Small-Pox* has now entered the Town."[6] For the minister to speak with such certainty about a worsening smallpox problem at a time when the official word remained that only one man was sick and safely contained—and with the revelation of eight new cases still three days off—suggests either that he had sniffed out the truth himself or had been vouchsafed inside information, perhaps from his friend the governor or his daughter Elizabeth, who was still at the Clark house and might have overheard the doctor discussing the matter. His first impulse was to exult. Late the previous year, his father, enraged by the disrespect and indignity that had been visited upon his son, the clergy in general, his church, and himself, had issued a scathing jeremiad (also referred to as "an awful sermon") warning that "an heavy judgment was impending over Boston, that would speedily be executed." Early in 1721 Cotton Mather had followed suit with a nearly identical warning, foretelling "the speedy Approach of the destroying Angel."[7] Now the punishment they had predicted (and, in a sense, called down from Heaven) was at hand and their visions had been validated. But Mather quickly chastised himself for his hubris. "It becomes me," he wrote, "to humble myself exceedingly, and ly [lie] in the Dust. Lest the Vanity of mine upon seeing my poor praediction accomplished, should provoke the holy One to do some grievous Thing unto me."[8] Perhaps he remembered that he had at least two children at risk of infection.

But there was more to Mather's excitement than having been proven right about "the destroying angel." For nearly five years he had been waiting for the inevitable return of smallpox to "do good" for his community by proposing what he believed was a surefire way to rob the disease of its lethality. He had stumbled upon it in the summer of 1716, in the same issue of the Royal Society's *Philosophical Transactions* that had contained his very first contribution. The article was titled "An Account, or History, of the Procuring the SMALL POX by Incision, or Inoculation; as It Has for Some Time Been Practised at Constantinople."[9] It had been sent to the Royal Society by Emanuel Timoni, a Greek-born physician who was the son of Italian parents. He had received a university education at Oxford and medical degree in Padua, and he now practiced medicine in Turkey. Timoni described how matter extracted from a smallpox vesicle on the body of a person with a full-blown case of the disease was implanted in a series of incisions cut into the arm of a healthy person, who subsequently developed a mild and nonlethal case of the disease followed by lifelong immunity.

The Timoni article had so excited Mather that almost immediately he had penned a letter to his main correspondent at the Royal Society, John Woodward. Timoni's account had affected him profoundly, he told Woodward, because months earlier he had heard the story of a nearly identical procedure from a very different source—one of his family's slaves. The young African man had been with the family since Mather's congregation had made a present of him in 1708. Mather had named him Onesimus, after the biblical slave who had been converted to Christianity by the imprisoned apostle Paul. The name was the Latinized version of a Greek word meaning "beneficial or profitable."

Mather wrote that he had asked Onesimus, whom he described as "a pretty Intelligent Fellow," whether he had ever had smallpox. Onesimus had answered "both *Yes*, and *No*," going on to explain that as a young boy in Africa he had, in Mather's words, "undergone an Operation, which had given him something of ye *Small-Pox*, & would forever Praeserve him from it." The slave's description of that procedure and the scar Onesimus showed him on his arm, he told Woodward, "made it the same" as the procedure reported by Timonius.[10]

It was bold enough to gush enthusiasm for the claim of a "primitive" African in a letter to an esteemed member of the English medical establishment. But Mather, in his excitement, had gone a step farther, chastising English doctors—and, by extension, the notoriously touchy Woodward—for failing to test inoculation in the mother country, where outbreaks occurred more frequently than in New England. (An epidemic in London in 1710, for example, had killed more than three thousand persons.)[11]

"How does it come to pass," he wrote, "that no more is done to bring this operation into experiment & into Fashion—in England? When there are so many Thousands of People that would give Thousands of Pounds to have ye Danger and Horror of this frightful Disease well over with ym [them]?" Perhaps sensing that he might have pushed his point a little too far, he copped a more obsequious tone, flattering Woodward by comparing him favorably to the towering English physician Thomas Sydenham, the "English Hippocrates" whose "Cool Method" for treating smallpox, devised decades earlier, had boosted survival rates. "I beseech you, syr," he continued, "to move it, and save more Lives than Dr. *Sydenham*." And then he vowed to do likewise if and when circumstances warranted:

> For my own part, if I should live to see ye *Small-Pox* again enter into or [our] City, I would immediately procure a Consult of or [our] physicians, to Introduce a Practise which may be of so very happy a Tendency. But could we hear that you have done it before us, how much would That embolden us![12]

NOW, HAVING DETERMINED that the "grievous calamity" of the smallpox had returned, Mather harkened back to that letter and its vow. "The Practice of conveying and suffering the *Small-pox* by *Inoculation*, has never been used in *America*, nor indeed in our Nation," he wrote in his diary. "But how many Lives might be saved by it, if it were practised? I will procure a Consult of our Physicians, and lay the matter before them."[13] He believed—indeed, he was certain—that he held the secret to stopping a catastrophe. The question was whether anyone would listen to him.

He was realist enough to know that it would take more than his synopsis of the Timoni letter and the corroboration of a solitary black man to overcome the Boston medical community's near-certain skepticism.

At the very least he needed the *Philosophical Transactions*—ideally the volume of collected issues that included both the Timoni letter and another, more recent account of successful inoculations by a physician named Giacomo Pylarini. For whatever reason, Mather had no copies of the journal in his library. Indeed, in all of Boston—and, as far as Mather knew, all of Massachusetts—there was only one copy of the issue in question. That copy belonged to Dr. William Douglass.

Mather and Douglass had met in 1716, shortly after the then–twenty-five-year-old Scotsman arrived in Boston. The young physician's cocksure haughtiness and intellectual arrogance, and his habit of comparing Boston unfavorably with London and the great cities of Europe (he wasn't in town long before some Bostonians pegged him as "a snarler"), had caused the minister to develop a dislike for him.[14] More recently, he had also come to distrust Douglass for his friendship with Boston's most radical anti-Puritan, the Anglican evangelist John Checkley, who, Mather was convinced, was bent on making the Church of England the official state religion of the colony. Douglass was just as disdainful of Mather. He resented what he considered the minister's pretensions as a medical man and scientist, his boastfulness over his Royal Society membership and laughable contributions to the organization's journal, and his chronic meddling in politics. He tolerated Mather because he remained a powerful personage with a connection to the governor. Mather tolerated him because he was the most credentialed physician in Boston—the only one to have received university training and earned an "M.D." after his name—and because he let the minister borrow the occasional book from his sizable medical library.

Mather didn't tell Douglass why he wanted to borrow volume XXIX, number 347 of the *Philosophical Transactions of the Royal Society*. The doctor loaned it to him without asking; probably he assumed that the vain minister simply wanted to linger lovingly over one of his published observations—what Mather called his "Curiosa Americana." With the book in hand, Mather had the most compelling evidence for inoculation he could hope to offer the medical community. Four days after stating his intention to approach the town's physicians, however, he had yet to act. On June 2 he resolved to ask the ministers to turn the following Thursday's lecture day "into a Day of Prayer, that we may prepare to meet our God."[15] But he remained silent on inoculation. It's possible that, having predicted (and fairly welcomed) God's wrath against Boston a few months earlier, he now wondered whether sparing anyone, even his own children, constituted a sinful defiance of God's will. In his diary he agonized over whether he should send his son Sammy and daughter Elizabeth out of town to escape possible infection. At the same time, though, he was making forays into the town's African community, searching for corroboration of the efficacy of inoculation. When those inquiries turned up at least half a dozen persons who bore inoculation-type scars and the story of having had smallpox implanted in their skin "while they were yet in Barbary," he began drafting an argument and an appeal for an inoculation experiment.[16]

The underlying premise of Mather's appeal was that if inoculation seemed drastic (as he knew it would) the far more drastic consequences of the spreading smallpox outbreak warranted its trial. The problem—one of them, anyway—was that the town's newspapers were still minimizing the threat. On June 5, the same day that the town announced the Latin School's move to the Town House, the *Boston News-Letter* nonchalantly declared that there had been "but one Person taken Sick of the Small Pox since Saturday last, and those that were then Visited with that Distemper are all in a likely way to recover, most of them being up and about in their Chambers."[17] But readers must have noticed that the newspaper's reassuring line did not convince the Massachusetts General Court to cancel its plans to relocate out of Boston.

The next day, as the House and Council resumed business across the river in Cambridge, Mather delivered two handwritten copies of his finished address to Nathaniel Williams, who was both a physician and the headmaster of the school near the epicenter of the burgeoning outbreak. Neither copy survives. But the historian George Lyman Kittredge believed that most of the letter's content can be extrapolated from later

Mather books and pamphlets. "There has been a *Wonderful Practice* lately used in Several Parts of the World which indeed is not yet common in or Nation," Mather likely began, going on to explain that he had been "first instructed in it" by his "*Guramantee*-Servant [Onesimus]" who, he wrote, "shewed me the Scar of the Wound made for the Operation; and said, That no Person ever died of the Small-pox in their Countrey that had the Courage to use it." Mather had since met with "a considerable Number of these *Africans*" whose testimony he attempted to re-create exactly, utilizing their patois for authenticity. The "Juice" of smallpox had been placed in a cut in their skin, making them "a little Sicky, Sicky" but keeping them from dying. "Thus in *Africa*," Mather wrote:

> where the Poor Creatures dy of the Small-Pox like Rotten Sheep, a Merciful GOD has taught them an *Infallible Praeservative*. Tis a common Practice, and is attended with a *Constant Success*.[18]

Next he probably offered a description of the procedure according to the "learned Foreigners" Timoni and Pylarini.[19] Twelve or thirteen days into a case of naturally acquired smallpox, a needle was used to prick some of the larger sores on the body of "as Healthy a Young Person as they can find." The fluid from those pustules was deposited into a vessel that had been washed "very clean" with warm water. The container was sealed with a stopper and carried close to the body for warmth as it was transported to the chamber of the person awaiting inoculation. The operation began with two or more cuts, each deep enough to draw a trickle of blood, in the arm of the subject. Next, a "drop" of the smallpox matter was inserted into each wound and mixed with the blood pooling there. The wounds were covered with part of a walnut shell or some other concave object secured in place so that "the matter may not be rubbed off by the garments, for a Few Hours."[20] Usually the incisions ran with pus for several days without complication, and the few smallpox that came out—generally no more than ten or twenty, although some persons had as many as one hundred and others had none—dried quickly, the scabs falling off without leaving a permanent mark. Timoni, Mather wrote, had seen this procedure performed "on Persons of all *Ages*, both Sexes, differing *Temperaments*, and Even in the Worst Constitution of the *Air*," and maintained that no one had died of it, while nearly half of those infected in the "common" way succumbed to the disease.[21] Moreover, the inoculated were "hardly sensible of any Sickness" and had no scars or pits in their skin from the slight outbreak. The procedure's "*Happy Success* on Thousands of Persons for Eight Years," he wrote, had "putt [*sic*] it out of all Suspicion."[22] Pylarini's account varied from Timoni's only in the number and placement of incisions; he had witnessed success with a single incision in the arm, the same method described by the Boston Africans. He also reported that a harmless sprinkling of inoculated pocks usually appeared on the seventh day after the operation. Initially a skeptic himself, Pylarini had become convinced of the operation's safety and efficacy after years of observation and insisted that it had come to be accepted by everyone "except here and there a few *Cowards* that are afraid of their *Shadows*."[23]

The minister concluded with his own endorsement and an appeal that an inoculation experiment "be WARILY proceeded in." The next step, as he saw it, was for the Boston doctors to meet and consult so that "whoever first begins the practice, (*if you Approve it should be begun at all*) may have the countenance of his worthy Brethren to fortify him in it."[24]

Mather asked Dr. Williams to read the letter himself and then to arrange for it to be circulated among his colleagues—Doctors Clark, Cutler, Cooke, Archibald, Gibbins, Boylston, White, Steward, Halkerston, and Perkins—and perhaps a few prominent apothecaries as well. The second copy was to go directly to William Douglass. Mather might have hoped that the act of gratuitous flattery would assuage the physician's possible resentment over a minister's meddling in medical affairs. Probably his main reason for giving Douglass his own copy, though, was to indemnify the initiative against the even greater possibility that the incensed Scotsman would destroy the letter before the rest of his colleagues could read it.

8

THE EXPERIMENT

On June 10 Boston bathed in the light of a full moon. William Douglass later wrote that sometime between that day and the gibbous moon four days later the smallpox, which had been "skulking about" for many weeks, exploded.[1] Within two weeks the disease had spread to so many households in different areas of Boston that the authorities abandoned their attempt to contain it, removing the guards who had been posted at homes flying the red quarantine flag. There was a rush of evacuees, mostly well-off Bostonians who had the money and leisure to relocate themselves and their families to the still-uninfected countryside for weeks or months until the town was safe again. They numbered about one thousand. The remaining ten thousand inhabitants hunkered down, cowed by a sense of approaching catastrophe. Mather spoke for many of them when, on June 20, he wrote: "Oh! what shall I do, that my family may be prepared, for the Visitation that is now every day to be expected!" In his neighborhood several cases had appeared almost spontaneously. His son Sammy, who was due to return to Harvard, was afraid to leave the house, and his daughter Elizabeth was "in greater Fears" than her brother.[2]

The newspapers continued to understate the magnitude of the crisis. One week after its overly upbeat assessment of the situation on June 5, the *News-Letter* made no mention of smallpox. On June 19, while evacuees streamed from the town, it referenced the epidemic only tangentially, concluding its report of the accidental drowning death of Dr. James Halkerston, a onetime master surgeon for the Royal Navy who had established a practice in Boston five years earlier, by commenting that his loss was "At this Conjunction much Lamented because [he] may be much wanted in case the Small Pox (a Distemper generally fatal to New-England) should prevail." Halkerston's demise was one of several strange or sensationalistic Boston deaths—"remarkable Providences" they were called—that the newspaper lumped together in what seems to have been an effort to distract readers from the spreading pestilence. Perhaps on the theory that nothing diverts attention from bad news like more bad news, the newspaper also resurrected the specter of the now-infamous South Sea Bubble, whose bursting had wreaked economic disaster on England the previous year. It reported that a British official named John Aislabie had been convicted and imprisoned for using his government position to scheme the artificial inflation of the value of the South Sea Company's stock "with a View to his own Exorbitant Profit," thereby helping to bring misery to "great Numbers of His Majesty's Subjects, and the Ruin of the Publick Credit and the Trade of this Kingdom."[3]

Two weeks after he had delivered his address to the physicians, Mather was still waiting for a response. On or about June 21 he approached John Perkins, who practiced in the area of the North Church, and offered to "recommend him unto the Use of the Neighborhood, in the Calamity of the Small-pox coming upon us," if he would confide what he knew about the status of the inoculation proposal.[4] The news was not good. Although the address or some synopsis of it had been communicated to most or all of the doctors, Perkins told him, William Douglass had rejected it and had effectively preempted discussion of its merits.

Mather was disappointed but not deterred. His first inclination was to rework the letter into a pamphlet, "a little Treatise on the *Small-Pox*" he called it, and distribute it widely in the hope that public pressure would force the recalcitrant physicians to act.[5] When he completed a draft on June 22, though, he thought better of it. A direct challenge to the authority of the physicians might backfire, causing them to dig in their heels against the practice simply out of professional conceit. Instead, he drafted a new letter. This time he narrowed down the list of recipients to a few doctors he believed most likely to receive it fairly and openly and personalized it for each. Although this letter, too, has been lost, it likely offered to show the physicians the relevant volume of the *Philosophical Transactions*, which was still in his possession, William Douglass having apparently decided that since he had quashed the minister's crackbrained inoculation scheme there was no pressing need to reclaim it.

Douglass changed his mind the moment he learned about the new letter. He sent a note or perhaps a messenger to the minister's Ship Street house with a demand that the journal be surrendered immediately. By June 23 it was back in his home, where it would remain under symbolic lock and key for the remainder of the epidemic, off-limits to everyone who asked to see it, even, several months later, the royal governor.

None of the new letter's recipients responded immediately. And then on the evening of June 23 or the morning of June 24, the minister received a reply from a man who, although successful as a general physician and an apothecary (he owned the biggest shop in Boston), was best known as a surgeon. In 1718 Zabdiel Boylston had performed the first recorded mastectomy in American history, saving a woman's life by amputating her cancerous breast.[6] The forty-two-year-old doctor asked to see everything Mather had to recommend inoculation. As quickly as he was able, the minister gathered his notes, copied them, and forwarded them, along with a note calculated to ingratiate. "*You* are many ways endeared unto me, but by nothing more than the very good which a gracious God employs you and honours you to do to a miserable world," Mather began. It was a "testimony" of his "respect and esteem" for Boylston that he was providing him with all the information he had. The doctor's decision to attempt the procedure, he wrote, might "save many lives that we set a great value on. . . . But see, think, judge; do as the Lord our healer Shall direct you."[7]

Mather's familiar, almost affectionate, letter must have struck Boylston as odd inasmuch as the two men, although not strangers, had no history whatsoever. The fact that one of Boylston's closest friends was Mather's onetime nemesis, the Brattle Street Church's minister, Benjamin Colman, had precluded a friendship. Mather knew Boylston chiefly by reputation—as the surgeon who, in addition to boldly (some said cruelly and irresponsibly) cutting off a woman's diseased breast, had removed stones from the bladders of several children, all of whom had survived (a small miracle in an era when post-operative infection killed many of those who managed to survive the shock and pain of surgeries performed without anesthesia). He was also somewhat infamous for charging higher fees than his colleagues and for bringing suit against any patient who failed to pay his bill. But the doctor's willingness to entertain an appeal from outside the medical community—especially after all of his fellow doctors had either rejected that appeal or been bullied out of considering it by Dr. Douglass—had automatically endeared him to Mather. His charm offensive was also calculated: Although Boylston's enthusiasm for performing surgeries (which, during this era of medicine, many gentlemen physicians eschewed as manual labor and therefore beneath their dignity) and lack of a Harvard degree had, in the minds of many, relegated him to the second tier of Boston practitioners, he was known to have a high opinion of his own ability. Mather's letter, noted the doctor's biographer, "played on his vanity and appealed to his daring."[8]

THE NEXT DAY was the Sabbath. As always, Cotton Mather was in the pulpit. Boylston seems to have spent the day researching inoculation as thoroughly as circumstances permitted—reading what Mather had provided, interviewing some or all of the Africans who had related their experience with the procedure, and perhaps even visiting William Douglass in a failed attempt to gain access to the original Timoni and Pylarini accounts in the *Philosophical Transactions*. Without access to those articles, though, he found himself essentially where he had started, wholly dependent upon the word of African slaves and a minister who had a long history of mistaking the truth or twisting it to his purposes. And even if Mather's interpretation of the *Philosophical Transactions* was entirely accurate to the original, Boylston was still putting his faith in practitioners of Greek folk medicine. The notion of giving someone a disease in order to save him from dying of that disease was so preposterous that every other doctor in Boston had refused to discuss it. Then again, the same men had believed that it was impossible to stop a cancer by cutting it from the body.

Nearly three weeks had passed since Mather's first address to the physicians. At that point he had advised them to proceed "warily" in an inoculation experiment. Now the increasing pace of the infection's spread made caution an unaffordable luxury. Death was closing in on nearly every family in Boston, Boylston's included. One hundred and fifty years before the acceptance of germ theory, there was, to put it mildly, only a vague sense of what caused disease. But nearly everyone accepted that somehow smallpox was transmitted from person to person. Boylston and his wife had survived earlier epidemics and were immune. But their six children—three boys and three girls—were all vulnerable; and with Boylston's increasing visits to the chambers of the sick there was an increasing probability that he would carry the infection home to them. The writer Jennifer Lee Carrell believes that his instinctive and somewhat obsessive emphasis on cleanliness (one reason for the better-than-average survival rate of his surgical patients) might have helped protect his children during the early days of the epidemic: She speculated that after visiting infected patients he had taken precautions to cleanse himself by changing clothes and scrubbing his body.[9] Still, it was just a matter of time before he or someone else inadvertently caused his children to be infected. Not long before he had received Mather's second letter he had sent his wife and their girls, aged nine, eight, and four, out of Boston to the comparative safety of Roxbury, where they planned to wait out the danger at the home of Boylston's brother. The boys, though, had remained behind. Fourteen-year-old Zabdiel Jr. was attending college in Cambridge, where no cases of the disease had been reported, and was in no immediate danger. But the same could not be said for thirteen-year-old John, who probably ran the family's apothecary shop in his mother's absence, or six-year-old Thomas, who had been left with his father and brother simply, it appears, because there was no room for him in the country. It was clear that if Boylston hoped to do something to safeguard the lives of his sons he would need to act soon, before the infection found them.

Late that Sunday evening he sent a message to Cotton Mather informing him that he had decided to make an inoculation experiment. Since time was of the essence, he had resolved to act immediately. Early the next morning he would gather smallpox matter from an afflicted patient and implant it in the skin of three healthy subjects. One of them, he had determined, would be his youngest son.

THE PROCEDURE BOYLSTON had decided to attempt was not new. In one form or another it had existed since at least AD 1000, when the Chinese had procured immunity by snorting finely ground smallpox scabs through a thin, hollow tube made of bone. In parts of Asia, Asia Minor, and northern Africa, smallpox scabs had been swallowed rather than snorted. In Russia, the method had been to give the subject a steam bath and then whip his flesh with birch twig brooms covered with smallpox pus and lymph. Whether the more efficacious incision method described by Timoni and Onesimus had developed independently on both the western edge of Asia and in Africa or had been brought from the former to the latter is unknown. But by the time Onesimus underwent the procedure in about 1700 it had been common practice in parts of central and southern Africa for at least two decades.

That year the Royal Society had received its first account of inoculation, a description of its use in China. At least one additional account had reached the Society in the years preceding the publication of the Timoni letter in 1714 and the Pylarini letter in 1716. Had the London medical establishment wanted to test the merits of the mounting evidence of its efficacy it could have done so on at least two occasions prior to 1721: during the 1710 epidemic and a less widespread outbreak in 1719. Prejudice, not lack of opportunity, had prevented a trial. Westerners simply couldn't accept that "heathens" and "primitives" had hit upon so profound a discovery.

As the nearly unanimous rejection of Mather's appeal for an inoculation trial in Boston demonstrated, New Englanders, as a group, were no more open-minded than their counterparts in the mother country. Informed that Zabdiel Boylston had decided to attempt the procedure, William Douglass would conclude that he had ignorantly mistaken the Royal Society's publication of the Timoni and Pylarini accounts of inoculation—to his mind a "far fetched and not well vouched Method" offered simply as an amusement for subscribers—as its endorsement.[10] He simply could not conceive of any other rationale for attempting something so preposterous.

Boylston would say relatively little about the reasoning behind his decision, other than that he had been "very well pleas'd" with Cotton Mather's communication of the Timoni and Pylarini procedures and was convinced by the Africans he had interviewed that inoculation had been "attended with *Success*" in their part of the world.[11] What those laconic statements don't reveal is the extent to which his upbringing, training, and life experience had contributed to that decision. Boylston's father, a physician whose practice in the wilderness beyond the Boston peninsula brought him into regular contact with Indians, had passed on to his son both a respect for native medicine and a considerable number of Indian treatments. Indeed, Boylston himself would draw a direct line from his respect for Indian medicine—some of whose treatments and medicines most colonial doctors grudgingly acknowledged as efficacious—to his willingness to consider a treatment from another source outside the European tradition. "I don't know why 'tis more unlawful to learn of *Africans*, how to help against the *Poison* of the *Small Pox*," he would write, "than it is to learn of our *Indians*, how to help against the *Poison* of a *Rattle-Snake*."[12]

Boylston's perspective had also been shaped by his exceptionally horrific personal history with smallpox, which had struck Boston near the end of his apprenticeship to Dr. John Cutler, the man who had taken over his training after the sudden and premature death of Boylston's father. The old doctor had given his apprentice permission to remain behind when he visited the homes of the infected. But knowing that the disease was certain to return and that he would need immunity in order to treat its victims, Boylston had deliberately exposed himself early in the outbreak, hoping to pass through his sickness and recover soon enough to gain experience treating the disease. Rather than the mild case he had hoped for, however, he had become mortally ill—so ill, in fact, that Cutler had given him up for dead. The recuperation he had envisioned would take weeks had dragged on for many months. He had been lucky to survive and even luckier to have been spared the blindness, lameness, and mental impairment that often resulted from near-fatal cases of the disease. With one exception—a severely pitted and pockmarked face—he had emerged physically whole. But his psyche had also been scarred. The horror and vividness of the battle he had waged for his life were still fresh years later when he offered one of the most graphic and harrowing descriptions of severe smallpox ever written:

> Purple spots, the bloody and parchment Pox, Hemorahages of Blood at the Mouth, Nose, Fundament, and Privities; Ravings and Deliriums; Convulsions, and other Fits; violent inflammations and Swellings in the Eyes and Throat; so that they cannot see, or scarcely breathe, or swallow any thing, to keep them from starving. Some looking as black as the Stock, others as white as a Sheet; in some, the Pock runs into Blisters, and the Skin stripping off, leaves the Flesh raw. . . . Some have a burning, others a smarting Pain, as if in the Fire, or scalded with boiling Water. . . . Some have been fill'd with loathsome Ulcers; others have had deep, and

fistulous Ulcers in their Bodies, or in their Limbs or Joints, with Rot-
tenness of the Ligaments and Bones: Some who live are Cripples, others
Idiots, and many blind all their Days.[13]

Smallpox had been cruel to Jerusha Boylston as well. At age nine or
ten she had lost both of her parents and three of her four brothers to the
disease. Twelve years after she had been taken into the family of her uncle
Stephen Minot, a prosperous merchant, the next epidemic killed two of
Minot's sons, her surrogate brothers. In that epidemic or the one previous,
she, too, had come down with smallpox. Whether she had been as close
to death as her future husband is unknown; but her marriage to Boylston
at the relatively late age of twenty-six suggests that she, too, might have
been severely scarred as a result. (Despite how common facial scarring
was during this time, it remained a severe stigma for women. Lamenting
the ruined beauty of Frances Stewart, King Charles II's mistress, Samuel
Pepys wrote: "It would make a man weep to see what she was then, and
what she is like to be, by people's discourse now.")[14]

Given that attempting inoculation constituted an almost complete leap
of faith for Boylston, he spent surprisingly little time agonizing over it. He
decided to go ahead, he later wrote, "well remembering the Destruction
the Small-Pox made 19 Years before, when last in *Boston*; and how narrowly I then escap'd with my Life."[15] Both he and his wife had nearly had
their lives destroyed by previous epidemics. They had no reason to think
that their children would be spared by this one. The best and perhaps only
hope for the couple's sons—and, if the epidemic spread, for their three
girls in the country as well—was inoculation. For reasons even he probably couldn't explain, he believed it would work. And at least he was doing
something. For Boylston, doing nothing had never really been an option.

IN BOSTON AND vicinity, Commencement Day was "the great summer holiday," one of only two days a year when the Puritan pious put

work and worship aside and indulged freely in celebration and frivolity.[16] (The other was Election Day.) Held in Cambridge on the first Wednesday in July, its official purpose was to send a new batch of Harvard graduates into the world. But in the years since 1684, when it had been opened to the public, Commencement Day had become, much to the displeasure of some persons connected to the college, a giant party. Thousands of persons with no direct connection to the college flooded into the town, joining graduates, instructors, alumni, and government officials. The event, which had "the color and noise of a local fair," attracted "hundreds of eligible women from all the surrounding towns" and a "motley assortment of opportunists" including hawkers and street performers.[17] Vendors sold roasted, boiled, and baked meats and plum cake, which were consumed with large quantities of wine. Public drunkenness was tolerated if only because trying to prevent it was futile.

For decades Commencement Day had taken place rain or shine, regardless of the challenges facing the town and the colony. But on June 26, 1721, the *Boston News-Letter* announced the cancellation of the public celebration of the college's commencement "by reason of any Danger that may arise from the Small Pox's spreading."[18] This was perhaps the most stunning smallpox-related news yet because it affected a huge swath of the populace and shattered any remaining illusions of normalcy. Two months earlier no one would have imagined that anything could prevent this year's celebration from taking place. Now the only thing more surprising than its cancellation was that no one raised a voice in protest.

By the time that issue of the *News-Letter* began circulating in Boston, Zabdiel Boylston had already begun his experiment. At first light he had gone to the sickroom of a smallpox patient approximately twelve days into a regular or "distinct" outbreak of disease—one whose vesicles were fully formed and ripe but still white and fluid, not yellow and malodorous—and, using a "fine cut sharp Tooth-pick" instead of a lancet (because, he explained, the toothpick "will not put the Person in any Fear, as a Lancet will do many"), he had sliced open several fully emerged blisters at the side and pressed them so as to express their matter into the end of a quill.[19] When the quill was full he released its contents into a clean, dry vial and closed it with a stopper. Then, following the directions of Timoni, he tucked the vial inside his shirt, holding it close to the skin so that its contents would remain near body temperature, and headed back to his home in Dock Square, where his slave Jack, Jack's two-and-a-half-year-old son, Jackey, and Boylston's youngest son, Thomas, were waiting.

Boylston's decision to make little Thomas part of the initial test would outrage many Bostonians. But it was logical. As the youngest of the three Boylston boys, Thomas required the most personal attention from his father, especially with his mother away in the country. Close, regular contact between father and son dramatically increased the odds that Tommy would be infected before his more self-sufficient older brothers. As Boylston later admitted, he also inoculated Tommy at the outset "for Example sake."[20] He knew that when the word got out that he was implanting smallpox into the skin of perfectly healthy subjects, charges that he was acting impulsively and with a cavalier attitude toward the well-being of his patients (accusations he had likely encountered after performing the mastectomy) were certain to follow. The surest way to convince the people of Boston that he was not embarking on his experiment lightly and that the procedure had merit was, he believed, to successfully inoculate his own son. Practically speaking, he could not expect parents to submit their children to a procedure he had been afraid to perform on his own.

He had practical and mercenary reasons for including his slaves in the experiment. They were, on one level, valuable property he didn't want to lose. He also wanted Jack immune so that he would be able to help with the coming rush of smallpox cases. (The slave likely acted as his master's medical assistant when the doctor was between apprentices.) But here again, Boylston seems to have understood the necessity of making an example. In the aftermath of several slave uprisings in the colonies, including a particularly infamous New York ambush in which two dozen slaves had murdered eight white men and wounded seven more, Bostonians had become increasingly wary of the thousand or so black persons living among them. Many whites had begun to read ominous significance into every illegal or immoral incident involving a slave or free black. It didn't help that the first man acknowledged to be sick with the disease was black—and therefore, in the eyes of some, the person who had "caused" the burgeoning outbreak. The historian Margot Minardi noted that with those thoughts roiling in the minds of white Bostonians, "the idea that slaves had concocted inoculation as a scheme to kill off their masters may have seemed plausible."[21] She also pointed out that Cotton Mather had unwittingly contributed to the suspicion by alluding to the rebellious tendencies of blacks in his recent execution lecture for Joseph Hanno. Indeed, that lecture might have helped undermine his first letter to the physicians, written just one week later, wherein he had argued—in seeming contradiction to the sermon—that the Africans who vouched for inoculation had "no Conspiracy or Combination to cheat us."[22] All Boylston could do to undermine the inevitable charges that inoculation was a murderous African plot was to include Africans in the experiment.

He inoculated Thomas first, pinching some skin on the boy's upper arm and making an incision a quarter of an inch long and deep enough into the "true skin" of the dermis that in theory the opening could accommodate a pea. After wiping away the blood, he inserted a full drop of the smallpox "variole" into the wound and mixed it with the new blood seeping in. To protect the wound while simultaneously exposing it to air he covered it with a walnut shell and secured the shell in place with a strip of cloth. Then he made a second cut on Thomas's upper leg near the buttocks and repeated the procedure. When he got to Jack he made the second cut on his neck near the shoulder, possibly, as Carrell has suggested, so that the expected smattering of smallpox around the incision wouldn't inhibit the slave from riding a horse or mule when accompanying him on patient visits.[23]

In the space of a few minutes all three subjects were inoculated. Little Jackey, who was too young to understand the pain of an operation performed, like all surgeries of the era, without anesthesia, must have been inconsolable. After a little while, though, he was up and playing with Thomas, both boys oblivious of their incisions and the heat of the room, whose windows Boylston had shut as a precaution. If the symptoms produced by the inoculation proved as mild as Mather's account of Timoni suggested, the surgical discomfort they had just experienced might prove the worst part of their journey to immunity. But for Boylston the period of discomfort had just begun. For the next several days he could only watch, wait, and wonder whether he had saved his son and the others from the horrors of full-blown smallpox or planted the seeds of their deaths.

The sun had been up for only a few hours, but already the day was "sweltering." At ten o'clock in the morning the roar of gunfire from the HMS *Seahorse* startled the town out of its torpor. The warship had returned to Long Wharf from Bird Island nearly three weeks earlier without authorization from the town officials, Captain Durrell apparently having decided that he had been quarantined long enough. Asked to explain the unscheduled and jarring discharge of fifteen of the ship's guns on the morning of June 26, Durrell would claim that he had ordered it to commemorate the birthday of King George's young granddaughter Caroline.[24] But most Bostonians probably sensed that it had been motivated in part, at least, by malice; that the captain knew they were already on edge over smallpox and wanted to see them jump. About a week later his second-in-command, Lieutenant Hamilton, would exhibit his own brand of insensitivity, taking on a black slave as his personal servant and naming him "Cotton Mather" in mockery of what he considered the minister's ridiculous trust in the Africans who had told him that inoculation was safe.

It didn't take nearly that long, though, for Bostonians to discover that inoculations had been performed and to react. "By sunset," wrote one historian, "the entire city knew what [Boylston] had done and the immediate reaction was shock."[25] Four days later the town was thoroughly up in arms, even though the subjects had yet to exhibit symptoms. Mather, whose role in the medical trial was now generally known, referred to it as "an horrid Clamour, which Occasions new Cares upon me."[26] Boylston ignored the uproar and kept a close watch on his son and slaves. When Thomas and Jackey began running a fever early on July 1 he darkened the room, ordered them to bed, and limited their diet to toast and water and "a Thimble-full of oatmeal."[27] Throughout the next day the boys were "a little hot, dull, and sleepy." That night, Thomas's fever spiked, causing him to experience delirious "twitchings" in his sleep.[28] On the eighth day following the inoculations both boys were still running fevers. Jackey seemed to be tolerating his well. But Thomas's fevered dreams had grown more frequent and intense.

The temperature of public outrage had also continued to rise. Boylston could feel it when he left Thomas to make his rounds. The "Clamour, or rather Rage of the People," was "so violent," he wrote, that he was "put into a very great Fright."[29] That fear might have been for his physical safety. What frightened him more, in all likelihood, was the possibility that the people shouting and pointing fingers at him were right: that he *had* acted unconscionably in attempting a dangerous, unsubstantiated procedure on his own son, whose death, if it came, would be unforgivable.

Without an experienced inoculation practitioner to consult, he "had nothing to have Recourse to but Patience." He canceled his other appointments and sat vigil at Thomas's bedside, waiting, he wrote, "upon Nature for a Crisis (neither my Fears nor the Symptoms abating)." When Tommy awoke on the morning of the ninth day still burning with fever, he decided to act. He gave the boy a "vomit," hoping to bring down the fever. Several anxious hours later Thomas's delirium eased and his temperature began to fall. Late that day both he and Jackey broke out in "a kind and favourable Small-Pox," with each boy showing about a hundred distinct blisters. From that point forward, Boylston wrote, "their Circumstances became easy, our Trouble was over, and they soon were well."[30] Jack, meanwhile, had hardly gotten ill at all. After two or three days of low fever and few complaints, "a few Pustules" had broken out at the site of one of his two incisions.[31] His symptoms were so much gentler than those experienced by the boys that Boylston concluded he had already had smallpox, perhaps before he was old enough to remember.

THE NEWSPAPERS IGNORED inoculation. Smallpox itself barely earned a mention. The July 10 *News-Letter* devoted more than half of its expanded four-page layout to the first and second parts of a three-part series on the nature and prevention of contagious disease. But once again the distemper was the plague, not smallpox. The next day, the Massachusetts House prepared a bill aimed at keeping plague out of the colony. It called for "all Vessels coming from infected Places to perform their Quarantine,"[32] an order that might have prevented the smallpox outbreak had the government seen fit to impose it on ships coming from Barbados a few months earlier. Only once in the three weeks following Boylston's inoculation experiment did the newspapers print a direct and significant mention of the disease that was overtaking the town. It announced the governor's order of a special fast day on July 13, at which time the people would gather in churches and express their "most solemn and sincere Humiliation" and "penitent Confession" for the sins and iniquities that had "stirred up the Anger of Heaven" and caused smallpox to be visited upon them.[33]

When inoculation did appear in the paper, it was only because its practitioner forced the issue. Frustrated that he was still being harassed in public even though it was clear now that all three of his subjects would recover fully, and resentful at having been secretly called before town officials and chastised for putting his son and the others in danger, Boylston sat down on July 15 and drafted a letter defending inoculation and his decision to attempt it. Two days later the letter appeared in the *Boston Gazette*. Boylston wrote that he had "patiently born with abundance of Clamour and Ralary [raillery] for beginning a new Practice here (for the good of the Publick) which comes well Recommended from Gentlemen of Figure & Learning, and which," he added, was eminently sensible "when try'd & duly

consider'd." He discussed the details of the three inoculations, admitting
that his son's high fever together with "the rage of the People" had caused
him anxious moments, but insisting that once the pocks themselves had
come out neither Thomas nor the other patients had required "one grain
or drop of Medicine" to aid their recovery. Having found the accounts of
Timoni and Pylarini "just and true," he hoped to give the public "some
further proof of their just and reasonable Account" in the weeks to come.[34]

As that statement implied, he had already begun his next round of
inoculations. On July 12, and in defiance of both the townspeople who
spewed epithets at him on the street and the town fathers, who had warned
him against continuing with the experiment, he had performed the operation on thirty-nine-year-old Joshua Cheever, one of his closest friends.
Then on July 14 he had inoculated two more persons, Jack's wife, Moll,
and thirty-four-year-old John Heyler, another personal friend who was
also a member of Mather's North Church.

On the morning his letter appeared in the *Gazette*, Boylston inoculated his middle son, John. Shortly thereafter he was summoned for a second private meeting with the authorities, who issued him a more insistent
order to cease and desist. On or about July 18, three persons approached
him asking to have the procedure performed. Only one of the three was in
good health. Boylston described the other two, a sixty-seven-year-old man
and a forty-three-year-old woman, as "weak infirm Persons."[35] Refusing
their requests meant that they would probably die if they came down
with smallpox naturally. Going ahead with the operations significantly increased the likelihood that he would lose a patient and open himself to
more dangerous repercussions from the public and the government. He
tried to discourage them. But seeing they would not be dissuaded, he relented, performing the procedure on all three on July 19. It would be his
policy moving forward to not refuse anyone, no matter how old or infirm,
if they were determined to be inoculated.

9

MALIGNANT FILTH

The General Court session that resumed in Cambridge on June 6 proceeded with comparative calm until June 20, when a letter from the colony's London agent, Jeremiah Dummer, was read to the House. It was another warning along the lines of one he had sent in 1719. That earlier letter had informed the House that the Lords of Trade were "very angrey" over its treatment of royal surveyor Jonathan Bridger and were censuring it for its obstruction of the royal prerogative.[1] Dummer's new letter informed them that a growing number of the Lords, angry that Massachusetts continued to make its royal governor "uneasy in his government," were convinced that the colony's inhabitants "would have no governor at all from hence, but want to be independent of the crown." Dummer added that although he considered the accusation a "strained and most injurious inference," what mattered was that the British ministry wouldn't "easily be persuaded out of it."[2] Indeed, there was already a movement afoot within the Board of Trade, he reported, to cancel all of the New England charters and bring the various governments under stricter and more centralized English control.

The agent's letter had a dramatic effect on the House, albeit not the one for which he had hoped. It's unlikely that a message so dire and threatening would have been received with equanimity no matter who delivered it. But coming from Dummer, who had remained suspect in the eyes of Cooke and his friends ever since he had helped bribe the man originally appointed to Samuel Shute's position into relinquishing it, the letter was instantly and automatically branded a fabrication (or at least an exaggeration) and a con, a pathetic attempt by Dummer to do the bidding of the governor by frightening and intimidating the House into capitulation. Before the day was done the deputies had voted to remove Dummer as their agent after eleven years of decidedly meritorious service. If in 1715 Dummer had made a poor decision in doing the Dudleys' dirty work by smoothing the way for Shute's appointment, he had also exercised almost flawless judgment and diplomacy ever since, repeatedly serving as a buffer between the colony and the Crown and defending Massachusetts—even the policies with which he personally disagreed—at his own peril. That was the Council's argument in refusing to go along with the House's decision to fire him. Whatever Dummer had or had not done in the past, this time, its members insisted, he was telling the truth. It was in the interest of all concerned to heed his warning and keep him close to the situation. But by June 1721 there was no seeing shades of gray when it came to allies of Samuel Shute. When the Council blocked its attempt to fire Dummer outright, the House exercised its power of the purse and voted simply to eliminate his salary.

With the scent of political blood in his nostrils, Elisha Cooke turned his wrath on a more unabashedly radical partisan of the governor, rallying his supporters to call for the ouster of Joseph Dudley's son Paul, who, Cooke's party now charged, lacked the residency qualifications to sit on the Council as a representative from the Maine territories, a seat he had held, unquestioned, since 1718. Governor Shute—whose anger had been festering since the day earlier in the session when the House had casually declared that any complaints he had made to the Board of Trade about its actions were irrelevant inasmuch as Massachusetts, by its charter, was "no ways answerable to that Honorable Board, for any Matter or Thing done here, Relating to Acts of Government"—became enraged at the two-pronged attack against Dummer and Dudley.[3] Casting about for some way to retaliate, he insisted that the House pay his salary immediately rather than waiting until the end of the session, as was customary. When the House refused he became even more frantic in his determination to avenge its impertinences. Now, with the smallpox-inspired July 13 fast day approaching, he held the House hostage, refusing to let them leave Cambridge and return home to spend the day praying with their families. He would release them only after they paid him and retracted their disloyal insult against the authority of the Board of Trade.

Shute was trying to project strength and assert his dominance. But it was a blunder to think that forcing the deputies to remain in session on a fast day he himself had ordered would be seen as anything but gratuitously cruel and scandalously impious. As Thomas Hutchinson later noted, the move "further alienated the minds of the people" from their governor.[4] And deep down Shute must have realized that, formally or otherwise, he would be defied. Yet when, at the very last minute, Speaker John Clark adjourned the House and sent its members home—overstepping his authority—Shute claimed shock and disbelief. He was still livid on July 19 when the House members resumed business in Cambridge. He waited for the deputies to send up their first piece of major business for the Council's concurrence, the award of a little over £19 to Timothy Clark for piloting the infected HMS *Seahorse* to Bird Island, and then pounced, calling the House leadership to his chamber and subjecting them to one of his most vitriolic outbursts yet. The power to adjourn the General Court, he reminded them, was "wholly Vested" in the governor. In self-adjourning, they had not only violated the charter and insulted him; they had also, he now claimed, endangered the province, since he had meant to keep the

House in session so that it could pass "some effectual Measures to prevent the Plague coming amongst us," a danger he declared imminent given the "the French Silks and Stuffs" brought into Massachusetts in violation of British law.[5] (This was a dig against the many House members who either turned a blind eye to the contraband or imported or purchased it themselves.) But now, having vented his ire, he promptly shut down the session, preventing the Court from enacting the measures he had just claimed were critical. By the next time the Court gathered he would have forgotten this emergency legislation altogether.

ON THE MORNING of Friday, July 21, Zabdiel Boylston was ordered to report to the Town House at noon. He arrived to find a large and dour assembly. Selectmen Cooke, William Clark, Ebenezer Clough, Thomas Cushing, John Marion, Nathaniel Green, and Isaiah Tay were all on hand, as were the justices of the peace, assorted other town and provincial officers, and all of the town's physicians and major apothecaries. The completeness of the turnout suggests that, although Boylston seems to have been caught by surprise, the inquest had been in the works for several days if not longer. Clearly, the opponents of inoculation were set on generating a demonstration of force. Much of what followed resembled a show, carefully blocked out and rehearsed.

With the town still in the grip of a heat wave, the upstairs chambers of the Town House must have been extremely uncomfortable, particularly if at some point the windows were ordered closed to prevent the raised voices from carrying to the eavesdroppers gathered on the cobblestones outside. Indeed, it didn't take long for the combination of withering heat and frayed nerves to turn the inquiry into a shouting match. According to Jennifer Carrell, the physician George Steward (or Stewart), who was present at the inquiry, "recorded that the first part of the meeting devolved into a morass of squabbling during which Boylston was repeatedly asked whether inoculation was infallible, or whether people 'might not die by it'—to which he repeatedly replied 'that persons might die by a vomit or a purge' too.'" After "a long debate" and perhaps a break at the customary dinner hour of two o'clock, the inquiry resumed.[6] Finally at four o'clock the opponents of inoculation brought forth the star witness they had been holding in reserve. Dr. Lawrence Dalhonde was a former French military surgeon who claimed to have observed the deleterious and deadly effects of inoculation on three occasions. The first, twenty-five years earlier in Italy, had involved thirteen soldiers, four of whom, he claimed, had died of inoculation, with six more suffering extreme side effects, including "Parotidal Tumors," and three experiencing neither a bad reaction nor the desired prophylactic result. An autopsy of one of the dead men, Dalhonde claimed, had revealed his diaphragm infected, "the Glans of his Pancreas tumify'd, and the Caul gangrened."[7]

Dalhonde's second account concerned a captain suffering from smallpox who claimed to have been inoculated "five or six times" but who had nevertheless been "so violently seized" with the disease that it had produced "several Ulcers on his Body, especially one on his Arm, which occasion'd a Lameness thereof for Life." Lastly, Dalhonde had seen two Muscovite soldiers inoculated in Spain. One had recovered. The other, who was thought to have received "no Impression" from the procedure, had been fine until six weeks afterward, when he was "seiz'd with a Frenzy, swelled all over his Body," and died.[8] The man's autopsy had revealed severely ulcerated lungs, which Dalhonde attributed to the poisoning effect of inoculation.

Nothing said against him or inoculation that day angered Boylston more than the testimony of Dalhonde, whom he subsequently branded a fraud and Cotton Mather called a "*French* Fellow of a very vicious Character."[9] The carefully orchestrated presentation of the surgeon's testimony—including the decision to have him present it in his native tongue, thereby preventing the non–French-speaking Boylston from challenging him directly—smacked of an attempt to manipulate the opinions of the authorities. Dalhonde's description of plague-like symptoms allegedly caused by inoculation tapped directly into the town's highly tuned anxiety over that other great pestilence and appears to have had a noticeable effect on the men in the room, producing something on the order of a collective gasp. Several years later Boylston would refer to the Frenchman's attempts to tie inoculation to the plague with scorn and mockery, writing that "the knowing Part of Mankind now believes as little of them as if he [Dalhonde] had said that their Heads had dropt off, or that Inoculation had turn'd Men into Women, or any other strange Tho't that might have come into his Head."[10]

Standing alone against this marathon onslaught of criticism, ridicule, and damning but unverifiable evidence—most of which he was hearing for the first time—Boylston refused repeated calls to disavow the procedure. Instead he reiterated its safety and efficacy as he had experienced it to that point. He had brought three subjects through inoculation safely and had performed the operation on several others, all of whom were progressing according to plan. He challenged his fellow physicians to put aside Dalhonde's fantastical assertions long enough to visit his inoculation patients and "judge of and report their Circumstances as they found them."[11]

Everything he said fell on deaf ears, the town having apparently decided to condemn inoculation before the meeting had begun and regardless of Boylston's arguments or appeals. One day after the meeting it formalized that condemnation in a resolve whose language nearly parroted Dalhonde's testimony, citing the "numerous Instances" in which inoculation had "prov'd the Death of many Persons soon after the Operation, and brought Distempers upon many others which have in the End prov'd deadly to 'em." It went on to state that inasmuch as "the natural tendency of infusing such malignant Filth In the Mass of Blood, is to corrupt and putrify it," and since inoculation appeared to provide "a Foundation for many dangerous Diseases," the town firmly opposed its continued practice.[12] The statement concluded with a demographic breakdown of the seventeen acknowledged smallpox deaths to that point. The juxtaposition of that modest total with the potentially horrendous consequences of inoculation as described by Dr. Dalhonde sent the message that Boylston's alleged cure was a far greater threat than the smallpox it was intended to prevent.

The numbers, though, were misleading. The dying had only begun. Looking back on this resolution five years later, Boylston would write: "It is a thousand pities our Select-Men made so slight and trifling a Representation of the Small-Pox, that had always prov'd so fatal in *New England*, as they seem to have done in this Advertisement."[13]

AS FAR AS Dr. William Douglass was concerned, the July 21 inquiry could not have gone better had he scripted it himself. Indeed, he seems to have done everything *but* script it, first pushing the government to stage a formal hearing into inoculation and then setting the meeting's agenda and serving as both its moderator and Lawrence Dalhonde's interpreter. It's reasonable to assume the opinions he voiced on his own behalf that afternoon mirrored the content of a letter that appeared in the *Boston News-Letter* on the Monday following and was dated July 20, one day *before* the inquiry. Writing under the pseudonym "W. Philanthropos," Douglass declared inoculation a "Wicked and Criminal Practice" that would not keep someone from suffering from smallpox in the future. Publicly, at least, he was willing to forgive Mather, "a Learned Gentleman of this Place," for his wrongheaded attempt to force the hands of the town's medical practitioners, which he excused as the minister's "Pious & Charitable design of doing good." All of the town's medical practitioners, he wrote, had sensibly refused that proposal, save for "a certain *Cutter for the Stone*, who this, without any serious thought undertakes." The moniker, which alluded to Boylston's fame for bladder stone surgery, was meant to evoke the infamous "stone cutters" of Europe, itinerant charlatans who set up shop in a town square, performed incompetent and reckless bladder stone operations, and then cleared out before the patients died. Douglass's supposed proof that Boylston was no more competent than those frauds was that his son had "*narrowly escaped* with his Life," having suffered a fever "so violent," he wrote, that "our Operator was obliged to have recourse to a confused course of Methods and Medicines." He charged Boylston with being *"illiterate"* and *"Ignorant"* and having completely misinterpreted the Timoni and Pylarini accounts. Boylston also had almost no experience caring for smallpox victims, the letter said, and had published a *"Dangerous quack Advertisement"* in his defense.[14]

It was disingenuous for William Douglass to accuse Boylston of being too stupid to understand the fine points of letters that he, Douglass, had refused to let him read. And if Boylston's lack of experience with smallpox patients somehow disqualified him from providing competent care, the same was true of most of the town's physicians, since for nearly two decades there had been no cases to treat. (Douglass's failure to tout his own smallpox experience by way of contrast suggests that he had not treated all that many cases himself.) The Scotsman wasn't content, though, to paint Boylston as a dolt and would-be propagator of smallpox. In keeping with Dalhonde's testimony, he raised the possibility that the inoculating doctor was fostering the outbreak of a second deadly disease. "Sometimes Inoculation *occasions troublesome Ulcers* in the glandulous parts of the Body, like PLAGUE SORES," he wrote.[15] (In the entire letter the only other word printed entirely in capital letters was "GOD.") The imputation that, by inoculating, Boylston might cause the plague to break out was a wild extrapolation of circumstantial evidence—the coexistence of plague and inoculation in Turkey. As Carrell has pointed out, the fact that Douglass "carefully excised it [the suggestion that inoculation caused plague] from the anti-inoculation tracts he published in London" at a later date indicates that he knew he was playing loose and free with the facts, using the fear of the plague to demonize both inoculation and the doctor practicing it.[16]

But he wasn't finished. Late in his letter he asked leadingly whether Boylston might find himself charged with a felony if one of his inoculation patients died—even if the death had resulted from smallpox contracted "in the common way" prior to the procedure. Douglass claimed to hope this scenario—which neither the selectmen nor the judiciary had felt

obliged to broach—would not come to pass, inasmuch as it would constitute "an additional Misery" to the town.[17] But in raising the possibility of
criminal charges and cleverly preempting the inoculator's one plausible
defense against conviction—that the inoculated person had died from
natural smallpox, not his procedure—he had all but assured that someone
would call for Boylston's prosecution if and when an inoculation patient
died. Douglass's coy refusal to name the felony did not make it any less
obvious. The charge would be murder.

William Douglass had a duty to exercise his skepticism and medical
judgment to safeguard the public. But under his influence a town meeting
that ought to have been a responsible inquiry into the safety of inoculation
had degenerated into a kangaroo court. Instead of refuting inoculation on
its merits, he had resorted there and in the letter that appeared afterward
to ad hominem attacks on Boylston's character and intelligence. Indeed,
his insults were so excessively venomous and his rhetoric so overheated
that it's not difficult to conclude that Douglass wanted to stop Boylston for
reasons that went beyond his concern for the public health.

To understand how William Douglass might have had an ulterior mo-
tive, it's important to understand how exasperated he was with Boston.
Five years after setting foot in the town for the first time, Douglass was
still waiting for it to prove its worth to him. In 1716 the London physician
had turned down a promising opportunity to start a practice in the English city of Bristol in order to come to the Massachusetts capital, where
he hoped and expected to join the administration of the newly appointed
governor, his friend Elizeus Burgess. Burgess had intimated that he would
provide Douglass with a sinecure similar to the one Douglass's fellow
Scots physician Cadwallader Colden had received from the governor of
New York: a cushy salaried position that would allow him to give up the
full-time practice of medicine and live the life of a gentleman, spending
the majority of his time developing his other interests and his estate. He
had reached Boston and begun to establish himself when he learned that
Burgess would not be assuming the governorship after all. The news that

Burgess had resigned, and that Samuel Shute would be taking his place, so upset and embittered Douglass that he sailed out of Boston Harbor shortly thereafter and spent most of the next two years roaming the colonies to the south and the islands of the Caribbean, returning to Boston only when he had decided that, dull though it was, the colonial backwater offered the best chance for him to make his name and his fortune. After three years his opinion of the town had not improved. The vigorous, now thirty-year-old bachelor, whom at least one contemporary referred to as a "blade," continued to find it substandard in nearly every respect.[18] He was appalled by its lack of sophisticated scientific instruments ("I know of no Thermometer nor Barometer in this place," he complained to Colden, with whom he shared an interest in meteorology) and resentful over having to bill his patients the American way, on a per-visit basis rather than by retainer.[19] He hated the cold weather and the Indians, whose "natural temper," he believed, was "cruel and vindictive," and he disliked the government's "long and tedious disputes" in general and Governor Samuel Shute in particular, declaring Shute so lacking in merit as to make him "the reverse" of the "Gentlemen of Genius and Learning" who governed Pennsylvania and New York, the colonies Colden had called home.[20] Although the inoculation controversy had led him to single out Zabdiel Boylston for derision, he was privately contemptuous of all of his colleagues, chiefly (though not solely) because they had been educated through an apprenticeship system and lacked the benefit of his medical college education. (It would be nearly half a century before an American medical school was established.) In response to Colden's complaint that medicine was "undervalued" in his town, Douglass responded that things were "not much better in that respect in this place," where, he wrote, "we abound with Practitioners, tho no other graduate than my self." Indeed, he refused to call his colleagues "Physicians," stubbornly referring to them as "Practitioners" instead. Douglass would sustain that contempt for the rest of his life; thirty years after his arrival in America he would still insist that American medical apprenticeships constituted "an impudent delusion and fraud."[21]

Disappointed or underwhelmed by Boston at nearly every turn, he had adopted a utilitarian view of the town. It had value only insofar as it held the potential for producing value. In a letter to Colden written a few months before the smallpox outbreak, he had declared it "no better than a factory as to my interest." He told his correspondent that he managed to live "handsomely" by the income he derived from his practice and "save some small matter" besides.[22] But in order to make life in Boston worthwhile he needed his "factory" to significantly step up its production.

In letters written after the onset of the smallpox outbreak he suggested that he had been waiting for that or some other epidemic to strike so that he could manufacture an international reputation by observing it and accumulate a windfall profit large enough to finance real estate investments by treating it. One week after the July 21 meeting, Douglass penned another letter to his New York colleague suggesting that he had a smallpox study well under way. He was keeping "an account of all intricate incidents," he told Colden, adding that he had the "prospect of being well acquainted with the mazes of that distemper, having at present a large share of that practice" and noting that "there are seven or eight thousand expectants of that disease in Town."[23] By studying the behavior and spread of smallpox he was continuing the work of the legendary Dr. Sydenham, who half a century earlier had rejected the accepted notion that "illness" was a single affliction with many different manifestations and had begun parsing it into discrete diseases, which he had also begun describing and classifying. Boston, as Douglass must have realized, was a perfect setting for that kind of scientific study. When an epidemic struck, thousands of persons became ill in the space of a few miles and on a peninsula remote enough that contamination from the overlay of a second, similar disease (as often occurred in large metropolitan centers like London) was unlikely. It was the perfect laboratory for someone attempting to understand the fine points of a disease's progression and the efficacy of its treatment.

After three years, William Douglass finally had the raw material for his "factory" and was committed to "making hay while the sun shines," as he phrased it to Colden.[24] But his plan had not taken into account inoculation, which threatened it in every way. Boylston's refusal to follow his lead in rejecting Mather's appeal for a test of the procedure had already sullied Douglass's otherwise triumphant debut as the new head of Boston's medical community. If allowed to continue, Boylston's inoculations would contaminate the "mazes" of naturally proliferating smallpox and ruin his research. And if patients flocked to Boylston believing he could save them from death by smallpox, Douglass might even find himself losing pounds and patients to the inoculator. Viewed through the lens of inoculation's imminent personal threat to Douglass, his histrionic and vindictive reaction to Boylston is easier to understand. From his perspective, the man practicing inoculation had to be stopped quickly, completely, and by extreme means if necessary.

JOSHUA CHEEVER BECAME extremely ill the day after Boylston received his humiliating reprimand at the Town House. "Lusty and strong," he was the last person the doctor thought would have difficulty tolerating inoculation. Six days after being inoculated and right on schedule he had developed the expected light fever and shivering, which had continued throughout the following day. One day after that, his fever had vanished and his incisions had stopped running, leading Boylston to conclude that the inoculation had failed to take. Cheever was feeling well enough on the evening of July 21 that when the town's fire gong sounded he had run from his house to help battle a neighborhood blaze. But by the time he had returned home late that night, he was drenched with sweat and "very ill and full of pain." When Boylston visited him on the morning of July 22 he found the patient in what appeared to be the early stages of deadly confluent smallpox. His skin was inflamed, his pulse was hard and quick, and his fever was climbing. As the day wore on and the selectmen's resolution condemning inoculation circulated Boston, the symptoms worsened. By evening Cheever's condition was so dire that, as in Thomas's case weeks earlier, the physician felt compelled to take action. He bled the sick man, "blistered" him, and administered a vomit of ipecac. Several hours later Cheever's symptoms "went off" and a smattering of smallpox of "a kind distinct Sort" emerged. The next morning, as *News-Letter* subscribers read William Douglass's letter damning Boylston's incompetency and suggesting that the loss of an inoculation patient ought to bring a charge of murder, Cheever emerged from his crisis. Boylston wrote that he rallied quickly, and "his Pains, and our Fears, were soon over, and in a short time he was well."[25]

At the end of July the Boston selectmen issued a report on the status of the smallpox outbreak. A relatively modest 168 persons were sick with the disease. Only 18 had died. Among those, several, they claimed, had been "lost by Carelessness and not by the Distemper."[26] Their report seems to have been an effort to prove to the public—and themselves—that they had acted prudently in putting a stop to inoculation. Insofar as stopping Boylston was concerned, they appeared to have succeeded. After a busy second round of inoculations during which he had performed the procedure seven times in as many days—the last three operations coming two days before the fateful meeting at the Town House—the doctor had performed no additional operations. Nor had he responded to the accusations made in William Douglass's scathing letter. The temperature of the outrage was simply too high. As he later wrote, the resolution against inoculation alone had been "sufficient to inflame and set almost the whole Town and Country against me and this Method."[27] In protest against his embrace of inoculation, a number of his regular patients had defected. Sensing that the rising sentiment against the doctor was a threat to his livelihood, if not his safety, his friend the minister Benjamin Colman drafted a rebuttal to William Douglass's attack and rallied Cotton Mather and four other clergymen—including John Webb, whose father Boylston had inoculated on July 19—to sign on. Colman's letter, which appeared in the *Boston Gazette* on July 31, declared the besieged doctor "a Son of the Town" whose "Gifts for the Service of his Country" were apparent to all.

Even if one disagreed with his decision to conduct the experiments, he did not deserve the "injurious Reflections" of Douglass and others. It was particularly "unworthy and unjust, (not to say worse)," Colman noted, that Douglass would attack Boylston for his surgical prowess. The doctor, he wrote, had been "Inestimable to them that have been snatch'd from the Jaws of Death by his happy hand."[28] He also took Douglass to task for presuming to judge inoculation a violation of God's will. If prudent and godly ministers like the undersigned decided after careful deliberation that inoculation was safe, he argued, who was to say that it was not God's will for Boylston to use it? But Colman stopped short of insisting or even urging that Boylston be allowed to resume the inoculation trial in Boston. Nor in the days following its publication did anyone else take up Colman's argument that God might actually be smiling down on inoculation and urge Boylston to continue. Even the procedure's supporters seem to have concluded that the mood of the town was simply too hostile to abide more inoculations.

IN ADDITION TO Colman's letter supporting Boylston, the *Gazette* published a brief contribution from the doctor himself. In it, he invited the town's justices, selectmen, and other men of distinction to visit his recovering inoculation patients "in order to prevent any further False Reports being spread about them."[29] Most readers probably interpreted it as an appeal for leniency, an attempt to salvage his reputation. But as developments would soon show, the doctor had a very different intention. By this point he could say without reservation that his most recent operations had been successful. Of the seven persons under inoculation at the time he had been dragged in front of civic and medical authorities, only Cheever had given him a scare. John Heyler had developed a mild case of inoculated smallpox. Boylston's slave Moll, like her husband, seemed to have already been immune. The doctor's son John had developed "a small sprinkling of a kind Sort" of smallpox, his symptoms "gentle." Joseph

Webb and his wife had developed fairly unworrisome cases of "distinct" smallpox on or about July 29. John Webb had experienced "an ill turn of Faintness and Oppression of Spirits, at the coming out of the Pox," but like the others he now seemed on his way to complete recovery.[30] To Boylston's way of thinking there was no reason not to resume the procedure. His notice was simply an offer to prove that to the authorities before he did so.

His identical offer to the town physicians weeks earlier had been ignored by all but one man, Dr. White. Now, after several days, he had still not heard from a single town official. Finally he decided he could wait no longer. Joseph Webb's nineteen-year-old daughter, Esther, who had nursed both of her parents through their inoculated smallpox and was fearful of having contracted the disease, was pleading to undergo the procedure. Early on the morning of August 5 Boylston inoculated her and three other persons, including Joshua Cheever's sixteen-year-old son.

IO

AMERICA'S FIRST
INDEPENDENT
NEWSPAPER

homas Fleet and James Franklin were friends as well as competitors. Over the years they had forged a bond built upon their common experience as printing apprentices in England and their mutual tribulations as competitors with the all-powerful Green family. Both men were innovators; in 1719, the same year James produced "Teach," Fleet apparently invented "Mother Goose," a character inspired by his prattling mother-in-law, whose name was, in fact, Elizabeth Goose. As printers who had come of age in the rowdy world of London publishing, they also shared an appetite for cheekiness. Twice before 1719, Fleet had been reprimanded for printing objectionable political pamphlets. Early that year he had been summoned a third time and ordered to stop work on a pamphlet suspected of being stridently anti-Puritan. All it had taken for the authorities to order the first pre-publication censorship in Massachusetts in more than two decades was the unconfirmed suspicion that John Checkley had written the pamphlet.

By that point Checkley had firmly established himself as Boston's most radical High Church Anglican and the Puritans' most vocal detractor. Later that same year, after the publication of another objectionable religious pamphlet he had supposedly authored (this one printed in England to escape pre-publication detection), the Massachusetts General Court had passed an act empowering two or more justices of the peace to tender "an oath of allegiance and abjuration" to "any person they suspected of being disaffected to his Majesty or to his Government."[1] Almost immediately, Checkley had been ordered to take the oath. He had refused, as defiant in the face of a certain fine and possible imprisonment as he had been earlier when ordered to divulge the author of the suppressed tract, whereupon he had turned the tables on his inquisitors by audaciously demanding proof that Governor Shute had "any authority or Instruction referring to the Press."[2]

Targeted by the censors, Checkley had become too hot for Fleet, who was on shaky ground himself. But the end of their professional collaboration did not prevent Fleet from remaining Checkley's friend and a sometime member of his social group, which gathered regularly at the Checkley's place of business, located "at the Sign of the Crown and Blue Gate over against the West End of the Town-House." Part apothecary shop, part bookshop, part toy emporium, it seemed mostly to exist for the purpose of the mysterious meetings that were a source of ongoing concern for Puritan Boston. Almost no one believed that Checkley was simply hosting a "literary coterie," as his biographer would subsequently claim.[3] By the time Fleet introduced James Franklin to the group in 1720 or early 1721, many Bostonians were convinced that the shop was either a forward operating base for the Anglican invasion of New England, the headquarters of a demonic cult, or both.

Checkley's physical resemblance to the Devil added to the suspicion. Extremely short, and with an unnaturally high forehead, his appearance was off-putting. He embraced his homeliness with gusto, sitting for his only known portrait (painted by the artist John Smibert and since lost) at least partly as a joke, to give those who viewed it a laugh at his expense. He had a sense of humor about everything except his religious faith. His devotion to the Church of England was dogmatic and unsmiling. He loved picking theological fights. He wore a large gold cross around his neck as much to offend Puritans—who considered it a blasphemous icon—as to declare his religious devotion.

In the heyday of the Puritan theocracy thirty years earlier a religious troublemaker like Checkley would have been arrested and banished, his followers forced to scatter. If he had kept up his crusade he would have been put to death. Now, though, the government was forbidden from overtly persecuting those who espoused religious views the Puritans considered devilish and dangerous. Nor was there unanimous consensus that Checkley ought to be silenced. The town's growing Anglican population welcomed some pushback against the Puritan establishment. So did a number of intellectually curious young Puritans, who, impatient with the rigidness and narrow provincialism of their cloistered upbringing, found Checkley's boldness intoxicating. They also found him a charismatic figure, fascinating in his worldliness and cultural sophistication. He had spent years traveling through Europe, studying languages and art and collecting books and manuscripts. He offered restless young men a glimpse of a world most had not experienced and a thrillingly contrary perspective on the one they thought they knew. They were titillated by his "keen sarcasms, his pithy humor, and his caustic wit" and by his willingness to scandalize the better sort of Puritan.[4]

For a time, Checkley's acolytes had even included a member of Puritanism's first family, Cotton Mather's nephew Thomas Walter. Scandalized by Walter's association with Anglicanism's chief radical, the young man's parents had enlisted Mather to stage an intervention. It had taken many months for him to break Walter's bond with Checkley. Once freed of the Anglican's influence, however, Walter had become his most vocal enemy. The impression created by Mather that Checkley's hold on Walter had been a kind of demonic possession—an impression Walter, who not only had come back into the Puritan fold but had become a Congregational minister to boot, did nothing to discourage—had gone a long way toward creating the perception that the little Anglican was an agent of Satan.

Shortly after the government had charged Checkley with disloyalty, Walter had published a pamphlet celebrating the charge and predicting that it would finally make his former friend the pariah he deserved to be. Walter felt certain that Checkley would be treated "with abhorrence" by "Every Body" in Boston.[5] Checkley's coterie, though, had remained largely intact. Although Walter was gone, John Gibbins and George Steward, two Anglican physicians, remained. Gibbins was a former member of Benjamin Colman's liberal Puritan congregation and had a convert's fanatical devotion to his new religion. Steward, who at forty-one was the same age as Checkley, was restrained and circumspect, more concerned with promoting the Church of England than with vanquishing Congregationalism. Occasional visitors included Henry Harris, the associate rector of King's Chapel, Boston's only Anglican meetinghouse; and Fleet, who, though a Church of England man, was drawn to the group more for its Anglophile sensibilities in philosophy, art, and culture than out of enthusiasm for Checkley's polarizing religious beliefs. The same could be said for William Douglass, who lacked Checkley's enthusiasm for strident Anglicanism but shared his resentment of the Puritan religious leadership and its intrusion into the civic affairs of Boston.

James Franklin was the group's token Puritan. He cared little about religious battles, but admired Checkley for his gumption, the way in which he had proven himself, in William Douglass's words, "not afraid to own his Principles."[6] The radical and the printer were similar in that respect; it would be said of James that he had a "stubborn, literal honesty about him that rejected any shadings or conditions."[7] They were alike in other ways as well. Both were clever, argumentative, and magnets for those who hungered for edgy discussions and debates about literature, philosophy, religion, and politics. Both had left their native Boston for England and returned transformed—Checkley as a cultural aesthete and a diehard Anglican evangelist, and James as an evangelist for an Enlightenment sensibility, the elevation of colonial taste and thinking. If the Anglican was disappointed that he could not convince James to renounce his father's church and join the Church of England, he was still happy to have a bright young Puritan in his circle, particularly since the young man also had a printing press. Despite the government's attempts to intimidate him into silence, Checkley remained determined to undermine Puritan influence in Boston and New England. What he needed to resume the fight was a printer willing to put ink to paper on his behalf and a way to sidestep the censors, someone to front his war on Mather and Walter and the rest of the Calvinist dissenters. It struck him that James Franklin might offer both.

BETWEEN MARCH AND the beginning of August 1721, James and Benjamin Franklin produced only one imprint, an instructional singing book noteworthy for its sixteen pages of musical notation—the first musical bars printed in America. They were not the only printers to experience a sharp drop in output. In the immediate aftermath of the controversy over "A Letter to an Eminent Clergyman" and "News from the Moon," fatigue with the currency debate and the chilling effect of the House's threat to out-censor the Council censors—coming down hard on the next politically objectionable work as a way of proving pre-publication censorship as desired by Shute was unnecessary—had combined to stifle the production of pamphlets. By June, though, smallpox had also become a factor. Preoccupied by its mounting threat, people had lost interest in the usual topics of debate and discussion. For James, whose struggling enterprise had finally seemed to be coming into its own, it was more bad luck and a possibly insurmountable challenge. Smallpox threatened not only his life but also his livelihood. He simply did not have pockets deep enough to wait out a long and severe epidemic.

Like the rest of the townspeople he had been stunned by the news that a doctor had infected his own son with smallpox in an experiment based on the testimony of African slaves. He had watched with interest as the doctor and his minister supporters had taken to print to defend the experiment and as William Douglass, a casual acquaintance through John Checkley, had responded with attacks on both the practice and the practitioner. What fascinated James almost as much as the debate itself was that it had taken shape in the town's newspapers and not in pamphlets, as had been the case with the currency debate and other recent controversies. The inoculation debate appeared to be responsible for an unprecedented increase in newspaper readership and sales.

John Checkley, meanwhile, was overjoyed to learn that Cotton Mather was behind inoculation. A few months earlier, after discovering that the title page of the minister's new book, *The Christian Philosopher,* claimed his membership in the Royal Society, he had written to the Society's secretary, Edmond Halley, asking for help catching Mather in what he felt certain was a lie. (His letter played to Halley's fervid dislike for dissenters, pointing out that by exposing Mather he would be helping a fellow Anglican "defend" himself from the New England Puritans, "these Sons of Strife, Schism & Sedition."[8]) But now the controversial practice had given him a far more potent opportunity to humiliate the minister and undermine Puritan authority in Boston. Not since the Salem trials had Mather made himself so conspicuously vulnerable to charges that he was vainly delusional, impulsive, and irresponsible. Corroborated by the minister's supposed authority in the supernatural, the witch judges had put twenty persons to death. Now ten times that number might be killed if the procedure he had forced on the town was permitted to continue. Checkley viewed inoculation as a golden opportunity to ruin Mather's reputation— and the reputations of the Congregational ministers who supported him— once and for all. The question was how to exploit it.

One line of thinking holds that the idea to launch an anti-inoculation newspaper was Checkley's: that he dreamed up the idea expressly to "persecute Mather and the Puritan clergy" as part of a larger strategy "to establish the Anglican Church on the ruins of Puritanism."[9] His chief confederates were several affluent members of the High Church party in

King's Chapel, William Douglass among them. James Franklin, the think-ing goes, was a bit player, important only for the printing press he owned and interested in nothing beyond the steady work of producing a news-paper.

But both that hypothesis and another that attempts to explain James Franklin's involvement in the initiative by positing that he was a secret Anglican convert dedicated to Checkley's mission against the Puritans (there's no evidence that James, who a few years later would be married in a Congregational church, cared enough about religion to change his alle-giance) underestimate the young printer's business savvy and journalistic ambition. One of his goals since returning to Boston had been to publish a newspaper inspired by the groundbreaking periodicals he had encoun-tered in London, especially the *Spectator*, which had been published for a middle-class audience and had become, during its short existence, "the first periodical to enjoy true mass readership" in England.[10] The perpetually shaky health of his printing business and his inability to rationalize, from a financial standpoint, a third newspaper in a town apathetic about the two already being published made moving ahead too much of a risk, even for someone with his daring. Now, though, the inoculation controversy had shown itself capable of supplying a robust audience to any newspaper that fully exploited its potential. James also had willing confederates and inves-tors in Checkley, who needed a mechanism to smite Mather; and William Douglass, who needed even more urgently to discredit Boylston. His view of the opportunity at hand, though, was very different from theirs. Check-ley and Douglass saw the paper as a way to further their agendas. James saw their agendas as a way to bring a newspaper into being and give it the running start it needed to survive. As Ben Franklin biographer Leo Lemay put it, James believed that "he could produce a better paper" than either of the two being published in Boston and that he had "a splendid opportunity to begin a paper by espousing a popular position."[11]

Not everyone was convinced. "I remember his being dissuaded by some of his Friends from the Undertaking, as not likely to succeed, one

Newspaper being in their Judgment enough for America," Benjamin Franklin wrote decades later.[12] (It's not clear whether by that point Franklin had forgotten that in August 1721 there were already three papers in America and two in Boston, or he was simply expressing the consensus opinion at the time that any newspaper beyond the first was extraneous.) Josiah Franklin, too, tried to talk his son out of the venture. But James would not be discouraged. As Checkley and Douglass drew him into their plan, he drew them into his. If the radical and the doctor believed that the printer was their pawn, their lackey, a mere front man for their partisan attacks, they would soon learn otherwise.

ON AUGUST 7, 1721, two days after Zabdiel Boylston resumed inoculating in defiance of the town meeting condemning it, America's fourth newspaper, the *New-England Courant*, hit the streets of Boston for the first time. Its name evoked a London publication called *The Daily Courant*, which in 1702 had become the first daily newspaper in England. The new Boston paper was not a daily—initially James expected it would come out only every other week—but like its namesake it was intended to be a significant departure from the norm. The decision to go with "New-England" rather than "Boston" hinted that the paper would be more ambitious in scope than its competitors. In its general configuration, though, it was similar: a single sheet twelve inches tall by eight inches wide, with two columns of type on each side and datelines rather than headlines. If anything, its appearance was a little more pedestrian than that of the *Gazette*, which retained its James Franklin woodcut illustrations in the masthead. With Checkley and Douglass pushing him hard to get the first issue on press, James might not have had the time to carve anything for his newspaper. It's more likely, though, that the omission was intentional—that James wanted to copy the simple, spare look of his beloved *Spectator*.

The most conspicuous difference between the new newspaper and its two competitors was in the masthead. Both the *News-Letter* and the *Gazette*

had come into the world with the words "Published by Authority" prominently featured there. Not being the postmaster, James had no right to the
government imprimatur. Simply by daring to launch a newspaper without
the pretense of the government's approval, he was striking out in a new
and bold direction. But as the town was about to discover, the omission
was more than obligatory; he had little interest in doing the government's
bidding or meeting with its approval. Instead he seems to have decided
from the outset that his paper's mission would include remedying what
Benjamin Harris, in his ill-fated attempt to start America's first newspaper, *Publick Occurrences both Forreign and Domestick*, had called "that *Spirit
of Lying*, which prevails among us," an objective incompatible with complete and unquestioning acceptance of the government's official version of
things.[13] His belief that he might actually get away with producing a newspaper that candid had been bolstered by news from Philadelphia, where,
a few months earlier, the *American Weekly Mercury*, the third newspaper in
the colonies, had published "the first American newspaper statement critical of British colonial policy"—a stinging protest of England's decision to
transport felons to America—and in doing so had managed to avoid severe
repercussions.[14] But James also wanted to entertain his readers, a goal that
did the government no practical service. Entertainment value had proven
crucial to both the success and survival of the great innovators of English
journalism in the years since the end of licensing—publications like the
Spectator and the *Tatler* and authors and editors like Addison and Steele,
Trenchard and Gordon, and Defoe and Swift, who had managed to comment on and critique English politics and society obliquely with wit and
satire and remain (except for Defoe) one step ahead of the jailers. They offered James a way forward, one that would permit him to offer more than
the news mongering of his competitors. The fact remained, however, that
no paper since *Publick Occurrences* had attempted to begin publication without at least a veneer of official approval. The mere absence of "Published
by Authority" was likely to raise the hackles of the censors.

John Checkley, who penned the first issue's opening salvo, wasted no time confirming the suspicions raised by the absence of those three words. In a graceless imitation of Joseph Addison's clever introduction to the first issue of the *Spectator*, he poked fun at Boston's provincial rudeness. Then he got down to his real purpose, employing a short, snide stanza of verse to attack the irresponsibility and hypocrisy of the pro-inoculation Puritan clergy, "Who like faithful Shepherds take care of their *Flocks* / By teaching and practicing what's Orthodox/ Pray hard against *Sickness*, yet preach up the POX!"[15]

The *Courant* was already a minor scandal by the time readers reached the bottom of the first column. William Douglass took over at the top of the second. His contribution, "A Continuation of the History of Inoculation in Boston," resumed his attack on Boylston and inoculation where the letter he had published after the Town House meeting left off. Now he reminded readers that Boylston was carrying forward "the Practice of Greek old Women" against the wishes of the selectmen. He mocked the fulsome praise the doctor had received from the ministers, saying that they regarded Boylston as though he were "some Romantick Character," and declaring their plaudits so preposterous that most Bostonians took them for a joke. His erstwhile deference toward the clergy—actually toward Mather as a member of the clergy—was gone. "Six Gentlemen of Piety and Learning, profoundly ignorant of the Matter," was how he described Boylston's minister supporters. He warned them that in staking their reputations on so unworthy a medical procedure they risked doing permanent damage to their standing in the community. He called the ministers' insistence on the safety and propriety of inoculation an "Infatuation" as likely to be "as Epidemick a Distemper of the Mind, as at present the small Pox is of the natural Body." It would not be the last time Douglass and others attempted to discredit Mather by invoking the word "infatuation," with its overtones of the Salem witch crisis.[16]

James Franklin wrote the rest of the issue. Although hardly as inflammatory as the paper's first two offerings, his dispatches and editorial choices departed boldly from the norm. Whereas the *News-Letter* and the *Gazette* were dominated by English and European news, partly out of a belief that those stories were intrinsically more important than domestic news and partly because domestic and local stories risked offending local officials, James focused exclusively on Boston. He editorialized freely on a report that a military expedition had been launched to put down the hostilities of the "Eastern" Indians on and near Arrowsic Island, in what is today Maine, calling it a "well-timed" initiative against the "Menaces of those treacherous Barbarians," a position that aligned with Elisha Cooke and the Popular Party and subtly against the governor, who wanted a diplomatic solution.[17] He also reported the results of the August 2 town meeting at which John Clark, Elisha Cooke, William Hutchinson, and William Clark had been chosen "by a great Majority," as the town's representatives to the next General Court, making the *Courant* the first newspaper in America to publish the results of a local election. Finally, he followed up the insults Checkley and Douglass had penned against the ministers and Boylston with a preemptive swipe at Boston's other two newspapers, sarcastically promising that out of "meer Kindness" the *Courant* would occasionally be "(like them) very, very dull."[18]

One week later, in the *News-Letter*, John Campbell sputtered indignation at his new rival's "very, very frothy fulsome Account of himself" and defended his newspaper against the charge of dullness by the odd strategy of admitting it was true but claiming that, by dedicating himself to giving simple factual accounts of the news and committing "no offence, not meddling with things out of his Province," he was, in essence, *trying* to be dull.[19] No one was sure whether Campbell was being sincere or failing in his attempt at sarcasm—at age sixty-eight, an old dog unable to emulate the new trick that the *Courant* was performing.

Another sign that the first issue of the *Courant* had struck a nerve was that the second issue appeared a week later, a full week ahead of schedule. James reported that due to the paper's favorable reception it would continue to be published weekly. To help meet the increased demand for content, he invited readers to submit "some short Piece, Serious; Sarcastick,

Ludicrous, or otherways amusing." In response to what must have been criticism or outrage over the first issue's shoddy treatment of Mather, Colman, and the other ministers, he also promised that "nothing shall here be inserted, reflecting on the Clergy (as such) of whatever Denomination, nor relating to the Affairs of Government, and no Trespass against Decency or good Manners."[20] Only James could say whether the pledge was genuine or mere lip service to a discomfited establishment; but the conspicuous hedge of "as such" must have left some readers suspecting the latter.

The lead essay for this second issue went to William Douglass. "A project for reducing the Eastern Indians by Inoculation" was another attack on Boylston's experiment, this time in the form of satire. With tongue in cheek, the physician suggested that a second expeditionary force be sent against the Indians, this one comprised entirely of inoculators with incision lancets as weapons. Under the command of "a Major General Inoculator" (Cotton Mather), a subordinate to the great "Captain General Timonious" ("our Inoculator General's good Friend and intimate Acquaintance," Douglass mocked), the force would attempt to kill as many of the enemy as possible by inoculating them.[21] A bounty of £5 would be paid for every Indian exterminated. If the Indian survived but spread his inoculated smallpox to several of his people, the bounty would be doubled.

Douglass's colleague George Steward also contributed a letter attacking inoculation. Its centerpiece was an "Abstract of a Letter from a Physician at Marseilles," which painted a gruesome picture of the plague's ongoing ravages in France, where the air was filled with the stench of dead dogs and cats, the streets were lined on both sides with people dead and dying, and there were serious shortages of bread, wine, meat, and medicine. Like Dalhonde and Douglass before him, Steward suggested that a similar fate might befall Boston. A quarantine on vessels coming from plague-infected locations would be futile, he wrote, if nothing was done to stop "a Practice that may breed it [the plague] among us."[22]

On the same day that James published that issue of the *Courant*, he also put out a sheet that, at a glance, bore an uncanny resemblance to it. A closer examination revealed that the masthead read *The Anti-Courant*. Its purported author, "Zechariah Touchstone," was actually the Reverend Thomas Walter, John Checkley's former protégé and now enemy. Outraged by Checkley's insult of his uncle and the other pro-inoculation Boston ministers in the first *Courant*, Walter had fired off a letter savaging the Anglican by mocking his "Self-conceit" and his pretensions as an author, wit, and intellectual. Walter wrote that Checkley completely lacked "the Talent of Satire." He was dull and his admirers were "stupid."[23]

John Checkley was "shocked," wrote one historian, that Walter "devoted practically his whole *Anti-Courant*, not to Douglass's serious, open, but nonpersonal attack on the minister [Mather], but to his, Checkley's, rather good-natured rambling."[24] James, though, was ecstatic. By publishing Walter's letter in a featured form and as its own counterpoint "newspaper," he was exploiting the feud between Checkley and his former friend to raise the profile of the *Courant*, making it a "must read" for Bostonians. He was the only man in Boston who would have conceived so outlandish a publicity stunt. What he didn't anticipate was that the vindictiveness of John Checkley's counterattack would nearly cost him his newspaper.

II

THE CUP WHICH I
FEAR

Z abdiel Boylston's inoculation of his youngest son and two slaves
on June 26 had brought to life a plan Cotton Mather had been
contemplating since 1716 and had spent nearly a month trying
to sell to the doctors of Boston. Yet it somehow went unmentioned in
the minister's diary that day and for the three days that followed. Mather
mentioned a "horrid Clamour" on June 30, adding that it was related to
"The Affair mention'd this day Se'nnight [a week earlier]," but he still
refused to reference the experiment by name.[1] He remained silent for two
more weeks, through the period of the boys' fevers, Thomas's scare, and
the appearance of "kind and favourable" inoculated smallpox. It wasn't
until July 16, after the boys' pocks had been out for about ten days and
both had passed the point when a second, post-outbreak fever sometimes
took a smallpox patient's life, that he finally discussed inoculation with his
erstwhile bravado. "At this Time," he wrote, "I enjoy an unspeakable Consolation. I have instructed our Physicians in the new Method used by the
Africans and *Asiaticks,* to prevent and abate the Dangers of the Small-Pox,

and infallibly to save the Lives of those that have it wisely managed upon them."[2]

Notwithstanding his claim that inoculation was infallible, Mather showed no indication that he planned to have it performed on his own children—this despite the more than two dozen mentions in his diary of their fears of coming down with smallpox. In a July 7 entry he came close to admitting that he was struggling with his doubts, writing that he would "beg . . . the Lives" of the children in his prayers and also ask for "a Direction of Heaven, what I may do for their Welfare in that, and . . . in all Regards." The townspeople's fury toward inoculation unnerved him and exacerbated those doubts. "They rave, they rail, they blaspheme; they talk not only like Ideots but also like *Franticks*," wrote a rattled Mather. He seemed shocked to have discovered that in addition to Boylston, he, too, had become "an Object of their Fury; their furious Obloquies and Invectives." Now, in his first direct reference to inoculating family members, he all but dismissed the possibility, writing that the "cursed Clamour of a People strangely and fiercely possessed of the Devil, will probably prevent my saving the Lives of my two Children, from the Small-pox in the Way of Transplantation."[3] Why the minister felt prohibited from having Sammy and Elizabeth inoculated when, despite the public fury, Boylston had gone ahead and inoculated his second son, he didn't say. Probably by that point he knew or suspected that a formal hearing on inoculation was only days away. He might have reasoned that the town would order the procedure halted. But there was still time for Boylston to perform the procedure on his son and daughter. His failure to act suggests that he was looking for the government to let him off the hook of his own bluster. It was one thing to call inoculation infallible and another to put his loved ones in harm's way. Haunted by the ghosts of ten dead children, he discovered that he simply didn't have the stomach for it. It was easier now to blame their non-inoculation on a people possessed by the Devil than to admit he was afraid. When Boylston stopped performing the procedure following the July 21 inquisition, he probably felt a mixture of relief and dread. Spared a decision he did not want to make, he could only hope and pray that his children would also be spared a terrible and painful death.

Mather's failure to have his children inoculated was far more condonable than his failure to come to Boylston's defense. If anyone should have stood behind the doctor during and after the July 21 town meeting it was the man who had urged him to attempt inoculation in the first place. Instead, Mather spent that day at home, praying for his children on the assumption, it appears, that the town was determined to prohibit inoculation, leaving their preservation entirely to God. His diary entry that day made no mention of the ordeal Boylston had undergone at the Town House; he referred only to the "hellish Assault" on his own attempts to do good.[4] His next mention of inoculation six days later was equally self-pitying. He bewailed the "monstrous and crying Wickedness of this Town . . . and the vile Abuse which I do myself particularly suffer from it, for nothing but my instructing our base Physicians, how to save many precious Lives."[5] There was no indignation over Boylston's mistreatment or a determination to continue fighting for the cause that he had introduced.

Thirty years earlier, at Salem, he had helped foment a crisis and then backed away when things had begun to go badly, shirking his responsibility to those caught up in a fury partly of his making. Now he was doing it again. Having pushed inoculation on Boston with an urgency and certainty reminiscent of his former calls for vigilance against an invasion of witches—a similarity William Douglass, for one, had noted—he shrank from his obligation to defend the procedure and the physician accused of endangering the public with it. His dream of being hailed as a hero dashed, he had given up the inoculation campaign for lost.

THE *BOSTON NEWS-LETTER* published on the final day of July posted numbers of sick and dead lower than many readers might have expected. But it also subtly warned against a too optimistic interpretation of the data. "We have several good and experienced Nurses in this Town," it reported, "but the Number is not answerable to those that may be wanted if the Distemper should prove general."[6]

The next day Boston commemorated the seventh anniversary of King George's ascension to the throne with multigun salutes from the town's two batteries, from the fort on Castle Island, and from the HMS *Seahorse*, as well as by "other Demonstrations of Joy."[7] But with smallpox still spreading, the celebration was perfunctory and spiritless.

While the guns sounded from land and sea and Bostonians did their best to affect joyousness, Samuel Mather left his Harvard dormitory, caught the ferry from Cambridge to Boston, and hurried east across the peninsula toward Ship Street. His appearance at the front door of the family home was a surprise to his father, who could tell from the boy's agitation that something was very wrong. Sammy's Harvard roommate, a young man named William Charnock, had come down with smallpox. Now, hoping that the effects of his own possible infection might be preempted, Sammy made a desperate appeal to his father, who recorded it in his diary. "He begs to have his Life saved, by receiving the *Small-Pox*, in the way of *Inoculation*," Mather wrote.[8]

At that point the minister might have believed that inoculation was out of the question, given that Boylston had not performed the operation since the town meeting ten days earlier. But when the doctor resumed the procedure five days after Sammy's return, the young man was not among his subjects. Cotton Mather rationalized why it remained an impossibility. There were "People, who have Satan remarkably filling their Hearts and their Tongues," he wrote, who would "go on with infinite Prejudices" against him and his ministry if the boy underwent the procedure. If Sammy died, Mather's condition would be "insupportable."[9] But he also knew that if he refused to allow an operation his son had asked for and the boy died of natural smallpox he would never forgive himself.

Mather sought out his father's advice. Increase recommended inoculation, but with the caveat that it be conducted secretly in case the outcome was unfavorable. Even with that hedge against accountability, though,

Cotton Mather dithered. Three days after Sammy's return he had signaled a reengagement with the inoculation cause by committing himself to writing something supportive of Boylston—"some further Armour, to conquer the Dragon."[10] But he had backtracked from there, withholding his approval when Boylston performed the operation again a week later. On August 9 he resolved to press "Lessons of Piety"—not inoculation—on undisclosed members of his family who were in "continual Fears of being seized by the *Small-Pox*."[11] The appearance of a new testimonial to Boylston by four of the men he had shepherded through inoculation—Cheever, Heyler, and John and Joseph Webb—in the August 14 *Boston Gazette* helped shift the minister back in the direction of approval. His indignation over the insults he and the procedure had received in the first two issues of the *New-England Courant* might also have helped spur him in the direction of action. What finally settled the matter, though, was the news that arrived at the family's home on August 15. In his diary that evening, after acknowledging that his son's inoculation had finally been performed, Mather revealed it: Sammy's "dearest Companion" and "Chamber-fellow" at Harvard was dead.[12]

Boylston was less worried that Sammy had already been infected—by this point he believed that inoculation after the fact could mitigate the severity of an infection already acquired by contagion—than about the two weeks that had elapsed between that possible infection and the inoculation. Mather tried to mask his own apprehensions about the possible consequences of the delay with bravado. "The Notable Experience I now have of this New Method, for the Saving of many Lives, yea, and for the Abating and preventing of Miseries undergone by many who do live, and survive an horrible Distemper," he wrote, "enables me to recommend the matter so, that I hope it may be introduced into the English Nation, and a World of good may be done to the miserable Children of Men." The next day he resolved to contribute some letters to the newspapers in order to "correct and restrain the Epidemical Follies of the Town."[13]

Before another week had passed, though, that optimism, ebullience, and renewed sense of mission had disappeared. On the evening of August 20 or the morning of August 21, Sammy broke out in a high fever. It wasn't the fever itself but the timing of its onset that unnerved his father. Typically, inoculated smallpox incubated for eight days before symptoms appeared. Sammy was only six days into his inoculation. In his diary Mather acknowledged what he had hoped and prayed had not been the case: that his son had "also taken the Infection in the common Way."[14]

Panicked at the thought that Sammy was sick with the same smallpox that had killed his roommate, and stricken with guilt for having delayed the inoculation so long, Mather did what he often did when overwhelmed by the consequences of his own action or inaction: He looked for someone else to blame. At least in his diary that person was Boylston. The problem wasn't that he had waited too long to have his son inoculated, but that Boylston had botched the procedure, making only one incision "so small as to be hardly worthy the Name of one." Deeply pessimistic, he began preparing for the likelihood that his son would "miscarry" Boylston's shoddy inoculation and die, and that in addition to losing the boy in whom he had vested all of his hopes he would be made to suffer what he called the "prodigious Clamour and Hatred" of the mob.[15]

12

THE HELL-FIRE
CLUB

W illiam Douglass kept after Boylston and inoculation in the
lead essay of the third *New-England Courant*. This time he
argued that inoculation didn't work. His evidence was a
testimonial from a British ship's surgeon who claimed to have encoun-
tered men who had been inoculated in Spain only to be afflicted later on
with cases of smallpox so severe that "they narrowly escaped with their
Lives." He also mocked the letter Joshua Cheever and his fellow inoculation patients had written in support of Boylston, calling it "silly" and a
"*Quack Recommendation* of the Operator." Finally, he attempted to por-
tray inoculation as an unnecessary risk by arguing that unlike "the *Plague*
at *Marseilles*," smallpox wasn't really "*a terrible Distemper*." This outbreak
in particular, he insisted, was a relatively minor one. "Few Epidemics or
Popular *Fevers* of any Sort, have been *more favourable*," he wrote. "Notwithstanding of its spreading, it becomes *more gentle*, the greatest Part
of our Patients at present having a *fair, large, distinct Sort*, and many not
requiring Confinement." The real threat posed by the current outbreak,

he opined, was that its danger would be blown out of proportion; that excessive fear might "tend to obstruct the Town's being supplied with Provisions from the Country" and interrupt its ocean trade.[1] To prove that the smallpox outbreak was minor, he employed a selective statistical analysis of the death toll so far, pointing out that the total number of Boston deaths in the months since the first cases of smallpox had appeared was no higher than during comparable smallpox-free periods. But he neglected to add that the number was trending upward. Officially, at least, only one person had died from smallpox in May. Eight deaths had occurred in June, followed by eleven in July. By the time August was over, twenty-six more people would be dead.

Although some readers doubtless took issue with Douglass's attempt to downplay an outbreak that had killed members of their families and threatened their own lives, his letter was not the talk of the August 21 *Courant*. Two other contributions, both in answer to Thomas Walter's *Anti-Courant*, created far more controversy. Dr. John Gibbins accused the young minister of being a drunk, citing his fragile constitution and "vicious" mind as proof. He also threatened to blackmail Walter with "Materials" that would offer "a Narrative of his mysterious Actions."[2] John Checkley picked up where Gibbins left off, labeling Walter an *"obscene and fuddling Merry-Andrew"* [a clown] and the *"Tom-Bully* for the Cause" advocated by his uncle Cotton Mather. He wrote that since the men defending inoculation argued that their prestige and reputations—"the naked *Merits* of their *Character*"—were reason enough to believe them about the procedure, those reputations ought to be fair game for skeptics. With that he revealed that during Walter's rebellious period he had written a scandalously insulting note to his uncle Mather, offering to give him, among other things, "a Kick on the Arse" and "a Slap on the Chops." Checkley also claimed that one evening Walter had been discovered

with another *Debauchee*, at a Lodging with two Sisters, of not the best Reputation in the World, upon the Bed, with them Several Hours, and this Spark sent for *Punch* to treat them with, and would have had the *Candle put out*, but they not having a Conveniency to light it again, it was *lock'd in a Closet, and——&c.*[3]

He ended with a short passage of verse echoing Gibbins's accusation that the young minister was nothing more than a scribbling drunk.

The third issue of the *New-England Courant* was scandalous, malicious, sophomoric, and offensive. For all of those defects it was also an exercise in press freedom unlike any that America had seen. Extending the themes introduced in its first two issues to shocking lengths, it "criticized the ulti-mate instrument of authority in the Bible Commonwealth: the ministers and the state church."[4] Unlike the *American Weekly Mercury*'s criticism of the English government, which had been polite and proper and fleeting—having stated its case, the paper had had the good sense to let the matter drop—the *Courant* was showing itself to be doggedly impudent. And the paper was offending men who lived right down the street, not on the other side of the vast buffer zone of the Atlantic Ocean.

No specific objections were recorded. But when the next *Courant* ap-peared on August 28, the final page of what was meant to be a four-page issue was blank. Presumably one or more persons had convinced James to cut material similar in type and tone to the attacks on Walter the pre-vious week. The pressure might have come from the Anglican pastors of King's Chapel, who believed that the hostility expressed by Gibbins, Checkley, and, to a lesser degree, Douglass was both untoward and coun-terproductive to the cause of expanding Church of England influence in Massachusetts; or it may have come from the government, which might have threatened libel charges. James later admitted that his own pastors, by which he most likely meant the ministers of his father's church, the Old South, had reproved him. Aghast at his son's complicity in attacks on the Puritan clergy, the pious Josiah Franklin must have weighed in as well, concerned both that his son might end up in jail and that his own investment of more than £200 in the printing house might never be repaid if James and his business were embargoed by Puritan Boston or censored out of existence by the government.

Instead of the snide, personal attacks of Checkley and Douglass, the fourth issue featured the Reverend Henry Harris, who argued that allowing oneself to undergo the possibly deadly inoculation procedure was inconsistent with self-preservation and therefore a violation of God's commandment against murder. His essay took up all of the paper's first page and nearly three-quarters of its second. It was followed by a James Franklin poem lamenting the death and misery caused by the smallpox outbreak. "On the Distress of the Town of Boston, occasioned by the Small Pox" was as uninspired as its title.[5] Probably James had written it quickly and at the last minute to help fill the gaping hole created by his decision to cut material.

Even with the cuts and the milder tone, the *Courant* still managed to push the boundaries of what was considered a newspaper's proper sphere. In the issue's final column James divulged that the Rhode Island assembly had approved a quarantine on all persons and goods arriving from Boston or any other smallpox-infested town in Massachusetts.[6] It was the first evidence Boston readers had seen that smallpox was causing a fearful, self-protective response among the town's trading partners, precisely the kind of development the Massachusetts authorities had been trying to prevent by downplaying the severity of the outbreak. Neither of Boston's "authorized" newspapers mentioned the Rhode Island quarantine.

CHECKLEY WAS FURIOUS with James for capitulating to the threats of censorship and most likely for cutting his contribution to the fourth issue. Douglass, who might also have had an essay cut, took his side. Neither man particularly cared what might happen to James or the newspaper if the *Courant* continued offending as it had in issue three. For them each issue was a bomb to be lit and lobbed into the camp of their enemies. They hadn't thought past their own objectives to what the paper might become if it survived its initial campaign.

James, though, had been thinking beyond the inoculation controversy right from the start. Whether he personally opposed inoculation at all is an open question, since at no point would he jump on the bandwagon and pen a screed against it. (It was Checkley, not James, who in issue three had written that the "chief design" of the *Courant* was to oppose inoculation.)[7] Certainly he was not so convinced of its malevolence that he was willing to sacrifice a perfectly good newspaper to fight it. And he was even less willing to sacrifice the *Courant* over the sectarian religious disputes that obsessed Checkley. His crusade was against the overbearing arrogance of authority in any form—especially, though not exclusively, the heavy hand of the Puritan theocracy. His focus was on his dream of an American version of the late, great *Spectator*, which had endeavored to "enliven Morality with Wit, and to temper Wit with Morality," and bring philosophy "out of Closets and Libraries, Schools and Colleges, to dwell in Clubs and Assemblies, at Tea-Tables and in Coffee-Houses."[8] Put another way, he wanted to educate and enfranchise the emerging middle class of American tradesmen, giving them a voice in the important issues of the day. That and ruffle a few feathers in the process.

Standing up to his two partners could not have been easy. Checkley was nearly twenty years his senior. Douglass was only six years older than James but every bit Checkley's equal in his ability to browbeat those who dared challenge him. Both men wielded their education and superior worldliness like knives. But James had the printing press. And he knew that no other printer in Boston would print for Checkley. When push came to shove, as it did at some point between issues three and five, he was the one who refused to back down. The charismatic Checkley, who had gone "too far even for James Franklin," was banned from his own newspaper.[9] He would never again appear in it. Douglass's direct involvement in the paper was also terminated for the present. It would be several months before James relented and printed another of his essays.

The fifth issue of the *New-England Courant* was the first created entirely as James intended it. He signaled a new beginning with an elaborate woodcut at the top of the first column of text. Tooled to hold an initial capital letter at its center, it contained two conventional newspaper images: a horn-blowing courier mounted on his horse, and a sailing ship. Its third image, a young winged angel or putto that represented poetry, love, and the muse, was new to Boston, a declaration that the *Courant* had literary aspirations. The story that proceeded from that ornate first letter confirmed the fresh start. It took the form of a letter from "Zerubbabel Tindal," who complained about the paper's coverage of inoculation, not because he disagreed with it, but because he was bored with having to read about the subject week after week. It was, he wrote, "a very insipid Theme to us, who have a most exquisitely nice and refin'd Taste, and not Superabundantly entertaining to your Common Readers." He told the publisher of the *Courant* that in order to print more interesting items he ought to avail himself of the services of a new group of contributors— a "clan of Honest Wags" of whom Tindal himself served as leader. He and the Wags, he wrote, were "Owners of a great Genius" who "without racking our brains, can Occasionally be at [*sic*] DULL as you please." The group included "excellent" poets, astronomers, and "Batchellers . . . well vers'd in the Theory of Love." He continued: "We are now Exhillerating our Spirits over a Capacious Bowl of Inebriating Liquor; and your Health is just going round." Teasingly he warned that if James didn't let inoculation drop, his group would "procure another Scourge for you from Little Compton [Thomas Walter], and lend J—n C—l [John Campbell] a hand to satirize you in his next."[10]

After the lacerating attacks of the first three *Courants* and the sober seriousness of the fourth, Tindal's tipsy and mildly irreverent playfulness surprised the paper's readers. Although a scold or a prude could find it objectionable—too undignified, too juvenile, too glib about a serious topic, unbecoming of a newspaper that expected to be taken seriously and apparently written by a man who was not only drunk but also unabashedly so—it was comparatively harmless, a vast departure from the offensive stuff of its predecessors. In the same issue and under the pseudonym "Timothy Turnstone," James Franklin replied to Tindal, poking fun at the comically extravagant way in which the letter writer had addressed him—"Most Hyperbollically Profound, and Superlatively Sagacacious, and Penetrating Sir"—by referring to himself as the "most noble, and superabundantly DULL Author of the New-England Courant," and by offering several rules Tindal and his Wags should follow in submitting their work, including one that stipulated they should drink no more than a "full Gallon" before contributing, and that each man refrain from discussing "State Affairs" until his drinking had rendered him "so far gone as to forget your own."[11]

Having established the lighter touch of the new *Courant*, James closed the fifth issue by addressing a more serious matter that had been gnawing at him for a week. A letter inserted in the *News-Letter* on August 28, one week after the *Courant* attacked Thomas Walter, had accused James and his associates at the newspaper of being an American version of a group of infamous English libertines reputed to be Satanists. The English Hell-Fire Club was said to conduct black masses and host drunken orgies. As an earlier *News-Letter* had reported, the royal government had committed itself to "detecting and prosecuting with vigour all the Profaneness, Immorality, and Debauchery" caused by such groups for fear that they would "Increase and draw down the Vengeance of GOD upon this Nation."[12] According to the August 28 *News-Letter* correspondent, the *Courant* had proven itself to be "Notorious" and "Scandalous" and "full freighted with Nonsence, Unmannerliness, Railery, Prophaneness, Immorality, Arrogancy, Calumnies, Lyes, Contradictions, and what not, all tending to Quarrels and Divisions, and to Debauch and Corrupt the Minds and Manners of New England." If the authors of "that Flagicious and Wicked Paper" failed to "clear themselves of and from the Imputation," the anonymous author warned, "People will take it for granted, they are a new club set up in New England, like to that in our Mother England."[13]

Three decades after the Salem witch trials, an accusation of Devil worship was still no laughing matter in New England. Writing as "W. Anti-inoculator" in the *Boston Gazette* (because James had shut him out of the *Courant*), a rattled William Douglass insisted that he could find nothing published in the *Courant* "to contain the least shadow for so high an Accusation." Even Checkley's reply to Walter, which he conceded had been offensive, had, in his opinion, been blown out of proportion. But he also distanced himself from his former newspaper, insisting that the members of his *real* club, the new physicians' group he and Checkley had formed to resist the encroachment of the clergy in medical matters, were "only accountable for their own pieces, and not for other Matters inserted by the Publishers of News-Papers." Unlike members of "that Blaspheming Hell-fire horrid Club in England," he and his fellow members of "the Society of Physicians Anti-Inoculators" did not attempt to conceal their identities (his use of a pseudonym in this case apparently notwithstanding). If a secret Boston Hell-Fire Club did exist, he wrote, the authorities ought to prosecute its members to the fullest extent, "that such execrable wickedness may be crushed in Embrio, and the said Men suffer exemplary punishment." But if the accusations were baseless and malicious, as he insisted was true in his case, the authorities ought to "brand the Authors of said Libel as infamous Libellers," since to be accused of so malevolent an intent was, he maintained, worse than having one's throat cut.[14]

James, too, was upset over the charge. He "was not sufficiently removed from the Puritan heritage and influence of Josiah, his father," wrote Arthur Bernon Tourtellot, "to regard [it] calmly or treat [it] lightly."[15] Unlike Douglass, though, he neither defended himself nor admitted the error of printing Checkley's reply to Walter. Instead, as "Peter Columbus," he took the offensive and claimed the high ground, declaring the Hell-Fire Club charges so patently preposterous as to be unworthy of a more particular response. "We dare not own *your Piece* for Publick Use / *When fill'd with private Spleen, & gross Abuse*," he wrote to his unnamed attacker, whom he accused of having "*Ill-natur'd Eyes*" and an "*envenom'd*

Brain.[16] Douglass had hinted strongly at the man's identity in his *Gazette* piece, describing him as someone who spread an "infatuation" of the mind when his proper role was "to cure indispositions of the mind."[17] It was the second time in three weeks that he had harkened back to Salem by trotting out the word "infatuation." James, too, seems to have been convinced that the man who had been infatuated with witches then and the one infatuated with the idea that the men behind the *Courant* were Devil worshippers now were one and the same.

13

A MAN ON A CROSS

T he rain began falling about the time of Samuel Mather's inoculation in August. After the dry, brutally hot days of June and July
it was a welcome relief. But when it persisted for days, the blessing turned to a curse. The drenching downpours flooded the streets and
threatened to drown the fields, ruining the crops and sending the diseased
town into winter with a catastrophic food shortage. When Cotton Mather
accused the authors of the *New-England Courant* of being a "Hell-Fire
Club" near the end of August he cited both the smallpox epidemic and
"the threatening Aspect of the Wet Weather" as evidence that the impious
acts of the people were inciting God's wrath.[1]

Mather's anxiety over the flooding probably contributed to his overre-
action to the *Courant* and the wild hyperbole of his ill-conceived and irresponsible Hell-Fire Club accusation. He was already frantic with fear that
he was on the verge of losing his son Sammy, whose post-inoculation fever
had broken out on the same day that John Checkley's attack on Thomas
Walter had been published in the *Courant*. Three days later the fever was

still raging. Mather described it as "dangerous and threatening . . . beyond what the *Inoculation* of the *Small-Pox* has hitherto brought upon any Subjects of it," and he seemed to hold the town responsible for the severity, declaring Boston "almost an Hell upon Earth, a City full of Lies, and Murders, and Blasphemies." Shortly thereafter Sammy broke out in smallpox. His father described the outbreak as "pretty full" and "not the best sort" and concluded that Samuel's condition was "very hazardous."[2] Boylston's description of Sammy's pocks as "near the filling" suggests that they were so densely packed as to approach a case of confluent smallpox, the type fatal in well over half the cases.[3]

With his son in agony and close to death, Mather retreated to the library on the top floor of his house. He latched the door, closed the shutters against the noise and dull gray light of another waterlogged day, and prostrated himself on the hard floor, where he remained, unmoving, for most of the day. With his mouth "in the dust" he repeatedly offered "to make a Sacrifice" of Sammy in emulation of the biblical Abraham, who had been willing to kill his son Isaac to prove his faith.[4] If God "would please to kill the Lad, even in such aggravating Circumstances of Sorrow, as his Death must now be attended with," Mather would "humbly acquiesce in His most sovereign, just and wise Dispensations." For most of the day, though, he subsequently wrote, he "beg'd for the Life of the Child, that he may live to serve the Kingdome of GOD, and that the Cup which I fear may pass from me."[5] Mather hoped that the angels would come to him with a "particular faith" that Sammy would survive his trial. But his concentrated meditations produced no such vision. When after many hours he pulled himself to his feet and descended the stairs from the library to the sickroom below, he found the boy's condition as dire as ever. For the next two days Samuel remained gravely ill. On August 27 Mather reiterated his willingness to sacrifice his son. Now he went even further: To prove his faith he would submit to being "stript" not only of Sammy but also of all his "worldly Enjoyments" including his wealth, his health, and his friends; he would "find in a glorious CHRIST alone, all the satisfactions which People vainly promise themselves in Creatures."[6] All would be made right, he was certain, in Heaven.

As Samuel Mather's ordeal dragged on, his father's emotions lurched from one extreme to the other. One day he was beatifically resigned to whatever trials and injustices life presented; the next he was wallowing in self-pity and bleating about his victimization by the combined forces of evil in Boston, which was a "miserable" town, "a dismal Picture and Emblem of *Hell*; *Fire* with *Darkness* filling of it, and a *lying Spirit* reigning there."[7] He devoted August 30 to another all-day prayer session. His intention was to once again give Sammy over to death to prove his love of God. This time, though, he found his spirit unwilling. In frustration he took up his Bible. It came to him, he later wrote, that if he opened it at random, God would guide his hand to "the fittest Matter for my Meditations." He landed on John 4:46–54, the story of Jesus's second miracle, his cure of a nobleman's son who lay close to death at Capernaum. The passage that immediately caught his eye was "Go thy Way, thy Son liveth."[8] It could have been luck or an exercise in muscle memory, his encyclopedic knowledge of the Bible combining with his desperate need for Sammy's survival to direct his finger to precisely the right spot. Mather, though, was convinced that he had received a sign from God.

Samuel's fever spiked that evening and the boy became delirious. At some point in the evening he cried out, begging to "have a Vein breathed in him" in a voice that his father described as coming from some "superiour Original."[9] Mather consented to the bloodletting. Within the hour Sammy's fever and his symptoms began to ease. He continued to improve the following morning and throughout the rest of the day. After ten days of near certainty that Sammy would die, Mather could allow himself to believe that he would survive after all.

The minister's trials, though, were only beginning. Five days earlier he had noted in passing that he had "other Children also at this Time, sick and weak and languishing, and in much Affliction." Now he elaborated. His daughter Abigail, who was pregnant and a few weeks from giving birth, was "very hazardously circumstanced with several Infirmities." Her husband, Daniel Willard, was also ill, delirious from an "unknown Fever."[10] Meanwhile, in his own home, his daughter Hannah had taken suddenly and violently ill with a fever. Whether some or all of them had smallpox is unclear. Twenty-five-year-old Hannah almost certainly had had the disease during its previous visitation, when Increase Jr. had also taken ill. Because Abigail was older by two years, her father might have mistakenly believed that she, too, had already survived it. (Mather had seen so much illness and death in his family that it was entirely plausible he had lost track of which children had suffered from which disease. Indeed, in the aftermath of the November 1713 measles epidemic, he had found it necessary to list his children on the back cover of his diary ledger and tally their fates: "Of 15, Dead, 9, Living 6."[11]) If Hannah was sick with something other than the pox, Abigail seems to have been its unfortunate victim.

Initially Hannah—or "poor Nancy, dear Nancy," as he referred to the disfigured girl—appeared worse off. Seeing "the plain Symptoms of approaching Death continually increasing upon her," he set aside another day to ask God to spare his besieged child. This time, though, there was neither a visitation by the angels nor reassurance from the Bible. "My two dying Daughters!" Mather wrote on September 1.[12] Two days later he was told that a delirious Hannah had only hours to live. He had given up hope for her survival when he experienced what he called "a strange Light" that she would survive. Not long afterward she regained her senses long enough to promise the same. She was still alive the next day, albeit no less "condemned" to death in the opinion of her doctors. "Nancy still a dying," Mather wrote on September 5 and again the next day. Abigail, too, remained "dangerously circumstanced."[13]

Hannah's fever broke unexpectedly on September 8, giving her father hope that she might pull through. Almost simultaneously, though, Abigail's condition began to worsen. Two days after delivering a baby girl on September 17, she became the Mather daughter in "Dying Circumstances."[14]

On September 24, Abigail's newborn daughter was brought to the North Church for baptism. In the midst of the ceremony, the little girl, whose baptized name was Resigned, suddenly died. The loss of his grandchild just as he was about to baptize her left Mather dumbstruck. "An Uncommon Occurrence!" was all he could manage in his diary. Two days later Abigail Mather Willard died a "long and hard Death" between ten o'clock and eleven o'clock in the evening.[15] She was the eleventh of Mather's fifteen children to die.

"A man hanging on a *Cross* . . . has little to say, unto anything that this *World* has to offer unto him," her father wrote.[16]

14

THE DEADLIEST
TIME

Four days after Esther Webb's August 5 inoculation—too soon for it to have taken hold—she developed confluent smallpox, her pustules so densely packed as to form a solid sheath of angry, inflamed skin. It was clear that the inoculation had come too late, that she had contracted smallpox in the common way, probably from one of her parents, not long after Boylston had been warned off inoculating at the July town meeting. Now, buried alive in her own necrotic flesh, she lay near death.

While he did his best to save her, Boylston kept inoculating. He performed the procedure twice on August 12, once on August 15, and once on August 22. On August 23 he inoculated five persons, including his oldest son. He worried that, like Esther Webb and Samuel Mather, Zabdiel Jr. might already have contracted smallpox in the common way, since he had spent two days in "an infected Chamber" at Harvard. But at about the eight-day mark the fourteen-year-old experienced the "gentle" symptoms of a textbook successful inoculation: the pain, fever, and outbreak of distinct pocks, all mild.[1] He returned to complete health shortly thereafter. There was good news about the Webb girl, too. Thanks to "a great deal of Care and Pains" on Boylston's part, she had passed through her crisis and now seemed destined to survive and recover with her vision and reason intact.[2] Her scarring, though, was severe and irreversible. Whatever beauty she had possessed was gone.

Esther's survival meant that Boylston had dodged a death his enemies would have been only too happy to blame on inoculation. But he still faced possible legal repercussions for resuming the procedure in defiance of its condemnation at the July meeting. He also faced a mob infuriated anew by the spate of recent inoculations. With his wife still in the country and his time taken up with patients, his younger sons roamed the streets unsupervised and probably the targets of abuse themselves. The Reverend Benjamin Colman, whose house faced the Boylston yard, worried that the boys were "too much exposed & neglected."[3] On one occasion he had seen young Thomas playing in the dirty water pooled in a street gutter.

Boylston's five inoculations on August 23 were the most he had performed in a single day. Outraged Bostonians hoped and anticipated that so flagrant a violation of the town's ban on the procedure would be the straw that broke the camel's back, resulting, finally, in an arrest and incarceration. When the next day came and went without so much as a new warning, they were flabbergasted. One reason for the government's inaction might have been that it had failed to explicitly outlaw the practice. The other was probably the identity of the young man Boylston had inoculated on August 22. Samuel Valentine was the nineteen-year-old son of John Valentine, who until recently had served as His Majesty's advocate general of Massachusetts and Rhode Island, a title that had made him the Crown's senior legal official in New England. (He had been one of the men present the night Elisha Cooke had called Samuel Shute a blockhead.) Young Valentine had powerful connections on the other side of his family as well: His mother was the daughter of the prominent Boston judge Samuel Lynde and the niece of Benjamin Lynde, a sitting member of the Governor's Council. If he survived his inoculation and emerged whole, those men were unlikely to abide Boylston's arrest since, by extension, the boy's mother would be party to an illegal activity. Conversely, the death of a young man with close ties to the government and the legal system made it all but certain that any retribution the family took against the doctor would stick.

Samuel Valentine broke out in "a kind distinct Sort" of inoculated smallpox on August 31 or September 1. The young man's symptoms were "gentle" and "he soon did well."[4] When it became clear that he would come through without incident, Boylston called his wife and daughters home from the countryside, inoculating all three girls immediately upon their arrival. Jerusha, Boylston's eldest daughter, fared well, with a total of forty or fifty pocks. Eight-year-old Mary and four-year-old Elizabeth were "pretty full in their Faces," but had "gentle" symptoms overall.[5] Boylston also inoculated Benjamin Colman's eighteen-year-old son, who likewise came through smoothly.

Word of Valentine's easy recovery spurred a rush of requests for the procedure. Among the twenty-five persons inoculated between September 7 and September 23 were members of two other prominent political families, one present, one future. The fourteen-year-old son of Councilor Thomas Fitch was the first immediate relative of a sitting member of the General Court to undergo the operation. And several days before performing that operation, Boylston had inoculated a thirty-two-year-old merchant and malter, his twenty-seven-year-old wife, and their four-year-old daughter. In the years to come, Samuel Adams Sr. would become a key figure in Elisha Cooke's Boston caucus. The son born to him and Mary Adams on September 27, 1722, a little more than a year after their inoculations, was destined to become the firebrand of the American Revolution. It's conceivable that Sam Adams Jr. owed his birth to the radical procedure—that his father might have been lost to naturally contracted smallpox had he not been inoculated. (His mother, who had no reaction to her inoculation, had apparently survived the disease as a young child.) If so, he was the first of many Founding Fathers who would benefit from the procedure.

In the three months since Boylston's first experiment on his youngest son and two slaves, he had operated on nearly sixty persons without losing a patient. That unblemished record deprived opponents like Douglass of their surest means of stopping inoculation. But there had been a number of close calls. A woman who had submitted to the procedure after having "lived in the Way of Infection above a Month" had developed confluent smallpox. At one point her face had been bloated nearly beyond recognition and she had barely had a pulse. Her eyes, swollen shut by the wild proliferation of pustules, had developed a "violent Inflammation" that had permanently destroyed the sight in one of them.[6] But she, too, had survived. Compared to that case and Boylston's earlier worries over his son Thomas, his friend Joshua Cheever, and Esther Webb, "Mrs. Dixwell" seemed destined for an easy recovery. She went a full nine days after her August 30 procedure before breaking out in inoculated smallpox, a strong indication that she had not been infected prior to the operation. The pocks that emerged were full but distinct in type, another good sign. But about seven days into the outbreak, the point at which a patient generally began to recover, her smallpox fluxed. On September 24, the same day Cotton Mather lost his daughter Abigail, she died.

IF WILLIAM DOUGLASS ever really believed his August 21 *New-England Courant* claim that the lethality of smallpox in Boston was both exaggerated and steadily diminishing, his own close monitoring of the epidemic in the weeks that followed offered incontrovertible proof that he was mistaken. From May until early July, he later wrote, the waves of the outbreak had occurred "in distinct parcels at about sixteen or eighteen days distance from seizure to seizure." (This described perfectly the incubation period of the naturally occurring form of the disease.) But after the third of those "parcels," the waves of infection had begun to overlap and meld. By late summer or early fall the disease had become, by his own confidential assessment, "universal." In a letter to Cadwallader Colden he admitted that as the number of cases increased, the severity of those cases became "more intense." Boston's smallpox epidemic was growing more lethal.[7] Halfway through September the death toll for the month was already higher than the totals for July and August combined.

Even as the growing terror of the epidemic became obvious, the government did everything in its power to hide and downplay its seriousness. On September 11 the General Court passed a law permitting towns to restrict funeral hours and the number of times a church bell could be rung for the dead. One week later Samuel Shute proclaimed a day of prayer and fasting to thank God "for giving so great a Measure of Health within this Province, and Moderating the Mortality of the Small Pox, so that a great Number of Persons are Recovered from that Distemper."[8] Possibly he reasoned that, after nearly six months, smallpox had to have nearly peaked and would be on the wane by the arrival of the appointed fast day five weeks later.

Among those who did not share the governor's optimism were the sloop men who supplied Boston with firewood for cooking and heating. Now, out of fear of contracting smallpox, they were refusing to land their boats at any of the town's docks. With supplies dwindling and temperatures beginning to drop, it seemed possible that those who managed to survive smallpox might freeze to death in the cold New England winter. A workaround was eventually devised whereby the sloop captains sailed their vessels only as close to Boston as Castle Island, where they turned them over to specially assembled smallpox-immune crews who sailed them the rest of the way to the mainland, offloaded the wood, and piloted them back. Before long a similarly ad hoc mechanism was created to keep food and other goods coming into the town. Country farmers and tradesmen afraid of infection would drive their wagons to a post set up at the George Tavern, just outside the gate at Boston Neck, and leave their butter, cheese, geese, eggs, beeswax, "or, in short, any Commodity that may be bought" for two Boston merchants to sell to the townspeople on consignment.[9]

These improvisations helped assure that Bostonians not killed by smallpox would survive its associated hardships. It was less certain that Boston's already anemic economy could hold out against an embargo that had grown to be universal and seemed destined to continue indefinitely. Contrary to the governor's implication that the worst was nearly over, every sign pointed to a continued burgeoning of the epidemic. The final September death toll was 101, nearly four times that of August. As Nathaniel Hawthorne wrote in a short story set during the 1721 Boston epidemic, smallpox was "stalking" Boston "with a fierceness which made it almost a new pestilence."[10] And still it had not come close to exhausting the supply of potential victims. Of the town's approximately 11,000 inhabitants, about 2,750 had contracted the disease so far. Assuming that an entire half of the town's total population had already gained immunity by surviving smallpox at an earlier point in their lives, and that another 1,000 remained evacuated to the country, the number of potential victims exceeded 1,700.

COMPARED TO THE brutally hot summer and an early fall so rain-soaked that the threat to the harvest seemed another punishment from Heaven, the weather in October 1721 was idyllic. William Douglass referred to it as "a fine Autumn month."[11] By almost any other measure, however, it was one of the worst months in Boston history.

The first indication that the month would be far more deadly than any preceding it came on October 6, when the selectmen received the results of a house-to-house canvass conducted by leaders of the town militia. It found that 203 persons had died from smallpox since the beginning of the epidemic. If both that number and Douglass's count of 156 smallpox deaths from the beginning of the epidemic through the end of September were accurate, 47 deaths had occurred during the first five days of October—nearly half as many as during the entire month of September. Another ominous sign was the huge jump in the number of written requests for prayers for the sick and dying that Cotton Mather received during those first days of the month. On October 1 the number was 202. Two days later it had climbed to 315. And it continued to rise. "Whole families were laid low at the same time," wrote historian Ola Elizabeth Winslow.[12] Benjamin Bronsdon, whose sister was married to the selectman and representative William Clark, lost three children to smallpox in October. In the second half of the month alone Samuel Sewall attended the funerals of ten persons and noted that "many more" of his acquaintance had also succumbed to the disease.[13] Like many government officials, though, he obstinately refused to acknowledge the immensity of the tragedy. The famously pious judge was put out when "by reason of the Distress of the Small Pox" most churches observed Samuel Shute's designated "day of thanksgiving" on October 26 with one sermon rather than the traditional three or four.[14]

According to the governor's proclamation, all businesses were to remain closed on the fast day. During a previous fast there had been at least one conspicuous act of defiance: A Popular Party man had opened his shop in protest of Shute's policies. But now, with Boston commerce at nearly "a complete standstill," there was no point in violating his order.[15] Activities of all kinds had come to a halt: The military companies had suspended their weekly drills and the meetings of all civic and religious societies had been canceled indefinitely. Boston had come to resemble a ghost town. The only signs of life, wrote Ola Winslow, were the "groups of mourners on their way to a funeral at one of the meetinghouses or waiting at the entrance to hold a service." Nighttime was silent except for the clacking wheels of the "dead cart" as it "rumbled over the cobbled streets."[16] Amid the dying and grieving, the townspeople tried to cling to a semblance of normalcy. An advertisement in the October 23 *Boston Gazette* invited people out of their homes to take in the town's newest curiosity:

> Just arrived from Africa, a very large Camel being above seven Foot high, and Twelve Feet long; and is the first of his Kind that ever was brought into America, to be seen at the bottom of Cold Lane, where daily Attendance is given.[17]

But the very next advertisement suggested that few people would likely risk infection for a glimpse of the exotic creature. It announced the postponement of an estate sale "for some time by reason of the Small Pox spreading in the Town."[18] In September, Samuel Shute had been willing to speculate that the epidemic would be over by late October. Now no one dared conjecture when the end would finally arrive.

THE DEADLIEST MONTH of the smallpox epidemic began with the one man capable of sparing people from death and permanent disability on an unexplained hiatus. Nearly a week into October, Boylston had gone almost two weeks without performing an inoculation. While it's possible that the death of Mrs. Dixwell had caused him to have a "crisis of conscience" regarding inoculation, it's more likely that he was reacting to a real or perceived threat tied to his first inoculation-related death.[19] Only about two months had elapsed since Douglass had suggested that Boylston could be tried for murder if any of his subjects died. He might have been waiting to see if a charge would materialize. The threat of mob violence also appears to have loomed large. Thomas Hutchinson wrote that Boylston's family "was hardly safe in his house" and that the physician himself "often met with affronts and insults on the street."[20] According to Boylston family legend, vigilantes "patrolled the town in parties with halters, threatening to hang him on the nearest tree." His "only place of refuge" was "a private place" in his house where at one point he "remained secreted fourteen days, unknown to any of his family but his wife."[21] Dismissed outright by some historians and considered an exaggeration by others, this claim fits roughly with Boylston's period of inactivity following Mrs. Dixwell's death. Probably the doctor spent twelve days lying low, waiting for the initial shock and outrage over her loss to dissipate, and worried enough by the possibility that those who had threatened his life would act on those threats that he had picked out a hiding place in case they came for him.

He performed one inoculation on October 6 and then waited another seven days. On October 13 he inoculated two persons. The next day he received a timely show of public support from a highly influential source when Councilor Thomas Fitch, who had entrusted Boylston with his son's inoculation during the previous month, summoned him to perform the procedure on his two daughters, aged sixteen and fifteen. Immediately thereafter, though, something—perhaps a new vigilante threat—caused the doctor to again stop performing the operation.

He was still in semi-seclusion nine days later when the *Boston News-Letter* delivered the stunning news that the king had authorized an inoculation experiment at Newgate Prison in London. The *Gazette* also reported that news. Only the *New-England Courant* was silent on the matter, instead publishing an account of the plague in Europe and a report of "a monstrous Fish, or Sea-Dog," that had been caught along the coast of Naples, weighed four hundred pounds, and was found to have half a man's skull and two legs in its stomach.[22] Although the results of the July Newgate experiment were yet to be determined—at least insofar as Boston readers knew—the simple fact that the royal family and the preeminent medical men in their employment had deemed inoculation worthy of a trial constituted a huge victory for Boylston.

Three days after the news of the London inoculation trial appeared, he resumed his inoculations. It was the governor's designated day of fasting and thanksgiving. With most of Boston gathered nervously in crowded churches, he rode out to Roxbury, where he inoculated four persons, including Sarah Boylston, the wife of his brother Thomas. All would fare well.

Boylston's month had begun in hiding and at the nadir of his inoculation campaign. It ended with another strong affirmation of the procedure from England. In the October 30 *Gazette* a London dispatch condemned the "notoriously false" rumors being spread about the Newgate experiment, referring to them as untruths "plainly intended to discredit the safe and universally useful Experiment of Inoculating the Small Pox."[23] In the same issue an anonymous author—almost certainly Cotton Mather, with Boylston providing the particulars—offered the first defense of inoculation published since August. It contained a glowing report on the success of the procedure and debunked as "malicious Inventions" rumors that inoculation patients gave off a "Particular Stench." Probably at Boylston's insistence the minister noted that inoculation was approaching the natural end of its usefulness. "The Air of Boston is now so generally infected . . . 'tis impossible to distinguish the clear from the Infected," he wrote. "But it is hoped . . . what has been done here may prove an Introduction to the saving of some hundreds of thousands of Lives, in other Places, where *Arts of Self-Destruction* will not hinder it."[24]

15

HONEST WAGS

"Zerubbabel Tindal" had promised that his "Clan of Honest Wags" would free the *Courant* from its "insipid" preoccupation with inoculation, offering readers "a *Charmingly Various*, as well as *Copious* Supply" of material, including political philosophy, poetry, and social commentary.[1] One week after his tipsy self-introduction, he and James Franklin began making good on that promise. The *Courant* featured a cautionary tale about the pathos of a miser, which was clearly inspired by one of its two models, London's *Spectator*. For the slightly more than two years the *Spectator* had been published every day except Sunday, it had offered "serious discussions of wit, poetry, and manners" in the form of a single narrative, usually an extended anecdote or an episode.[2] Generally, the intention was to edify the public. But the conversational tone and gossipy storytelling, complete with digressive asides and reproductions of short letters germane to the story being related, prevented it from seeming preachy. Readers also delighted in the *Spectator*'s cast of recurring characters, who represented a cross section of familiar English types. The so-called Spectator Club served as a prism through which co-authors Joseph Addison and Richard Steele shined their commentary on England's class system, manners, customs, and values. Addison, the poet, essayist, and author of the play *Cato, a Tragedy* (which George Washington would famously use to inspire his beleaguered army at Valley Forge) and Steele, his friend and fellow essayist, took turns writing as "Mr. Spectator," the publication's narrator and chief protagonist.

Together with the *Tatler*, which Steele had published previously with contributions from Addison and perhaps Jonathan Swift, the *Spectator* constituted "the first attempt made in England, or any other country, to instruct and amuse unlearned readers by short papers, appearing at stated intervals, and sold at a cheap rate."[3] Although the authors' Whig sympathies were easy to detect, they scrupulously avoided blatant political topics and partisan declarations. Their radicalism was socioeconomic rather than political. Mr. Spectator, wrote historian Craig Nelson, "was an apostle, bringing the ideas of the Enlightenment from the aristocrats and academics to the middle and working classes."[4] In the years since 1714, when it had been priced out of existence by a stamp duty aimed at curbing "the licentiousness of the press," the *Spectator*'s legend and influence had continued to grow.[5] By the time of the American Revolution, volumes of its collected issues would be fixtures of personal libraries throughout the colonies. One of the newspaper's fans was Thomas Paine, who assumed the role of "a real-world Mr. Spectator." Indeed, "a great many of Paine's 'radical' ideas," his biographer noted, "can be found, fifty years before, in the 'good and gentle' newspaper's columns."[6] Thomas Jefferson also owned a set of *Spectator* issues. Insofar as the English publication instilled in him an appreciation for the value of improving "the happiness of all through a system of urbane courtesies and ethics greatly inspired by the philosophies of Aristotle and Locke," it might have inspired the phrase "the pursuit of happiness," which for Jefferson, as for Addison and Steele, was tied to the accumulation of virtue, not material gain.[7]

James Franklin had been in England during the heyday of the *Spectator* and had returned to Boston one of its earliest and most fervent American fans. In his newspaper he would try to emulate what Addison and Steele had done, borrowing their tone and philosophy and sometimes their subject matter. Unlike those men, who had written nearly all of their publication's more than six hundred issues, James would open his publication to more than half a dozen contributors. But if any one "Honest Wag" played Addison to James Franklin's Steele, taking a lead in establishing the identity of the paper, it was Nathaniel Gardner, who as "Zerubbabel Tindal" had redefined the *Courant*, and who, as "Jethro Sham, Advisor General," had penned its first *Spectator*-like essay on misers. "No one writer better exemplifies the *Courant*'s ideas of independent reason, as opposed to reason ex cathedra; free speech, as opposed to censorship; and wit, as opposed to oppressive sobriety," wrote Joseph Fireoved.[8] In the paper's first forty-three issues Gardner would appear, under various pen names, at least thirty-five times, about twice as often as the second most frequent contributor, James Franklin himself. For a man who played so large a role in the controversial newspaper's success we know little about him, other than that at the time he started contributing to the *Courant* he was twenty-eight years old, married, the father of two children with another on the way, and a leather dresser by trade. He lacked the advantages of wealth and high public office, and probably of college and travel abroad as well. Yet somehow he would write with astonishing understanding, eloquence, sophistication, and prescience about politics, religion, and society. If all of that didn't make him enough of an enigma, he was also a devout Congregationalist who happily criticized the ministers of his own faith and loved telling a bawdy joke.

In addition to carrying its first *Spectator*-like essay, the September 11 *Courant* showed the influence of James Franklin's other major inspiration, an essay series called "Cato's Letters." It had debuted in the *London Journal* in November of the previous year, instigated in part by one of the biggest financial scandals in English history, the collapse of the South Sea Company. Granted a near monopoly on trade with South America in 1711, the company's stranglehold on a huge and untapped market thrilled investors, who, believing its close ties to the government indemnified it from failure, made it the era's preeminent get-rich-quick stock. In the first six months of 1720 alone, the stock's value had increased nearly tenfold. Contrary to all outward appearances, however, the company was grossly mismanaged and teetering on the edge of financial collapse. When its bubble burst, thousands of investors, wealthy and otherwise, were ruined. The men behind "Cato's Letters," John Trenchard and Thomas Gordon, were convinced that the government had colluded with the South Sea Company to keep its problems a secret—a suspicion that was later proved correct. Trenchard, a member of Parliament, and Gordon, a commissioner of wine licenses, claimed that the debacle was evidence of an epidemic of government corruption and greed that had been raging in England since the Glorious Revolution of 1688. Writing under the assumed identity of Cato, an incorruptible Roman statesman, they vented their indignation and urged vigilance against corruption they believed would result in tyranny. They also extolled the liberties and values that allowed Englishmen to sniff out corruption and that protected the people against political oppression. These included "natural rights, the contractual basis of society and government, the uniqueness of England's liberty-preserving 'mixed' constitution," and freedom of conscience and speech.[9] Although the general consensus among Englishmen was that the government was "less oppressive than it had been for two hundred years," Cato insisted that government "was necessarily—by its very nature—hostile to human liberty and happiness" and "could be, and reasonably should be, dismissed—overthrown—if it attempted to exceed its proper jurisdiction."[10] They were radical Whigs and inveterate skeptics, perpetually in the opposition.

"Cato's Letters" would prove the *New-England Courant*'s most frequently cited and reproduced source. Cato's insistence on the preeminence of liberty roused James and his fellow Couranteers in the same way he would galvanize America's Founding Fathers fifty years later. The historian Clinton Rossiter called the essays "the most popular, quotable, esteemed source of political ideas in the colonial period."[11] By 1755 six editions of the letters would have been published in the colonies; by the eve of the Revolution almost every man with a passion for politics would be familiar with them. As the first publisher in America to recognize their relevance and reproduce them in part or in their entirety for a general audience—in some cases just months after their original publication in the *London Journal*—James Franklin was decades ahead of his time. If Bernard Bailyn is correct that by 1728 "Cato's Letters" "had already been fused with Locke, Coke, Pufendorf, and Grotius to produce a prototypical American treatise in defense of English liberties overseas, a tract indistinguishable from any number of publications that would appear in the Revolutionary crisis fifty years later," James Franklin, a man never mentioned in discussions of the evolution of American political thought, deserves a share of the credit.[12] Without realizing it, he was introducing what would become one of the pillars of the philosophy justifying American independence.

The *Courant*'s inaugural Cato excerpt that Monday in September 1721 argued that the meaning of "libel" ought to be expanded to include "Libels against the People," which, for James and his friends, included Cotton Mather's imputation that any Bostonian who opposed inoculation was a liar and agent of the Devil.[13] Over two successive weeks in October, James published in full another Cato essay aimed at least partly at Cotton Mather's friendship with Samuel Shute. It denounced political flatterers as "constant and merciless Calumnators" who regarded every word they didn't like as a libel and "every Action that displeases them" as evidence of treason or sedition.[14] He followed that with two more weeks of Cato, parts one and two of an essay in which Gordon outlined his and Trenchard's political philosophy, opposing absolute government, embracing John Locke's concept of a social contract, and coming within a hairsbreadth of endorsing republicanism. (Gordon Wood argued that Trenchard and Gordon were intent on "desacralizing" the Crown and had no compunction about equating the king with the mayor of a town, inasmuch as "they both are civil officers."[15]) Cato insisted that the power of those in charge ought always to be limited, no matter what their station or how benevolent their rule. "The World," asserted Trenchard and Gordon,

> is governed by Men, and Men by their Passions; which being bound-less and insatiable, are always terrible when they are not controulled. Who was ever satiated with Riches, or surfeited with Power, or tired by Honours? . . . To conclude, Power, without Controul, appertains to God alone; and no Man ought to be trusted with what no Man is equal to.[16]

What James and the *Courant* had to say through "Cato's Letters" was bold; but it came with a measure of built-in indemnity. Since the authors were writing in London, there was no way the Boston newspaper's enemies could prove that James was "reflecting" on the Massachusetts government and clergy. (In fact, Trenchard and Gordon were using a similar dodge, cataloging the worst abuses of English government and then declaring—with a wink and a nod—how lucky England was to be free of them.) It was safer, noted Leo Lemay, "to reprint a London publication than to write an original radical statement that might be judged libelous."[17] But the October 30, 1721, conclusion of Cato's essay defining political liberty was the last time for six months the *Courant* printed Cato verbatim. By late the following month the newspaper would begin to venture beyond that safety zone.

For all of its lofty aspirations and conspicuous nods to the *Spectator* and "Cato's Letters," the *Courant* also quickly revealed itself to be coarser and blunter—more American—than its English models. Two weeks after promising it would delve into matters of love and marriage, it offered a letter complaining about the shallowness and hypocrisy of the young women of fashion who went to church pretending piety but spent much of their time silently flirting. For them to "smile and play with their Fans" during the religious service, wrote Nathaniel Gardner, was "an Indication of criminal Carelessness, and unthoughtfulness of the awful Presence they are in."[18] On one level Gardner was doing what he purported to be doing: expressing his disapproval for the impiety of the flirting girls. But his exaggerated indignation at the "criminal" offense was also a way of poking fun at the overseriousness of the ministers, whose sermons were so dull and droning that they not only encouraged this "playful courting ritual" but also caused *him* to pay more attention to the flirting than to the preaching.[19]

In the same issue, James Franklin chimed in with "A CAUTION to Batchellors," a verse that began with the decidedly unromantic lines: "Beware, fond Youths, of Nymphs deceitful Charms / Nor take the fair Affliction in your Arms."[20] In the October 2 *Courant* a woman named "Amelia" took issue with this unflattering portrayal of women, dismissing the author as a "DULL SWAIN."[21] The next week James retaliated with a poem that predicted his critic's spinsterhood.

> *Farewell, Amelia, stroke your Cat;*
> *This is your Fate, no doubt of that;*
> *In this a lasting Pleasure take*
> *No MAN is doom'd to be your Mate.*[22]

Generally speaking, young and eligible women fared poorly in the newspaper's pages. In another harsh poem titled "On SYLVIA, the Fair, A Jingle," James wrote:

> *A Swarm of Sparks, young, gay, and bold,*
> *Lov'd Sylvia long, but she was cold;*
> *In'trest and Pride the Nymph control'd,*
> *So they in vain their Passion told.*
> *At last came Dulman, he was old,*
> *Nay, he was ugly, but had Gold.*
> *He came, and saw, and took the Hold,*
> *While t'other Beaux their Loss Condol'd.*
> *Some say, she's Wed; I say, she's sold.*[23]

Marriage was mocked as roundly as true love. "Abigail Afterwit" bemoaned the fact that "so many of our Sex, after having overlook'd Offers to their Advantage from Gentlemen among our selves, should dispose of themselves to Strangers, who have little or nothing to recommend them but a gay Appearance in Idleness, or an uncommon Skill in the Art of Flattery," adding: "It is my Misfortune to be wedded to a Stranger of this Sort, whose Carriage perswades me he had no other Design in his Addresses than to make me miserable."[24] Gardner appeared in a brief letter as "S.B.," a husband "sadly fatig'd with a Scolding Wife" who was "such a Shrew," he wrote, "as I believe cannot be matched in all Christendom."[25] John Eyre, who at twenty-one was both the youngest Couranteer and the only regular contributor who had attended Harvard (he had recently received his master's degree but, according to Tourtellot, seemed more interested in dancing and drinking than in taking up an occupation[26]), also chimed in. Eyre would offer some of the *Courant*'s most scathing critques of Puritan arrogance in general and Cotton Mather in particular. Now, though, he wrote from "Cuckolds Point" that his wife and her friends made him "their laughing Stock and Ridicule."[27] In early 1722 Thomas Fleet would join the Couranteers, at one point writing as "Ann Careful" that her husband needed to spend less time obsessing over inoculation and politics and more time on his business.[28]

The newspaper's borderline misogyny was essentially a gimmick, an attempt to stir up a "war of the sexes" controversy and boost circulation—even if that controversy was almost wholly contrived, with men writing indignant letters in a female persona to keep the quarrel going. For James, Gardner, Eyre, and another contributor, Matthew Adams, a devotee of poetry who worked as a leather skinner or tanner and might have been in business with Gardner, the controversy was also great and titillating fun. They were all in their twenties or early thirties and feeling both their "oats" and rebellious toward the repressive religious, political, social, and sexual mores of Puritan New England. The gender war that they and Fleet (who at thirty-six was the elder statesman of the Wags) ginned up was fairly frothy stuff compared to the attack on Thomas Walter that had nearly cost James his paper. But there was a subversive subtext. Nowhere was this more apparent than in the newspaper's many subtle and not so subtle references to sexuality. Was James's prediction that the spinster Amelia would "stroke [her] Cat" a reference to masturbation? The newspaper's other sexual allusions suggest that it was. In what amounted to a forerunner of the advice columns that would become fixtures of newspapers of a later era, another *Courant* featured a letter from "Ben Treackle" (Gardner), a young man in love with "a brisk young Widow" whose charms included both a "good Temper, and natural Parts not inferior to any." Treackle wanted to know if it was appropriate to let a woman "pop the question" of marriage. The answer he received was that it would be entirely proper, especially, wrote the unnamed Couranteer (probably Gardner again), "since your Bashfulness renders you incapable of giving her one single Pop for all the good Manners and Pleasantness with which she treats you."[29] In the same issue that contained James Franklin's poetic "tribute" to Sylvia, the *Courant* "reported"

> That a certain Man at Stonington (who has a Wife and several Children) lately castrated himself; which has occasion'd [an] abundance of Waggish Talk among the looser Sort of the Female Tribe, who are so incensed against him, that some of them talk hotly of throwing Stones at him, if he lives to come abroad again. He is very much swell'd, but seems rejoyc'd at what he has done.[30]

In a society that venerated marriage and holy love, and that repressed discussions of sexuality, this kind of talk was a scandal. Occasionally the *Courant* dropped its salaciousness and cynicism and celebrated true love— as when Gardner, writing as "Corydon," sang the praises of "ELIZA," writing that "Her pleasing Smiles, her every grace Combin'd / Do feast the senses, and regale the Mind."[31] (And even then, noted Tourtellot, the poem likely unsettled some readers, containing as it did an "emotional intensity" and "physical fervor" that was "quite alien, if not to the Puritan spirit, at least to Puritan utterances."[32]) More often, however, the "women" complained that the men were lazy and unappreciative; while the men complained of being henpecked in marriage and that prospective wives were vain, shallow, insincere, and, in some cases, for sale to the highest bidder. Rarely had such thoughts been shared in polite company, never mind in the pages of a newspaper. Simply by printing them James Franklin was taking American journalism into uncharted territory. What made them more shocking still was that they appeared throughout the autumn and early winter of 1721—the very height of the smallpox epidemic. While Boston bowed its head in perpetual mourning for the dead, James Franklin and his friends snickered about sex. On Sundays the ministers stood in their pulpits exalting marriage and holy love as bulwarks against despair in a time of plague. One day later a new *Courant* appeared and mocked both. It was juvenile, crass, unfeeling, and in bad taste. But it was also another kind of rebellion: youth whistling past the graveyard, refusing to be cowed by the specter of death.

16

THE ASSASSINATION
ATTEMPT

O ctober 1721 was a horror that left Bostonians stunned and stag-
gered. In the space of thirty-one days nearly a quarter of the
town's population—twenty-five hundred people—fell ill with
smallpox. Four hundred and two persons—nearly half the total number
claimed by the epidemic—died, at the rate of about thirteen a day. The stories from Boston were so horrible that when the epidemic spread to New
London, Connecticut, partly, at least, by way of an infected man named
John Rogers, and when Rogers and his family refused to remain quarantined in their home, authorities not only posted armed guards at their door
but summarily rounded up and destroyed their dogs for good measure.

Terrified by the runaway proliferation of the disease and emboldened
by the survival of all but one inoculation patient and by London's vali-
dation of the procedure, Bostonians began flocking to Boylston in large
numbers. They came from every part of town and every religious denomination. They were Prerogative Party men and Popular Party men. They
shared a willingness to trust a still radical-sounding and counterintuitive

procedure and the ability to pay the roughly £4 the doctor charged to perform it. Increasingly now, the divide was between those who could afford the procedure and those who could not; the debate was focused not on questions of medical authority, morality, or God's will, but on whether inoculation was prolonging the epidemic and endangering those unwilling or unable to have it performed. Lacking the money to inoculate themselves and their sometimes large families, many leather-apron tradesmen and most common laborers felt isolated and exposed. For them the threat of inoculation was indistinguishable from that of smallpox itself. To the extent that the former perpetuated the presence of deadly disease in their midst, it also perpetuated the deprivations and economic hardships associated with the epidemic. While the wealthy—the same people who could afford inoculation—paid inflated prices for the food and supplies trickling into town, poor workers laid off because of the epidemic scratched and scraped for basic sustenance.

During the first days of November those class tensions were exacerbated by the sense that, at long last, smallpox had plateaued in Boston and was beginning to decline, and that the persons now streaming into town for inoculations from the places where the disease had migrated—Charlestown, Roxbury, and, to a lesser degree, Cambridge—were the equivalent of dry wood thrown on a fire that had nearly burned itself out.

The selectmen, fearful not only that the epidemic might somehow be reignited but also that vigilantes might attack outsiders coming to town for the procedure, proposed a law requiring anyone entering Boston for inoculation to return immediately to his hometown or submit to being transferred to Spectacle Island for quarantine until he was well. (Once again, the specter of an outbreak of bubonic plague generated by inoculation was cited.) As soon as the law was passed on November 4, the selectmen asked the justices to warrant the removal of any non-Bostonians who had recently undergone the procedure. Although they declined to cite any specific offenders, it was generally understood that they were targeting three Roxbury men known to be waiting out the onset of their inoculation symptoms at a house in the North End. The house belonged to Cotton Mather.

MATHER COPED WITH the deaths of his daughter Abigail and his granddaughter Resigned the same way he had coped with the previous losses of loved ones: He threw himself into his work. Two days after Abigail's death he fulfilled his commitment to preach the Thursday public lecture, where he presented a sermon dedicated to her memory. The day after her funeral he secluded himself and prayed for his surviving children. One day after that he preached a sermon at the New North Church, whose minister had lost his wife to smallpox. On September 30 he brought both sermons to the bookseller for printing.

He had devoted nearly all of October to service for the sick, the dying, and the dead, and to raising emergency funds for those hardest hit by the epidemic. By the end of the day on October 26, the provincewide day of prayer and thanksgiving, he was exhausted and feverish. He blamed his illness on too much time spent in the cold night air as he traveled from house to house, and on the "Poisons of infected Chambers."[1] He wondered whether the hour of his death had come—and claimed to welcome it. By the next evening, though, he was feeling optimistic that he would "speedily" conquer his illness and be back at work.[2] Not for the first time, the sense that he might be dying revived his appetite for life. Now, in addition to helping Boylston draft the defense of inoculation that appeared in the October 30 *Gazette*, he acted on an earlier resolve to help a "kinsman" undergo inoculation. On October 29 or 30 Mather summoned his nephew Thomas Walter to Boston. On the last day of the month Zabdiel Boylston came to the Mather home and performed inoculations on Walter and two other Roxbury men, Samuel Aspinwall and Mr. Dany, a young doctor.

Mather appears to have given little if any thought to the possibility that inviting three non-Bostonians into town for inoculations might anger the procedure's jittery opponents. When he learned of the town's decision to crack down on outsiders coming to Boston for the procedure he felt no culpability—only wounded indignation since, as Tourtellot wrote, he knew the action was "clearly directed" at him.[3] The judicious move would have been to send the men home or to the quarantine station in compliance with the town order. But three days later, when his guests broke out in inoculated pocks, they were still comfortably ensconced in his upstairs bedroom, which he had converted into a sickroom for their convalescence. In all three cases the pocks appeared "at the usual Time" and were "of a distinct Sort"; the symptoms in general were so mild that Walter and Dany teased Aspinwall about his panicky reaction to the first signs of inoculated illness, accusing him of having been "troubled with Vapours."[4] Immune to smallpox and headed for a smooth recovery, they could afford to be lighthearted. Their biggest concern now was how to allay their boredom until they were well enough to go home.

Their host was not so sanguine. Already rebuked by the town indirectly, he received a second and more pointed rebuke a few days later courtesy of the *New-England Courant*, ending an unofficial semi-truce that had gone into effect two months earlier, after he had branded the *Courant*'s contributors Devil worshipers and James Franklin had retaliated by describing his brain as "envenom'd." Since September 4 the paper had published only one direct reference to the inoculation controversy, a note comically exaggerating the safety of the procedure and the number of lives that might be saved by its acceptance, written in a voice that was an obvious imitation of Mather. But when the minister picked up the November 6 *Courant* he had found two items directed against him and his family. The first was a parody of his father's famous 1680 jeremiad "Heaven's Alarm," which had interpreted the appearance of a bright comet in the Boston night sky as a sign of "great Calamities at hand."[5] Then, after some international news, John Eyre had delivered a brief but scathing rebuttal to Mather's pugnacious defense of inoculation in the previous week's *Gazette*. As "Peter Hakins," he accused Mather of overreaching his proper authority in ways that made him an enemy not only to the people of Boston, but to God as well. Quoting from Dr. Gumble's biography of the seventeenth-century military figure George Monck, Eyre wrote that a clergyman,

> While he keeps within the Sphere of his Duty to God and his People, is an Angel of Heaven; but when he shall degenerate from his own Calling, and fall into the Intriegues of State and Time-Serving, he becomes a Devil; and from a Star in the Firmament of Heaven, he becomes a sooty Coal in the blackest Hell, and receiveth the greatest Damnation.[6]

With Walter and the others sequestered in his home and, at that point, on the cusp of suffering whatever sickness would be caused by their inoculated smallpox, and with the unhappy town already poised to relocate them, Mather could hardly afford to take on the *Courant* in public. But clearly he yearned to do so. Three days after the newspaper's attack he wrote in his diary: "The sottish Errors, and cursed Clamours, that fill the Town and Countrey, raging against the astonishing Success of the Small-Pox Inoculated; makes it seasonable for me, to state the Case, and exhibit that which may silence the unreasonable People."[7]

For the rest of the week he continued to hold his tongue. When the next issue of the *Courant* appeared on November 13 it contained no new attacks. But late that morning or early that afternoon, Mather received news that the town selectmen had met again and amplified upon their earlier order concerning out-of-town inoculation patients. They were ordering a "diligent Search" for all those who had already come into the town (that is, Walter, Dany, and Aspinwall) with the goal of turning them out.[8]

Mather left his house in a state of high dudgeon. At some point thereafter he encountered James Franklin on a Boston street. Generally described as a chance encounter, it seems at least as likely that, needing to vent his wrath on someone and prevented from confronting the town selectmen without effectively admitting that he had been hiding three inoculation patients, he had gone in search of his young nemesis. A public spectacle ensued. Mather bellowed at James with an "Air of great Displeasure" while James, either out of shock or discretion, remained silent. He later reproduced a version of Mather's outraged soliloquy from memory:

> You make it your business, in the paper called the Courant, to vilify and abuse the Ministers of this Town. There are many Curses which await those that do so. The Lord will smite thro' the Loins of them that rise up against the Levites. I would have you consider of it; I have no more to say to you.[9]

The story of the confrontation between the fifty-eight-year-old minister and the twenty-four-year-old printer and publisher would have been the talk of the town by the following morning had it not been for what transpired in the meantime. A few hours before sunrise on November 14, while most of Boston lay sleeping, an incendiary device in the shape of an iron ball crashed through Mather's bedroom window. It struck the floor and rolled to a stop without exploding. A few feet away, its fuse, which had been knocked loose when the ball had ricocheted off an iron window casement, fizzled and then extinguished. Had the "grenado" functioned as intended, the explosion and the ensuing fire probably would have killed Walter and his two companions—and perhaps, if it spread quickly enough, Mather, his wife, and his children as well. Even unexploded, the projectile had nearly proved lethal, missing the head of a sleeping Thomas Walter by inches.

The Governor's Council acted quickly, proposing a reward for information leading to an arrest and conviction. Neither Elisha Cooke nor John Clark made an effort to obstruct the measure, and the House passed it unanimously. The next day Samuel Shute issued a proclamation directing sheriffs, constables, and other officers to hunt down the person or persons responsible for the attack. The best evidence at their disposal was a note that been attached to the bomb:

COTTON MATHER, I was once one of your Meeting; But the cursed
Lye you told of—You know who; made me leave You, You Dog. And
Damn You, I will Inoculate You with this, with a Pox to You.[10]

Mather claimed to have "proofs" that there were "people who approve
and applaud the Action of Tuesday morning," and he predicted that they
would make a second attempt on his life.[11] But if he suspected anyone
in particular, the authorities were unable to tie that person to the crime.
Neither the promise of a pardon for an accomplice who came forward nor
the offer of a £50 reward for information leading to an arrest generated so
much as a single suspect. In a town of fewer than twelve thousand people,
a place where secrets were nearly impossible to keep, the person or persons who had attempted to kill the most famous minister in New England
would never be discovered.

BY ONE ACCOUNT, Zabdiel Boylston's house was also firebombed,
the attack occurring early one evening while the doctor was out visiting
patients and his wife and children were sitting in the parlor. According
to medical historian James Thacher, "a lighted hand grenade was thrown
into the room, but the fuse striking against some of the furniture fell off
before an explosion could take place, and thus providentially their lives
were saved."[12] It probably never happened. No record of the incident exists, and neither Boylston nor any of his friends ever mentioned it. (The
man who originated the story, Boylston's grandnephew Ward Nicholas
Boylston, was born more than twenty years after the inoculation controversy and might have mistaken the attack on Mather's house—where
disaster had been averted by a nearly identical act of providence—for
one on his relative's.) Even if the attack didn't occur, though, the doctor
must have worried that his home would be next, since between his inoculations of the Roxbury men and the November 4 town meeting he had
performed the procedure on eight more persons, including three who,

like Walter and his friends, had come to Boston from afflicted neighboring towns.

Given the ferocity of the epidemic in those places—in Roxbury smallpox had already killed ten of the first thirteen men who had come down with it, all of them heads of families, and in Charlestown all but ten or twelve families were destined to be affected—Bostonians probably doubted the early November orders would succeed in keeping desperate persons from flooding into their town for inoculations. But the tighter rules achieved their purpose. Boylston performed no inoculations at all for several days after the Boston town meeting and only four over the course of the next week. He was still ready, though, to accommodate anyone who came to him for the procedure. On the morning of November 13, the day the selectmen reconvened and authorized a house-to-house search for out-of-town violators, he performed two inoculations. The next morning, just hours after the attempted firebombing of Cotton Mather's house, he performed another.

Boylston's records indicate that everyone who underwent the procedure between November 15 and November 22 was a Boston resident, but the *New-England Courant* asserted otherwise, reporting on November 20 that some of the town's ministers continued to invite outsiders into Boston to undergo the operation. Perhaps because he feared that this accusation might prove the tipping point, provoking violence against the doctor, Boylston's friend and minister Benjamin Colman published his first pamphlet concerning inoculation. Adopting a calm and even conciliatory tone, the liberal minister gently debunked many of the most pernicious rumors about inoculation, including charges that subjects broke out in oozing, foul-smelling sores and suffered debilitating long-term side effects. He acknowledged that the procedure was unorthodox—"surprising," he called it—but insisted that, considered calmly, it was rational.[13] There's no question that his portrait of inoculation was idealized—he claimed, for example, that the procedure left many people in better health than they had been previously. But what distinguished it and gave it weight was that

Colman, unlike most of the procedure's critics, had observed inoculation and its results firsthand. Indeed, his pamphlet's only harsh words were reserved for the physicians and civic leaders who had provoked panic in the community without taking Boylston up on his appeals to visit his patients and assess the dangers or virtues of the procedure they condemned.

17

A DEATH IN THE HOUSE

Back in August, at the start of the first session of the General Court following the House's illegal adjournment for the July fast day, Samuel Shute had ordered a change of venue from the Town House, whose area of town was so infected that no non-immune representative could be expected to venture there, to the George Tavern, located just outside of Boston, beyond the gate at the end of the peninsula's neck. The House's first order of business had been to ask for another change of venue back to Cambridge, arguing that the tavern was too small to accommodate its membership comfortably and too close to the main thoroughfare into and out of Boston to provide an adequate buffer zone against the growing epidemic. The members quickly discovered, however, that the governor had chosen the George Tavern for precisely the reasons they disapproved of it. He wanted to punish them for their previous self-adjournment and make them squirm. He would consider a move to Cambridge, he told them, only after they admitted to wrongdoing in seating a speaker without his approval and in assuming the power to adjourn themselves.

The extortion attempt failed. "There was a quorum," wrote Thomas Hutchinson, ". . . who chose to risque their lives rather than concede that the governor had power, by his own act, to remove the court from Boston to any other town in the province."[1] Stubbornly, the House settled into the George, ordering guards posted at the tavern doors to keep potentially infected persons from gaining access. After two unproductive weeks, which included an unsuccessful attempt by the governor to get the House to recognize the validity of a London communication confirming his power to nonconcur in the choice of a speaker, the House issued an ultimatum: Either Shute moved them to the safety of Cambridge immediately or they would pick up and go home. In order to preempt the mutiny, the governor once again angrily shut down the session. Then, in another furious letter to the Lords of Trade and Plantations, he accused the Massachusetts House of disloyalty, citing as proof the August 31 appointment of Elisha Cooke as temporary speaker on what he called the "pretext" that Speaker John Clark needed a leave of absence to help his medical colleagues cope with the burgeoning smallpox epidemic.[2] Inasmuch as Cooke's elevation to the speaker's chair had come shortly after the arrival of the letter affirming Shute's right to reject him as speaker, it had constituted, Shute informed his superiors, an attempt "to elude the force of your Lordships' Instruction."[3]

NOW, AS THE November restart of the General Court approached, Shute realized that, after the public health catastrophe of October, no threat or strong-arm tactic would force the deputies back to the George Tavern. His only chance of assembling the government was to grant the deputies their earlier wish to meet in Cambridge. He announced the move before the House members could demand it, and with the caveat that the power "respecting the Removal of the General Court from place to place" remained his and his alone.[4] He was, he insisted, conceding nothing.

Months earlier, the college town had seemed safe, at least compared to Boston. But the proliferation of smallpox in Cambridge since then had destroyed that mostly illusory security. Only reluctantly and with trepidation did the members of the Court report as ordered to their assigned venue, the First Church of Cambridge, which sat across from the Harvard campus. The governor's short, session-opening speech on November 7 captured the jittery mood:

> Since it hath pleased God in his wise Providence to suffer the *Small-pox* to spread very much in this Province; and being also informed, that many Members of the Council, and the House of Representatives have never had the Distemper, I shall therefore only Recommend to you at this Session, the quick Dispatch of those Affairs, which will be absolutely necessary for the present Welfare of the Government.[5]

If only for safety's sake, some basic level of cooperation between the governor and the House was expedient. But the next eight days would prove that the fight for political control of the province had come to trump every other consideration, even self-preservation.

A few days into the session, the House demanded to know why the governor had canceled a military expedition it had approved in August. Shute had agreed to send three hundred soldiers to the headquarters of the Eastern Indians at Norridgewock, in order to deliver a proclamation commanding them "on pain of being prosecuted with the utmost severity" to turn over a French Jesuit believed to be inciting acts of vandalism and intimidation against English settlers along the New England frontier in Maine. If the Indians took up arms to resist, the soldiers were to "repel force by force."[6] This was the resolution that James Franklin's *Courant* had applauded. Not satisfied with the governor's explanation for suspending the operation—he had decided, he said, that autumn was unsuitable for it—the House on November 10 voted to reauthorize the expedition. For nearly a week the Council, on behalf of the governor, stalled. On the morning of November 16, the House again voted that the Indians should be held in check by a force of several hundred men; that the Jesuit, Sebastien Rale, should be apprehended and "Rendered to Justice"; and that the Indians should be cut off from trade.[7] Realizing that the deputies would not be deterred, the Council reluctantly concurred.

Although the issue had been brought to a kind of resolution, both sides emerged more embittered than ever. The deputies resented the governor's attempt to double-cross them by nodding his approval of the expedition and then canceling it while they were out of session. The governor was convinced that the House was attempting to usurp his authority as commander in chief. The revitalized enmity guaranteed that there would be no cooperation moving forward. When the Court took up the relatively straightforward matter of replenishing the province's treasury, a fight immediately broke out over the House's addition of a phrase restricting the governor's authority to spend provincial funds when the Court was in recess. Noting that no such restriction had ever been imposed before, and insisting that doing so now would tend to "clogg the Publick Affairs," the Council demanded that the phrase be removed.[8] The House refused. Two more times over the course of the next few days the Council repeated the request. In both instances it was rejected. On November 15 the deputies offered their rationale, arguing that since the charter empowered the House, not the Council or the governor, to levy assessments, rates, and taxes, it was "fully Reasonable that those that Grant Money, should have the disposal thereof."[9] The councilors sent a terse message to the House implying that Governor Shute would not bend on the issue and that, smallpox or no smallpox, the House would be kept in session until its members came around to his viewpoint. The House put the question to another vote but once again decided against withdrawing the disputed phrase. Its rationale this time—that its constituents had expressly forbidden it from giving the governor discretionary spending power—elicited scornful howls from the councilors, who pointed out that the governor had been exercising that power for years without any great hue and cry from the public. Flabbergasted by the House's audacity in claiming yet another power for which it possessed no clear precedent, they declared that they were washing their hands of any "ill consequence to the Government" that might result from its continued attempts to encroach upon the royal prerogative.[10]

Ten days earlier the members of the General Court had come to Cambridge, a river's width from the white-hot center of smallpox contagion, with great apprehension and expecting to remain for only a few days—a week at most. Now the session appeared destined to drag on for weeks, mired in retaliatory obstruction and producing little meaningful legislation. Indeed, the only things the House, Council, and governor had agreed upon were a reward for help apprehending those responsible for the attempted firebombing of the Mather house and a few measures aimed at easing the hardships of the smallpox epidemic, including the allocation of a thousand pounds for distribution among families that had lost their heads of household. With every passing day that Governor Shute held the assembly in Cambridge, the odds increased that the infection would find its members. By November 15 a large number of deputies had had enough. Twenty-six representatives, close to a quarter of the full membership, were absent, either because they had refused to come to the session in the first place or because they had packed up and left, convinced that, out of pure malice, the governor would keep them there until every vulnerable man was sick with smallpox. Those who remained despite the danger focused their attention on the liberties they were determined to protect and did their best to put the threat out of their minds. As catastrophic as the smallpox epidemic had been, it had thus far left their ranks untouched. It was still possible to see the General Court as an oasis safe from the threat of infection.

That perception was dashed permanently on November 16 when the House learned that William Hutchinson, the newest member of the Boston contingent, was gravely ill. His personal popularity and relative youth made the news especially devastating. His colleagues, who realized that they had been talking, eating, and drinking with him in the days prior to his "being seized," were so thoroughly terrified, wrote Thomas Hutchinson, that "it was not possible to keep them together and the governor found it necessary to prorogue them."[11] That afternoon, the House awarded Shute another £500 in compensation. The next morning he dissolved the session. William Hutchinson died thirteen days later. The brinksmanship over smallpox that had skewed the actions of the General Court for months had produced its inevitable result. Ironically, the man killed by extreme partisanship was the most moderate politician in Boston.

18

POINTED SATYR

L ate on the afternoon of December 2, 1721, several hours after what Samuel Sewall called "a great Funeral" for the deceased Boston politician William Hutchinson, a letter appeared at the Franklin printing house, where the proprietor and his apprentice were composing the next issue of the *Courant*.[1] James would refer to it as "my *Curse at Large*."[2] An introductory note, written by someone who called himself "Castalio," challenged the *Courant* to publish what followed, a supposedly full and true account of the confrontation between James Franklin and Cotton Mather on a Boston street three weeks earlier. The author was plainly Mather himself, whose diary entry for the day amounted to a single sentence: "Some very wicked Persons, must have suitable Admonitions dispensed unto them."[3]

Along with the rest of pious, respectable Boston, Mather had been offended by the paper's indecent treatment of marriage, and by its salaciousness and smirking impudence, its lack of proper respect for everything decent Bostonians held dear. What he resented most, though, was the mockery and satire it had directed at him and his father in the months since it had cut ties with John Checkley and repudiated the blunt-force assaults of its first several issues. On one occasion the newspaper had caricatured Mather's sometimes hyperbolic support for inoculation by having an impersonator proclaim it a discovery "More Worth than a World!" and insist that "Never one dyed in this Way; and 'tis probable, more than probable; never will," a fatuous boast made more so by its appearance soon after the death of Mrs. Dixwell.[4] The Couranteers had also made sport of the specious reasoning Mather and his father had employed in their arguments for the procedure. At one point, for instance, Increase had asserted that since ministers and magistrates were wise and judicious, and since many ministers and magistrates were for inoculation, therefore inoculation was wise and judicious. Cotton had then chimed in, asserting that since inoculation was "a most successful and allowable Method of preventing Death," it was not only "Lawful" but also mandatory; that man had "a Duty to make use of it." With an imperiousness that begged for retaliation, he had added that only "*very foolish, and very wicked People will deny* the Proposition *in this Argument*."[5] Nathaniel Gardner's response took the form of his own set of absurdly nonsensical syllogisms, one of which made comic fodder of both Mather arguments:

> Arg. IV: A method of preventing *Death*, which the Known children of the *Wicked One*, are fierce Enemies to, is not only lawful, but a Duty. *But* the known Children of the Wicked One, do fiercely Oppose Inoculation. *Therefore*, it is not only lawful, but a Duty.[6]

The young men of the *Courant* were pointing their fingers at two of the most powerful religious figures in the history of Massachusetts and laughing. The effect had been to deepen and intensify Cotton Mather's long-festering grudge against what three years earlier he had called a "wicked, stupid, abominable Generation; every Year growing rather worse and worse, under the Judgements of Heaven; drowned in all Impiety and

Perdition."[7] His issue with the "rising generation" (of which, ironically, his son Cresy was a prime exemplar) actually dated back more than a decade, to the point at which certain young men had begun singing insulting, drunken ballads beneath his window in the middle of the night and others had begun to cast an accusatory eye on his record at Salem and on other errors of the Puritan theocracy he represented. As the youthful publisher of the *Courant*, James Franklin was merely the latest personification of that generational wickedness, the new symbol of its "Impiety and Perdition."

IT JUST SO happened that when the Castalio letter arrived at the printing house, James was typesetting *his* version of the public run-in with Mather. The *Courant* that came out the following Monday included both Mather's letter and two letters from James, the one he had planned and a second, hastily written response to Mather's fresh attack. In the first, James conceded that he had exercised bad judgment in printing John Checkley's malicious response to the *Anti-Courant*. But he stood his ground on publishing the piece that had purportedly incited Mather to corner him on the street: John Eyre's indictment of the minister for, as James wrote, representing the greatest part of the town as "unaccountable Lyars and Self-Destroyers" simply because they disagreed with him about inoculation.[8] In the second, shorter piece, James charged Mather with cursing him in the street and again now in print without "proving any Thing against him."[9] The minister of the North Church, he wrote, had "no Business to curse any Body out of his own Congregation" and, in fact, ought to curse himself for endeavoring to defame the Couranteers.[10] For the first time since he had launched the *Courant* about four months earlier, James signed one of his letters with his real name. Indeed, he did it twice, affixing his full name in an oversized typeface and capital letters at the end of the longer, calmer letter and his initials after the shorter, hotter one.

Benjamin Franklin's biographer Tourtellot wrote that James "opened fire on the Mathers, over the curse incident, with a fury that neither he nor anyone else had ever shown before."[11] Although he claimed to be offended by the minister's suggestion that his chances for eternal salvation were slim to none, he probably felt more anger over the minister's slight of his newspaper. According to Castalio, Mather had begun his tirade against James on the street with: "You Entertain, and no doubt you think you Edify, the Publick, with a Weekly Paper, called *The Courant*."[12] Edifying while entertaining was *precisely* what James Franklin believed he was doing; and Mather's suggestion that he was failing surely galled him. (It probably wasn't an accident that in his version of Mather's lecture there was no mention of his supposed pretensions as a publisher.) The fury Tourtellot referred to, though, was about more than James Franklin's personal grudge against Mather. Its force was that of a generational desire to avenge the victims of Salem and all of the Puritan theocracy's abuses of power. Born five years after the witch trials, James had grown up in the oppressive shadow of a public shame always felt but never discussed. For him and others of his generation, Cotton Mather—the only living figure connected to that event who had neither apologized nor been held accountable— symbolized an evil that needed to be exorcized. Mather's evolution into a bogeyman had been under way since at least 1703, when someone had thrown a drawing of the minister in a hangman's noose over the front wall of his property. Nine years later the intoxicated sea captain had tried to hack him to death; the next year "knots of riotous Young Men" had begun gathering under his window to harass him.[13] But the emergence of a new generation less cowed by religious authority, together with Mather's ongoing political, religious, and civic indiscretions, had made the long-overdue reckoning inevitable. In the words of historian Perry Miller: "Nobody talked in public about witchcraft, not since Calef and Hale had published, but privately they had worked it out; James Franklin knew what people thought, saw his chance, and thrust home."[14] Indeed, by the time Mather confronted James on the street, the *Courant* had already begun to drag the minister's culpability for Salem into the light of day, having suggested on several occasions that inoculation was an infatuation no different from the minister's infatuation with witches at Salem. But now, in the aftermath of that confrontation, James took up the theme personally, condemning both Mather and the sometimes brutal tradition he represented in the most direct and unambiguous language yet. In the preface to a pamphlet he printed in January 1722, he wrote:

> All Countrys, or Bodys Politick, (our own Mother Country not ex-
> cepted) have been subject to *Infatuations*: These in this Country seem
> always to have proceeded from some of those who call themselves *Sons*
> *of Levi*. The *Persecution of the Quakers* about the Year 1658, the *hanging of*
> *those suspected of Witchcraft*, about the year 1691, &c. and *Inoculation*, or *Self-*
> *procuring the Small Pox*, in the Year 1721; and to speak like an Astronomer
> or rather in the manner of Dr. C.M. Infatuation seems to return to us
> after a Period of about Thirty Years, *viz*. from the *Massachusetts-Bay* being
> colonized *Anno* 1628, to the Persecution of the Quakers, Thirty Years;
> and so from Infatuation to Infatuation.[15]

Whether or not inoculation truly qualified as an infatuation mattered less to James than the opportunity to publicly condemn Mather's behavior from thirty years earlier. It was the minister's hubris and arrogance—his claim of divine infallibility, be it at Salem or now in Boston—that constituted the real evil. As another pamphlet printed by James put it, ministers were "Men, and but Men." The people would be better off if clergymen "kept their proper Sphere, where God hath set them," and didn't meddle in things outside of it.[16] By refusing to learn that lesson, Mather had condemned himself to a generation's wrath.

AT ABOUT THE same time the *Courant* declared war on Cotton Mather, it also began to take a more emboldened approach to questions of political liberty, moving beyond extended quotations from "Cato's Letters" to publish America's first homegrown essays on the subject. If James felt reluctant to lose the indemnity that came with being able to claim his criticisms were directed at some unnamed government across the ocean, his anger with Mather's attack seems to have fired his resolve and put him in a pugnacious state of mind. The first volley had come on the Monday after their confrontation and the subsequent firebombing of the minister's house. On that morning the lead story in John Campbell's *Boston News-Letter* had been the royal governor's proclamation authorizing a reward for the apprehension of the person or persons who had attacked Mather's home. The *New-England Courant* also announced a reward for "any Person that shall discover the Authors of the above said Villainy."[17] But it placed that notice near the end of the back page, just above the shipping news. The lead position went to a letter from "Hortensius," a pseudonym inspired by the famed Roman orator. The author, Nathaniel Gardner, began by offering a *Spectator*-esque definition of the purpose of James Franklin's publication. "One principal Design of your Paper (if I mistake not)," he wrote, "is to reform the present declining Age, and render it more polite and vertuous."[18] Then he urged the paper to fully adopt a second mission more in line with Trenchard and Gordon: the preservation of liberty and a check on the follies and abuses of the powerful. In a rallying cry to James and the rest of the Honest Wags, Gardner wrote:

> Go on; And let Impartiality be your constant Motto, and Truth the Compass by which you Steer. Go on and check the Follies and Extravagancies of a fantastick Age; Describe the Proud, the Envious and Ambitious in their odious Hue; and paint the Usurer and Oppressor in their Infernal Colours. Here let your Whips be turn'd into Scorpions, And—Let pointed Satyr speak for injur'd Right. . . . Briefly, promote Enquiries after Truth, quicken and rouze the Slothful, animate and inspire the Dull: And however the World has been impos'd on, it will soon appear, that Crimes are not lessn'd and sanctifi'd because committed by Men in High Station, or of Reverend Name; nor are they inhanced because they are perpetrated by the Obscure and Mean.[19]

Two centuries later, objectivity and a duty to expose corruption and help right the wrongs of society would be universally accepted characteristics of a free press. But prior to Nathaniel Gardner's letter, no one in America—or anywhere else, perhaps—had so specifically articulated the responsibilities and challenges of a newspaper operating outside of government authority. Tourtellot called Gardner's "prescient declaration of the high mission of the newspaper" and "realistic appraisal of the inevitable plight of the conscientious editor" the "most brilliant" work done by the Couranteers.[20]

On December 4 James took Gardner's appeal for a press that pursued truth even to the discomfort of "Men in High Station" a step further. He asserted that it was "wicked" to "anathematize a Printer for publishing the different Opinions of Men." The liberty to dissent was not only noble, he argued, but ought to be left unmolested by the church and government even if they were its unhappy targets. ("Even Errors made publick, and afterward publickly expos'd, less endanger the Constitution of Church or State, than when they are (without Opposition) industriously propagated in private Conversation," he wrote.[21]) Such reasoning ran contrary to the English legal standard for seditious libel, which maintained that any criticism of the government was a threat to its authority and therefore constituted a crime. Not only was truth no defense against conviction, but, as the saying went, "the greater the truth, the greater the libel." Asserting that public criticism of state or church was actually in the best interest of the people was a radical notion in the early eighteenth century. Over the next seventy years it would gradually take hold in America; and support for the idea that the press should serve as a Fourth Estate, with the authority to question the integrity of the government and protect the people from the tyranny of the powerful, would lead to the ratification of the First Amendment to the United States Constitution. Appropriately enough, it found its earliest expression in America's first independent newspaper.

19

AN EPIDEMIC'S END

By the middle of November 1721, Zabdiel Boylston had managed to inoculate 110 persons with only one death. But the 103 procedures he performed that month dramatically increased the odds that someone would miscarry. On November 21 he inoculated John White, the former longtime clerk of the Massachusetts House. The fifty-two-year-old White was "a weak infirm Man" who for some time had been both "consumptive and very splenetic."[1] Boylston had advised him to forgo inoculation and "remove further into the Country to avoid the Infection."[2] White, though, had insisted on the procedure. Nine days after his inoculation he seemed well save for his demeanor, which Boylston described as "splenetic and dull."[3] But after another three days a second wave of pocks unexpectedly appeared "slowly, and of but an indifferent Complection."[4] White's "splenetic Darkness" increased, and he refused to eat or be comforted.[5] "Thus he lay languishing," Boylston wrote, "and withering away like a Plant without Moisture (the Pock not ripe, and of a livid Colour) until the 12th of Eruption and 21st from Inoculation, when he died."[6] His December death was the third smallpox-related fatality of a man with ties to the House of Representatives in just under two weeks' time. (William Hutchinson had died on November 30 and the former House speaker John Burill had died in the town of Lynn on December 10.) After successfully sidestepping smallpox for months, the members of the General Court, past and present, now appeared as vulnerable as lesser men.

The odds seemed to have turned against Boylston as well. In the days leading up to White's death, he had lost two other inoculation patients. In November he had inoculated Edward Dorr, his six children, and two family servants. Dorr and the children had done well, but one of the servants, an Indian girl about seventeen years old, had become "very ill, the Pock sunk in, her Pulse too frequent and uneven."[7] He had ordered her moved from a cold, unheated anteroom to a position in the main room closest to the fire and had tried "many Means" to get the pock "out" again, but to no avail.[8] By the morning of December 8 she was dead. Three days later and just hours in advance of John White's death, another young woman, twenty-two-year-old Bethiah Scarbrough, had also died before her inoculated smallpox could fully emerge. According to her mother, Bethiah had been "a very sickly young Woman, and never well"; but Boylston held himself partly to blame, convinced that in his attempt to keep tabs on a large number of inoculation patients both in and outside of Boston he had neglected to make sure that she was properly cared for.[9]

Of the fifty persons Boylston inoculated in December, forty-seven would break out in a distinct and manageable case of smallpox and recover completely. Bethiah Scarbrough was the first of the three unfortunate exceptions. The second was Mrs. Wells, a "very weakly Gentlewoman," aged fifty-four, who was among the fourteen people Boylston inoculated on December 2, the day representative William Hutchinson was buried.[10] She died a little more than two weeks later. One day after her death, the physician George Steward published a letter in the *New-England Courant* reiterating that inoculation violated God's commandment against murder.

Now that several inoculation patients had died in the space of a month, the charge had a new resonance. In a pamphlet published shortly thereafter, an anonymous author who was probably William Douglass made a fresh assault on Boylston. By continuing to perform inoculations, he wrote, Boylston was casting abroad "Arrows and Death." Harkening back to the attempted firebombing of Mather's home in November, he asked ominously whether people who threw bombs into houses and those who "willfully bring infection from a person sick of a deadly and contagious Disease, into a place of Health" were not *both* guilty of a crime justifiably punishable by death.[11]

It was at about this point that someone—possibly someone motivated by Douglass's inflammatory analogy—tried to vandalize Boylston's saddle. The attempt failed only because the perpetrator mistook another man for the doctor and, according to someone with knowledge of the plot, "put a good quantity of Tar" on the wrong saddle, so that when Boylston's unwitting double left the house he had been visiting and mounted his horse he "spoil'd his Breeches."[12] Inoculation opponent John Williams, the man who witnessed the vandalism, added that the saddle incident did not constitute the only instance in which Bostonians had failed to act as "a quiet and peaceable People" in their opposition to Boylston. By his count there had already been "one or two more" acts of vandalism or harassment, both presumably successful.[13]

Boylston performed no inoculations between December 27 and January 27, perhaps because, as the tarred saddle incident revealed, public anger had again reached a boiling point. The January 3 death of "Mrs. Searle," who had been inoculated the same day as Mrs. Wells, certainly contributed to the hostility. The aforementioned John Williams seized upon her death to publish an anti-inoculation pamphlet that seemed to encourage a vigilante response. He informed Bostonians that in Germany a doctor had been *"whipt out of Town"* for performing five inoculations, while in Alexandria an inoculator had been *"mounted on an Ass, and at the Corner of every Street . . . bastinado'd on his Feet, in his way to the Place of Execution, where a Scaffold being built, he was executed.*" Even in London, Williams wrote, the College of Physicians had decreed that "if any Doctor, Quack, or any other Person, shall do any thing that may spread it [contagious disease], they shall suffer Death."[14]

William Douglass, too, kept pounding away. On January 11 he published a new anti-inoculation pamphlet that charged Boylston with inoculating pregnant women and thereby causing them to abort their fetuses. He asserted that murder charges and a guilty verdict were now inevitable, and he advised the practitioner's friends to convince him to submit to a trial "while so many judicious *Magistrates* and *Ministers* are in the Humour of Inoculation."[15]

A few weeks later a young Harvard man named Isaac Greenwood defended Boylston and attacked Douglass. Greenwood, one of several students Boylston had inoculated in Cambridge in November, indicted Douglass for his arrogance and disparaged his character, calling him "a Madman and a Fool" whose writing against inoculation and Boylston was "full of LYES and EQUIVOCATIONS."[16] Depicting Douglass as "Sawny," a generically derogatory term for a Scotsman, Greenwood penned a fictitious dialogue that ridiculed the doctor's heavy accent and portrayed him as pathologically conceited. (*"And if any Man is so brazenly impudent, as to whisper a good word for any Physician but my self,"* Sawny says, *"he shan't escape Scot-free: I'le be foul on him."*[17]) But the least gratuitous and most damning accusation in the pamphlet was that Douglass was a hypocrite who now admitted the merit of inoculation privately while publicly continuing to proclaim, Greenwood wrote, that it was *"a Felony, and that the Physicians ought to be hanged for it!"*[18]

Douglass fired back twice. In a pamphlet he took umbrage at the crassness of his depiction by Greenwood, first pointing out that in ridiculing "the Dialect of the *Northern Parts of Great Britain,*" his attacker was actually casting "an Aspersion on part of our *Mother Country*"; Douglass then scorned his use of satire.[19] "Burlesque is a kind of continued *Irony* representing the lowest abject Persons as *Heroes,* and on the contrary depressing

Characters of Distinction," he wrote loftily, apparently forgetting that he himself had dabbled in the genre in order to denigrate Mather, Boylston, and the Eastern Indians.[20] His more impassioned response was published in a letter that appeared the same day in the *New-England Courant*, where he was now welcome again. Clearly more outraged at the praise Greenwood had lavished on Boylston—who, the Harvard man had written, deserved the town's "highest Regards, and most public Thanks" for his "undaunted Resolution, and truly Heroic Courage"—than at the ethnic and character slurs directed at him, Douglass sneered at Boylston, dismissing him as *"Waltho Van Claturbank, Ulcocalculus, &c.,"* a self-pitying quack whose claims of miraculous cures were ludicrous.[21]

While the debate over inoculation continued to rage, the practice itself had just about reached the end of its utility. In a brief January 15 rebuttal to Douglass's first attack of the new year, Boylston pointed out that there was "not one Person under the Operation" in Boston.[22] Indeed, since the middle of November he had been spending most of his time performing the procedure in the outlying towns, where smallpox was now doing most of its killing. In two of those towns he now had confederates. A doctor named Thompson had been performing inoculations in Roxbury since November 30. In Cambridge, the scientist and physician Thomas Robie was also offering the procedure. Together, they would account for approximately thirty-five inoculations. In Boston, smallpox had nearly petered out. In December the town had seen only thirty-one new cases of naturally occurring pocks, one eighth the total for the previous month. By December 12 the improvement was noticeable enough that the selectmen rescinded an order limiting the ringing of funeral bells.

On February 26, 1722, the *Boston News-Letter* printed a statement from the selectmen declaring that Boston had no known cases of smallpox, inoculated or natural—the first time since the beginning of the epidemic eleven months earlier that the town was completely smallpox-free. When the month's deaths were tallied the total came to eighteen, about average for nonepidemic times. The sudden appearance of a smattering of new cases in mid-April, presumably among people returning from their extended evacuation to the countryside, caused a small panic. When a collar maker named Samuel Deming died of smallpox on April 22, the selectmen acted swiftly and decisively, ordering that he be buried the next day and with the least possible exposure to the populace. The urgency had as much to do with perception as with reality. True or not, a rumor that there was a new full-blown epidemic in Boston might mean a reinstatement of embargoes that had just been lifted.

In early May several more persons returning from the country were found to be sick with smallpox. Six other returnees underwent inoculation by Boylston. The aggregate number of the sick and the inoculated was high enough that fears of a new epidemic and anger over the new inoculations quickly escalated. It didn't help that the inoculated included members of Cotton Mather's extended family: his daughter-in-law Katherine; her husband, Samuel; and Katherine's sons George and Nathan Howell. Town officials stationed guards at the doors of the two houses where the subjects waited for their inoculations to take hold. They also moved against Boylston. On May 15, three days after he had performed the last of the six procedures, they ordered him to appear at a town meeting, where, after calling for a warrant to have the inoculated persons removed to the quarantine station on Spectacle Island, they demanded that he stop performing the operation. According to a published report of the meeting, the physician "did solemnly declare and promise, That he would not, either directly or indirectly, inoculate any Person within said Town for the Future, without License and Approbation of the Authority of the Town."[23] Later that day or early the next, Katherine Sewall and her family were transported to the pest house. Boylston was prohibited from traveling there to monitor their progress, apparently for fear that, his pledge to desist from further inoculations notwithstanding, he might secretly harvest smallpox matter from their pustules for use in future procedures.

The inoculations of the Sewall-Howell family and two others were the last Zabdiel Boylston performed during the 1721–1722 smallpox epidemic. The panicked reaction they caused ended his nearly year-long inoculation campaign on a sour note. He was amenable to halting the practice because the need for it had ended; but he was bitter over the kneejerk reaction of the town to these final few inoculations, and especially over the way officials had unnecessarily banished his patients to the pest house, segregating them from his care out of what he considered simple hysteria. His annoyance was still palpable several years later when he wrote that all six subjects had come through their inoculations well, "not withstanding the many Difficulties and hard Shifts they were put to . . . the Particulars too tedious to be related here, but well known in Boston."[24]

THERE WAS ONE final death by naturally occurring smallpox in May 1722. With that, the worst epidemic of that disease in Boston history was over. Twelve months after the first cases had been reported to the town selectmen, the full scope of the tragedy was apparent. Although the exact number of sick and dead varied according to the source—the most accurate estimate seems to have been 6,000 stricken and 844 deceased—every assessment agreed that roughly half of the town's people had taken ill and up to a tenth had been killed. (Tourtellot put the human cost into a contemporary context in pointing out that in a city of one million the number of afflicted would have been 600,000 and the death toll 90,000.[25]) Untold hundreds more had been left blinded, mentally disabled, debilitated with severe arthritis, or grotesquely disfigured. Like every other smallpox epidemic, this one had been indiscriminate in its ravages, claiming the lives of both the anonymous poor and the prominent and privileged. The latter group included the young wife of Samuel Shute's nephew John Yeamans, the man who had struck Elisha Cooke in Hall's Tavern. The number of persons who remained in Boston during the epidemic but somehow escaped infection might have been as low as a few hundred. Among them was Benjamin Franklin, who despite having to travel throughout town delivering newspapers every week had somehow dodged the deadly disease.

The final statistics bore out what Boylston and Mather had believed all along: that the 280 inoculated persons had significantly reduced their chances of dying compared with those who had contracted smallpox in the natural way. Although six of them—not nine or ten or more, as Douglass claimed—had died while under inoculation, their 2.4 percent death rate was dramatically lower than the 14 percent death rate of those who had contracted smallpox naturally. (Among the elderly and children, natural smallpox had been far more deadly, with a 50 percent fatality rate.) Inoculation's success was even more striking given the unfavorable circumstances of the trial. Boylston had performed the operation not only on those most likely to tolerate its effects but also on "the weak and diseased, the aged and the young" as well.[26] He believed that a fairly large number of his inoculation patients—"twenty-five, if not thirty"—had already been infected with naturally acquired smallpox at the time of their operations and that all six of the patients who had died after being inoculated had come to him in poor health from one affliction or another.[27]

As the months passed and the fears associated with the epidemic began to fade, many of the procedure's doubters began to acknowledge that Boylston's unwavering faith in it had been justified. Just as Isaac Greenwood had alleged, William Douglass was secretly one of them. In a letter to Cadwallader Colden on May 1, 1722, he offered a "general history" of the Boston smallpox epidemic and told Colden that while he remained essentially opposed to inoculation because of what he considered its risks and religious impropriety (and was confident that he still spoke for the majority), he could not ignore its merit. "But to speak candidly for the present," he wrote, "it [smallpox] seems to be somewhat more favourably rec'd by Inoculation than rec'd the natural way."[28] In epidemics to come he, too, would practice the procedure. But he would never acknowledge Boylston's contribution. The men were destined to be lifelong enemies.

Boylston's victory came at a significant price, one for which even the £950 he made by performing inoculations failed to compensate. "I have . . . suffer'd much in my Reputation and in my Business too, from the Odiums and Reflections cast upon me for beginning and carrying on this Practice," he wrote.[29] For nearly a year he had lived in daily fear for his own safety and his family's. He was exhausted from the stress and physical rigor of performing the controversial procedure on so many persons in various towns and in an environment of unrelenting hostility. He did not seek vengeance against Douglass and the other men who had mocked him, denigrated his ability and intelligence, and called for his arrest for murder. Neither, though, did he forgive and forget. Those who had "railed" against inoculation, he wrote, ought to "sweat it out with just Reflection and due Repentance."[30]

The Boston inoculation experiment was a victory for reason over both superstition and unquestioning obeisance to accepted scientific notions. From the start, Boylston had believed that empirical evidence should win the day, that there was "no better Way of judging between moral and immoral Methods of Medical Practice, than from the good or ill Success that does, or may attend them."[31] Now he added that if anyone could present him with "any other Method of Practice" that was more successful in combating smallpox, he would acknowledge it as such. Until then, he wrote, "I shall value and esteem this Method of inoculating the Small-Pox, as the most beneficial and successful that ever was discover'd to, and practiced by Mankind in this World."[32] What sounded to some of his colleagues like a grandiloquent boast would prove over time an understatement. In addition to being what John B. Blake called "the earliest important experiment in America in preventative medicine," Boylston's inoculation trial was also, wrote Gerald Mager, "the chief contribution to medical science from America prior to the nineteenth century."[33] The method he employed and validated would have profound ramifications not only for the battle against smallpox, but also for the fight against polio, measles, tetanus, rabies, and other deadly illnesses. The medical historians Otho T. Beall Jr. and Richard H. Shryock put it best: "The history of immunology, with all its ultimate values in overcoming infectious diseases began—above the folk level and on a meaningful scale—in the Boston of 1721."[34]

Among Boylston's contemporaries, no one captured the significance of what he had dared and accomplished better than the man who had put him up to it. Cotton Mather had introduced inoculation to Boston hoping to please God, earn the gratitude of the people, and expiate the sins of Salem. Reviled throughout the period of the experiment, he had the satisfaction of seeing himself exonerated in the months and years that followed its conclusion, as a growing chorus of medical and scientific authorities—including the illustrious Royal Society, the group he had spent decades trying to impress—pronounced it a resounding success. Mather had earned bragging rights. Certainly it would have been consistent with his character to declare himself the hero of the epidemic, just as he had envisioned doing at the outset. What no one could have anticipated was that the egotistical minister would mostly demur, freely and magnanimously lavishing Boylston with full credit in a voice absent of even a hint of his habitual bitterness and resentment. In December 1724, shortly before Boylston sailed for London to be celebrated for his accomplishment, Mather gave him a letter of introduction to Dr. James Jurin, secretary of the Royal Society and member of the Royal College of Physicians. After apprising Jurin of Boylston's uncommon talent as a surgeon, he turned to inoculation. "But that which will more particularly recommend him to your Notice," he wrote, "is that *This* is the Gentleman who first brought the way of saving Lives by the Inoculation of the Small-Pox, into the *American* world." He continued:

> When the rest of the Doctors, did rather the part of Butchers or Fools for the Destroyer, to our perishing people, and with Envious and horrid Insinuations . . . against him, this Worthy Man had the Courage and Conscience to enter upon the practice; and (generously beginning with his own Family) he alone, with ye Blessing of Heaven, saved the Lives of (I think) several hundreds; Yea, at our time, he saved a Whole Town from a fearfull Desolation.[35]

PART THREE

AMERICAN MONSTERS

The conviction on the part of the Revolutionary leaders that they were faced with a deliberate conspiracy to destroy the balance of the constitution and eliminate their freedom had deep and widespread roots—roots elaborately embedded in Anglo-American political culture. How far back in time one may trace these roots it is difficult to say, but I have attempted at least to illustrate . . . that the configuration of attitudes and ideas that would constitute the Revolutionary ideology was present a half-century before there was an actual Revolution.

—Bernard Bailyn, *The Ideological Origins of the American Revolution*, 1967

Could unrepentance have kept to this courtly tone (learned out of imported periodicals), respectability might have been confounded, but James Franklin was an American and therefore an angry man.

—Perry Miller, *The New England Mind: From Colony to Province*, 1953

20

SONS OF CATO, SONS OF CALEF

O f the three Boston newspapers, the *New-England Courant* published the majority of the news on the smallpox epidemic,
paying comparatively little heed to the government's desire to
downplay the size and severity of the crisis so as not to depress trade or
panic the populace. It was the only paper to report in detail on the extraordinary measures being implemented to keep the town from running
out of firewood, food, and other essentials and the only one to report
on Rhode Island's quarantine of Boston ships, which it did twice. It also
offered the most robust account of deaths by both natural and inoculated smallpox in and outside of Boston. On November 27, 1721, the
Courant announced that William Hutchinson was ill with the disease in
Cambridge; the *News-Letter* said nothing. (No copy of that day's *Gazette*
survives.) The newspaper's coverage of the late stages of the inoculation
controversy included what in later eras would be known as a "scoop" or
an "inside story": the revelation that following the November 4 town
meeting the selectmen had accused a group of ministers of encouraging

people to come to town for inoculations, resulting in "some hot Discourse on both sides."[1]

All three newspapers printed a final death toll for the epidemic. Only the *Courant*, though, offered a poetic reflection on the tragedy. It appeared in late November, well before the danger had passed but at a point when the cases of smallpox had finally begun to taper off. James Franklin placed it at the head of the issue. Titled "An Evening Retirement," it began with a deceptive bow to the tropes of the conventional fire and brimstone jeremiad: There was "an Angel flaming" who stood over the town "with an awful List / Of all our Crimes" for which "an angry God" prepared to issue "the Blows of his revenging Rod." Then the retribution began, with roaring thunder and flashing lightning and "infectious Clouds" rising with "sickly Gloom, to vail the healthful Skies." At this point, though, the poem took a surprising turn for the gentle and defiantly hopeful:

> Then let him fight that will, my Soul shall fly
> For speedy Shelter from the Storm so nigh:
> I'll hide me in Love's Chamber, till his Rage
> Is overblown, and Mercy mount the Stage.
> Then of his sparing Grace I'll gladly sing;
> My rescu'd Life to him a thankful Tribute bring.[2]

On its face an elegy, "An Evening Retirement" was also a subtle act of defiance, a rejection of the abject guilt and self-loathing that Puritans were expected to feel in response to disasters attributed to divine retribution. Like much of what the newspaper had already printed and would continue to print, it was a subversive act, a gesture of rebellion against an old-guard authority that few Bostonians had dared question.

IN 1722, THE role of the newspaper in English society was far from settled. Only about one hundred years had passed since the appearance of England's first paper. In the lead-up to the English Civil War there had been a flurry of candid newspaper reports concerning the struggle between King Charles I and Parliament. But following the beheading of the king in 1649, a victorious Oliver Cromwell quashed the movement toward a freer press. Books and pamphlets were subjected to strict licensing. Newspapers, which were believed to be the tools of revolt and sedition, were (with a few exceptions) prohibited outright. Sir Roger L'Estrange, the man charged with enforcing the Licensing of the Press Act after its passage in 1662, disapproved of a newspaper geared toward the general public because, he wrote, it made "the Multitude too Familiar with the Actions, and Counsels of their Superiours . . . and gives them, not only an Itch, but a kind of Colourable Right, and License, to be Meddling with the Government."[3] Not until 1695, when licensing was permitted to lapse, had newspapers begun to multiply and diversify and, in a few cases, test boundaries. Even then they could be (and were) taxed into oblivion when they made the government too uncomfortable. The omnipresent threat of prosecution for seditious libel, a conveniently catchall term for the publication of anything deemed derogatory to the government, also helped keep publishers in their place.

No newspaper published in the British Empire in the twenty-seven years since the end of licensing had been more successful in challenging the limits of press freedom than James Franklin's *Courant*. By early December 1721 he had already produced, in several installments, what amounted to a manifesto arguing for a press that operated free of the constraints of government and that had both a right and a duty to monitor the very government that would prefer to censor it. Quoting Cato's Thomas Gordon, he had further asserted that governmental and religious authorities should freely accept the promulgation of opposition ideas, because "to reduce all Men to the same standard of thinking, is . . . absurd in Philosophy, impious in Religion, and Faction in State."[4]

Later that same month, he and Nathaniel Gardner put those lofty principles to the test, employing the *Courant* to condemn a New Hampshire law intended to prevent riots by restricting assembly—a near duplicate of the riot act Samuel Shute had failed to force through the Massachusetts General Court in April. In the guise of a fictitious Portsmouth resident named "Tom Penshallow," Gardner wrote:

> Ever since the New Laws have been Enacted, there is not a private Man among us who dare open his Lips, unless it be to flatter. As for Freedom of Speech, it is utterly suppress'd among us, and I suppose quickly we shall be hang'd for our Thoughts: And that those Laws did not pass at B—n, I hear is owning to the Conduct of some brave men among you.[5]

He went on to claim that the *Courant* would probably be banned in New Hampshire because it "sometimes sets forth the Rights and Liberties of Mankind; Doctrines which are not calculated to our Meridian: And possibly, our People by reading them, may too boldly perswade themselves, that they are *Englishmen*, and under Priviledges."[6] The following week Gardner replied to his Penshallow letter as a Massachusetts man. He asked if the people of New Hampshire could not elect better men "instead of them who measure their own Greatness, by their Oppression of their Neighbours."[7] In response to Penshallow's inquiry about trials in Massachusetts—"Pray inform me," he had asked, "whether in your Province Criminals have the Priviledge of a Jury"—Gardner offered a provocative answer:

> I would say, We not only have *Juries*, but such as are of our own choosing, and not such are pick'd and cull'd by the high Sheriff at the Direction of his Superiors: But if you are pleas'd with being Ass-rid, I know not who will pity you. I suppose some of you would be content with a Law, *That you shall not lye with your Wives*, and to be stript of all your Priviledges but a Negative One, viz. *Not to be Sold for Slaves.*[8]

He closed with a postscript in which he facetiously asked whether the New Hampshire government would also outlaw *"Excessive Punch-Drinking,"* since the "immoderate Use (or rather Abuse) of that Liquor" had "a natural Tendency to make Men riotous and seditious."[9]

Nothing, not even the *Courant*'s own history of audacious comments, criticisms, and declarations, had prepared readers for the temerity of the newspaper's attack on a neighboring government—and one that just happened to be under the administration of the same man who served as royal governor of Massachusetts. It's a mark of just how radical these utterances were that they sound more like the exhortations of a Revolutionary-era patriot fifty years in the future than anything that had been written previously. Not surprisingly, authorities in New Hampshire were indignant. On January 22, 1722, the *Courant* reported that a "High Sheriff" in that colony had seized the newspaper "as a Publick Disturber, and (according to Custom) without any Legal Tryal, acted the Part of a common Hangman in committing it to the Flames" simply because he feared "it might infect the Inhabitants with a Desire of Liberty."[10] The report might have been factual; more likely it was hearsay or completely apocryphal, another ploy by James to drum up controversy to sell newspapers. What was accurate about it, in any case, was its suggestion of how severely the government would have lashed out against James and his newspaper had the letters been published in New Hampshire rather than Massachusetts. The genius of the exchange between Tom Penshallow and the Massachusetts man, of course, was that, although ostensibly targeted at New Hampshire, it was also unmistakably an indictment of the men who had attempted similar encroachments of liberty in Massachusetts, where the governor's supporters also included political cronies and flatterers who measured "their Own Greatness, by their Oppression of their Neighbours." James was borrowing a strategy from Trenchard and Gordon, protecting himself from legal repercussions by appearing to criticize a government other than his own and letting readers draw parallels between the two.

Emboldened by his success in outmaneuvering the censors, James began 1722 with a pledge to "expose the Vices and Follies of Persons of all Ranks and Degrees . . . without Fear of, or Affection to, any Man."[11] Now, in addition to publishing what he wanted, he was finally making money doing so. Despite the economic hardships produced by the smallpox epidemic (but thanks largely to the controversy over inoculation), 1721 had been his most productive and profitable year yet, with a tally that included twenty-one imprints plus the *Courant*. He and Benjamin (and probably a journeyman printer) were having so much trouble keeping up with the workload that some of their imprints were appearing a week or more after their advertised publication dates.[12] The frantic pace was probably to blame for a gaffe in the *Courant* masthead, which in one issue was set to read: "From MONDAY March 21, to MONDAY March 19, 1722."[13] A few weeks prior to the publication of that issue, James had announced that the *Courant* had added more than forty subscribers since the first of the year; and he had taunted his enemies by predicting that the next pamphlet or letter published against his newspaper would bring him forty more. Even the loss of an angry Increase Mather as one of those subscribers had been a boon to business, he wrote, because old Increase had found that he could not do without the *Courant* and so had been forced to send his grandson Mather Byles to pick up individual copies at the Franklin shop, which meant that he "paid more for the Paper, and became more of a Supporter of it" than if he had remained a subscriber.[14]

As those boasts suggest, the Mathers had not sat by quietly after James had attacked them in December. In January 1722, the aforementioned Mather Byles published a letter in the *Gazette* labeling the *Courant* "Vile" and charging that its "main intention" was to "Villify and Abuse the best Men we have, and especially the Principal Ministers of Religion in the Country."[15] (The *Gazette*'s Musgrave was happy to assist in the counterattack, since the *Courant* had also attacked his performance as postmaster, accusing him of failing to deliver letters out of sheer laziness, of opening private letters, and even of stealing money from them.) Byles, the Harvard student and former Latin School classmate of Benjamin Franklin, reminded readers that the contributors to the *Courant* had been declared a Hell-Fire Club, and he threatened to divulge their identities. If that didn't end their "wickedness," he and other like-minded men would, he wrote, "pluck up our Courage, and see what we can do in our way to stop it."[16] James laughed off the threat, ignoring Byles and accusing Cotton Mather of using his "hot-headed Trumpeters" in an attempt to "spoil the Credit of the Courant, that he may reign Detractor General over the whole Province, and do all the Mischief his ill Nature prompts him to, without hearing of it."[17] Separately he charged that the minister had "thrown Praise in his own Face" so much that he had become "blind to his own Failings."[18]

Old Increase Mather issued a public appeal for someone to stop the *Courant*. He helped the only way he could by calling down God's wrath and warning James that inasmuch as he might meet an untimely demise, he had best atone sooner rather than later for printing things so "vile and abominable."[19] If James was unnerved he didn't show it. "I expect and Hope to appear before God with safety in the Righteousness of Christ," he replied a week later.[20]

Cotton Mather's response took the form of a fable about a man who took a long walk down a tree-lined road and was pelted with sticks thrown by monkeys who perched in the trees. Although he was confident he could kill several of the "wretches," the man suspected that all of them together might overwhelm him. Realizing that their *Impotent Sticks . . . did him little Damage*," he chose to ignore them, a decision, the fable noted, that was heralded by others as noble and wise.[21]

The Couranteers jumped on Mather's attempt to dismiss their criticisms the next week, declaring the fable's hero, whom they knew was Mather, a baboon to the monkeys assaulting him. William Douglass, writing from "Halls' Coffee House," added that Mather was "very modest in comparing them, and the whole Town, to a Parcel of *Monkeys*, seeing it is not long since (in his Letter to his Friends at Portsmouth) he was pleased to call them *Dogs*, and worse than the *Monsters of Africa*."[22] The minister, he declared, was a "peevish Mongrel," who barked and snarled and showed its teeth but didn't dare bite.[23] Elsewhere Mather was referred to as a "dunghill cock."[24] For all the indignities he had been made to suffer, this was perhaps the most humiliating. The crudeness and disrespect were breathtaking. It was fitting that at about this time an advertisement for a new edition of Robert Calef's *More Wonders of the Invisible World* appeared in the *Boston News-Letter*. What Mather's biographer Levin wrote about Calef—that in *More Wonders* and elsewhere his aspersions against Mather's methods, motives, and moral character were in some ways "unfair" but also "entertaining and infuriating"—was true of James and his newspaper as well.[25] In 1693 Mather had had Calef arrested for "scandalous libel."[26] When Calef's book had arrived in Boston seven years later, Increase Sr. had reputedly had it burned in Harvard Yard. But now the Puritan theocracy lacked the clout necessary to suppress that book or the *Courant*'s vitriol. What, if anything, the Mathers could do about this new Robert Calef remained to be seen.

From time to time James took a break from his attacks to defend his newspaper and offer a nod toward the impartiality he claimed to embrace. He illustrated the injustice of the repeated charges that he and his fellow *Courant* authors were a demonic cult by reprinting a London article on the real Hell-Fire Club, which revealed that its members gave themselves blasphemous names like "God the Father" and had an altar at which they prayed to the Devil.[27] He also praised a lecture on "Regular Singing" by the paper's first enemy, Thomas Walter, declaring it "excellent."[28] When the Mathers charged him with reneging on his promise to reprint a pro-inoculation article from the *London Mercury,* he effectively conceded that he had too hastily accepted William Douglass's claim that the article was fraudulent, and he promised to "take Care for the future, not to insert any thing in the Courant upon the Word of another."[29] Mostly, though, his newspaper reveled in its success and in the haplessness of its enemies. In February, the Couranteer Matthew Adams asked why, if the *Courant* deserved the "horrid Names which some have given it," its severest critics were "with Egg to read it (tho' *Incognito*) every Monday, and can hardly digest their *Chocolate*, till they have swallow'd a Dose of *Courant Hellbore!* 'Tis strange," he added, "it shou'd be too vile and scandalous to be printed, and yet full good enough to be faithfully perus'd as often as it appears."[30] That same month James wrote and published verse that epitomized his growing sense of empowerment and his cocky contempt for his hypocritical enemies. Its title, "THE LION, KING OF BEASTS, IS TO BE SEEN HERE," was a reference familiar to every newspaper reader—the headline to an advertisement that for more than a year had been inviting Bostonians to view the caged lion on exhibit in a Boston home. Just past halfway down the poem's single, long stanza, he wrote:

Couranto's Friends can write on Subjects new,
Without contending with such Fools as you.
Their biting Satyr will each Fop expose,
And every Vice their boyling Anger rouse.
By Dreams and Visions they'l detect the Great,
And show th' Oppressors politick Deceit.
No stingless Lashes (such as your's) presage
Couranto's Downfal. Your confined Rage,
But imitates your Lion, growling in his Cage.[31]

By April 1722 James had become intoxicated with his crusade. He was coming dangerously close to crossing a line that would force the hand of the censors. But he couldn't or wouldn't stop. Perhaps he believed his paper's success depended upon his willingness to go on shocking, delighting, and offending. Or it might simply have been a manifestation of his innate rebelliousness, a need to be, as his brother's biographers Lopez and Herbert put it, "systematically in the opposition."[32] But to others it seemed something more foolhardy and perverse. In late 1721 James had whistled past the graveyard, making fun of marriage and sexual mores while smallpox raged around him. Now, in spring 1722, he was whistling past the jailhouse, taunting the province's religious and political leadership and defying anyone to stop him. With a smirk, he advised the Mathers and their relatives "not to publish any thing more against it [the *Courant*], unless they are willing to have it continu'd."[33] In response to those who, like Increase Mather, called for a return to the days "when the Civil Government" had "taken an effectual Course to suppress such a *Cursed Libel*" as the *New-England Courant*, James argued that the proof he had done nothing wrong was that the government had taken no action against him.[34] It was the logic of a man begging to be arrested.

21

THE INVENTION OF
SILENCE DOGOOD

ames was not so obsessed with his crusade that he had lost his interest in—or ear for—material that would delight or titillate his readership. The issue that called Cotton Mather a peevish mongrel also
included the story of an apparently supernatural event in "Edgar Town,"
where a "Plain Indian Pudding, being put into the Pot and boil'd the usual
Time," had developed "a Blood-red Colour, to the great Surprise of the
whole Family."[1] A week later there was another story in the same vein but
even more chilling. A ghost had been spotted in a Narragansett, Rhode
Island, graveyard. Numerous persons had reported seeing "a bright Light,
as the Appearance of Fire" at "about 9 or 10 of Clock at Night." The light
was said to give off sparks and produce "the Likeness of a Person . . . wrapt
in a sheet with its Arms folded," which then moved great distances "in the
Twinkling of an Eye."[2] The apparition was believed to be that of a woman
who had died of smallpox the previous winter. That issue also included
another "war of the sexes " piece, a letter from a man who complained
about "the Insolence of an incorrigible *Virago* of a Wife, who (tho' she

denies herself nothing to put her upon a Par with the best in the Town, as to outward Apparel)," wanted her husband to dress more humbly and frugally, and nagged him about being a "*Sot* and *Drunkard*, and other such like opprobrious Expressions" if he had a "Glass" with his friend.[3]

But the most noteworthy item from the April 2, 1722, issue of the *New-England Courant* was a letter from a new correspondent: a middle-aged minister's widow and mother of three children who lived some-where in the countryside outside of Boston. She began by promising to treat *Courant* readers "once a Fortnight" with "a short Epistle" she hoped would "add somewhat to their Entertainment."[4] Most of the remainder of the letter offered salient facts from her youth and young adulthood—how she had been born on a ship sailing from London to New England and had lost her father when, in the throes of rejoicing over her birth, he had been swept overboard by a rogue wave. The letter writer's poor widowed mother had been forced by circumstances to apprentice her at a young age to a minister, who had instilled in her soul "vertuous and godly Principles" and had overseen her education, rewarding her love for books by giving her access to his library, which, although small, had been "well chose, to inform the Understanding rightly, and enable the Mind to frame great and noble Ideas."[5] After promising to tell more of her story in the near future, she closed with a show of cheekiness. "I am not insensible of the Impossibility of pleasing all," she wrote,

> but I would not willingly displease any; and for those who will take Offense where none is intended, they are beneath the Notice of . . . *Your Humble Servant*, SILENCE DOGOOD.[6]

Nothing the *Courant* had published was quite like this letter. On one level it was more ingratiating than anything that had come before it: Silence's story of her tragic and disadvantaged youth tugged on readers' heartstrings; and the story of her redemption by a kindly and wise minister affirmed their belief in the grace of God and the essential wisdom and

Elisha Cooke was the most dominant American politician of the early eighteenth century, and the political godfather of Samuel Adams and the Patriots. A "drinking man without equal," he utilized Boston taverns to build a political machine more powerful than the royal government. Exasperated English officials dubbed him "the idol of the mob" and "head of the scum."

By 1721, Boston was America's largest town and the British Empire's third most active seaport. Long Wharf, the centerpiece of its trade-based economy, extended nearly a third of a mile into the harbor and was the largest infrastructure project yet undertaken in the colonies.

When the people of Massachusetts arrested and deposed Governor Edmund Andros in 1689, they insisted they were rebelling against an abusive tyrant, not the royal authority he represented. But when Massachusetts rebelled again in 1721 and 1722, it was royal governance—and not simply the royal governor—they found intolerable.

Nearly thirty years after the Salem witchcraft trials, Puritan minister Cotton Mather was still trying to escape his reputation as one of the witch hunt's villains. He hoped to redeem himself by introducing a radical new medical procedure that he claimed would save thousands of Bostonians from death by smallpox.

Boston (off in the distance) as seen from a ship passing Spectacle Island, site of the town's "pest house." By quarantining diseased ships well offshore, officials hoped to prevent epidemics. But when a military frigate carrying smallpox slipped through the safety net in 1721, the consequences were catastrophic.

A Prospect of the Colledges in Cambridge in New England

Harvard in the 1720s. Commencement Day at the college was the "great summer holiday" for Massachusetts. Every year, thousands of people came from all over the area to eat, drink, and watch street performers. In 1721, the public celebration was canceled when an outbreak of smallpox began to worsen.

Cotton Mather's son Samuel was his father's last and best hope to continue the family's ministerial legacy. His ordination appeared a certainty until smallpox returned to Boston.

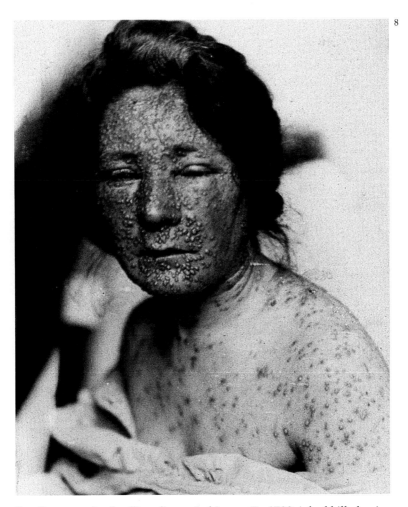

Smallpox was the deadliest disease in history. By 1702, it had killed, crippled, or disfigured nearly one-tenth of all mankind. The 1721 Boston inoculation experiment was a major milestone in its eradication, which is considered one of the greatest accomplishments in medical history.

Zabdiel Boylston was the only Boston physician to attempt inoculation against smallpox. He began by performing the procedure on his six-year-old son. Several years later he was honored in England, where, at Princess Caroline's urging, he wrote a book about his groundbreaking experiment.

AN

Historical ACCOUNT

OF THE

SMALL-POX

INOCULATED

IN

NEW ENGLAND,

Upon all Sorts of Persons, *Whites*, *Blacks*, and of all Ages and Constitutions.

With some Account of the Nature of the Infection in the NATURAL and INOCULATED Way, and their different Effects on HUMAN BODIES.

With some short DIRECTIONS to the UN-EXPERIENCED in this Method of Practice.

Humbly dedicated to her Royal Highness the Princess of WALES,

By *Zabdiel Boylston*, F. R. S.

The Second Edition, Corrected.

LONDON:

Printed for S. CHANDLER, at the Cross-Keys in the *Poultry*. M. DCC. XXVI.

Re-Printed at *BOSTON* in *N. E.* for S. GERRISH in *Cornhil*, and T. HANCOCK at the Bible and Three Crowns in *Annstreet*. M. DCC. XXX.

Boylston was accused of hiding inoculation deaths. But his book detailed the deaths by name and month. Of the 248 persons inoculated, only 6 died. Their 2.4 percent death rate was dramatically lower than the death rate of those who had contracted smallpox naturally, proof that inoculation was comparatively safe.

In 1718, James Franklin opened a printing house on Queen Street at the southeast corner of Brattles Street. Four years later, he would find himself incarcerated directly across Queen Street in the "gloomy pile" of the town prison. This detail from the Bonner Map (1723) also shows the printing shop's proximity to the Boston Town House ("a") and the First Church ("A").

The decapitation of the fearsome pirate Blackbeard was big news in early 1719. To boost his struggling business, James Franklin enlisted his thirteen-year-old brother Benjamin to write a broadside ballad dramatizing the gruesome event. It sold well, but their father, who considered such ballads tawdry, put a stop to the practice.

Benjamin Franklin's earliest portrait shows a prosperous young Philadelphia printer. He owed much of his early success to his Boston apprenticeship with his brother. The vibrant atmosphere of James Franklin's printing house—where "ingenious" young men discussed books, politics, philosophy, and more—spurred Benjamin to educate himself and perfect his writing. Ben's work on the newspaper his brother founded during the inoculation controversy of 1721 influenced him as an author, publisher, political philosopher, diplomat, and scientist.

Both James and Benjamin Franklin idolized the English essayist, poet, and playwright Joseph Addison. James modeled his *New-England Courant* after Addison's *Spectator*. The teenaged Benjamin worked tirelessly to emulate Addison's exemplary prose.

THE
New-England Courant.

From MONDAY July 2. to MONDAY July 9. 1722.

To the Author of the New-England Courant.
SIR, No VIII.

PREFER the following Abstract from the London Journal to any Thing of my own, and therefore shall present it to your Readers this week without any further Preface.

'WITHOUT Freedom of Thought, there can be no such Thing as Wisdom; and no such Thing as publick Liberty, without Freedom of Speech; which is the Right of every Man, as far as by it, he does not hurt or controul the Right of another: And this is the only Check it ought to suffer, and the only Bounds it ought to know.

'This sacred Privilege is so essential to free Governments, that the Security of Property, and the Freedom of Speech always go together; and in those wretched Countries where a Man cannot call his Tongue his own, he can scarce call any Thing else his own. Whoever would overthrow the Liberty of a Nation, must begin by subduing the Freeness of Speech; a Thing terrible to Publick Traytors.

'This Secret was so well known to the Court of King Charles the First, that his wicked Ministry procured a Proclamation, to forbid the People to talk of Parliaments, which those Traytors had laid aside. To assert the undoubted Right of the Subject, and defend his Majesty's legal Prerogative, was called Disaffection, and punished as Sedition. Nay, People were forbid to talk of Religion in their Families: For the Priests had combined with the Ministers to cook up Tyranny, and suppress Truth and the Law. while the late King James, when Duke of York, went avowedly to Mass, Men were fined, imprisoned and undone, for saying he was a Papist: And that King Charles the Second might live more securely a Papist, there was an Act of Parliament made, declaring it Treason to say that he was one.

'That Men ought to speak well of their Governours is true, while their Governours deserve to be well spoken of; but to do publick Mischief, without hearing of it, is only the Prerogative and Felicity of Tyranny: A free People will be shewing that they are so, by their Freedom of Speech.

'The Administration of Government, is nothing else but the Attendance of the Trustees of the People upon the Interest and Affairs of the People: And as it is the Part and Business of the People, for whose Sake alone all publick Matters are, or ought to be transacted, to see whether they be well or ill transacted; so it is the Interest, and ought to be the Ambition, of all honest Magistrates, to have their Deeds openly examined, and publickly scann'd: Only the wicked Governours of Men dread what is said of them; Audivit Tiberius probra queis lacerabitur, atque perculsus est. The publick Censure was true, else he had not felt it bitter.

'Freedom of Speech is ever the Symptom, as well as the Effect of a good Government. In old Rome, all was left to the Judgment and Pleasure of the People, who examined the publick Proceedings with such Discretion, & censured those who administred them with such Equity and Mildness, that in the space of Three Hundred Years, not five publick Ministers suffered unjustly. Indeed whenever the Commons proceeded to Violence, the great Ones had been the Aggressors.

'GUILT only dreads Liberty of Speech, which drags it out of its lurking Holes, and exposes its Deformity and Horrour to Day-light. Horatius, Valerius, Cincinnatus, and other vertuous and undesigning Magistrates of the Roman Commonwealth, had nothing to fear from Liberty of Speech. Their virtuous Administration, the more it was examin'd, the more it brightned and gain'd by Enquiry. When Valerius in particular, was accused upon some slight grounds of affecting the Diadem; he, who was the first Minister of Rome, does not accuse the People for examining his Conduct, but approved his Innocence in a Speech to them; and gave such Satisfaction to them, and gained such Popularity to himself, that they gave him a new Name; inde cognomen factum Publicolæ est; to denote that he was their Favourite and their Friend —— Lata deinde leges; —— Ante omnes de provocatione ADVERSUS MAGISTRATUS AD POPULUM, Lvii, lib. 2, Cap. 8.

'But Things afterwards took another Turn. Rome, with the Loss of its Liberty, lost also its Freedom of Speech; then Mens Words began to be feared and watched; and then first began the poysonous Race of Informers, banished indeed under the righteous Administration of Titus, Narva, Trajan, Aurelius, &c. but encouraged and enriched under the vile Ministry of Sejanus, Tigillinus, Pallas, and Cleander: Queri libet, quod in secreta nostra non inquirant principes, nisi quos Odimus, says Pliny to Trajan.

'The best Princes have ever encouraged and promoted Freedom of Speech; they know that upright Measures would defend themselves, and that all upright Men would defend them. Tacitus, speaking of the Reign of some of the Princes abovemention'd, says with Extasy, Rara Temporum felicitate, ubi sentire quæ velis, & quæ sentias dicere licet: A blessed Time when you might think what you would, and speak what you thought.

'I doubt not but old Spencer and his Son, who were the Chief Ministers and Betrayers of Edward the Second, would have been very glad to have stopped the Mouths of all the honest Men in England. They dreaded to be called Traytors, because they were Traytors. And I dare say, Queen Elizabeth's Walsingham, who deserved no Reproaches, feared none. Misrepresentation of publick Measures is easily overthrown, by representing publick Measures truly; when they are honest, they ought to be publickly known, that they may be publickly commended; but if they are knavish or pernicious, they ought to be publickly exposed, in order to be publickly detested,

Yours, &c,

SILENCE DOGOOD.

The *New-England Courant* was America's first independent newspaper. In July of 1722, sixteen-year-old Benjamin Franklin, writing secretly as Silence Dogood, protested the arrest of the paper's publisher—his brother James—who had offended the government in print. Ben quoted the radical Whig Thomas Gordon: "Whoever would overthrow the Liberty of a Nation, must begin by subduing the Freeness of Speech."

Judge Samuel Sewall, a member of the Governor's Council, was one of the most pow-
erful and ostentatiously pious men in Massachusetts. He led the effort to have James
Franklin arrested for "libels" against the clergy and the government. In response, the
Franklin brothers attacked him in the *Courant*.

The printing press that James and Benjamin Franklin used to put out the *New-England Courant*. James continued to use it when he left Boston for Newport, Rhode Island. It is on display at the Museum of Newport History.

Thomas Hutchinson was a Boston schoolboy when Elisha Cooke squared off with Governor Samuel Shute. Later he served as his colony's lieutenant governor and governor and wrote a history of Massachusetts. That work's acknowledgment of Shute's mistakes did not help Hutchinson avoid his predecessor's fate. Like Shute, he was driven from the colony by the political organization Cooke had created.

Samuel Adams, the firebrand of the American Revolution and the bane of Governor Thomas Hutchinson's existence, got his first lessons in political ideology and strategy from Elisha Cooke, who was a frequent guest at the Adams home during Sam's boyhood.

goodness of a clergy too often denigrated, particularly by the *Courant* itself. At the same time, the account of Silence's father's demise delighted readers in a very different way, pandering to their fascination with deaths that were both bizarre and poignant. And the letter's author had hinted at more provocative offerings in the future. It was impossible to be sure what she was aiming for but just as impossible to ignore her. After just one letter, readers were hooked.

So was James Franklin, who was a savvy enough publisher to recognize that, as one biographer wrote, the Silence letters were "a breath of fresh air in a pestilence-ridden town" too long "beset with anger, bitter recriminations, ugly epithets, and a dialogue of accusation."[7] When a second letter continuing Silence's biography with an account of her marriage and widowhood arrived a week and a half later, he gave it the lead position in the April 16 *Courant*.

James knew nothing more about Silence Dogood than his readers did. Her letters had appeared as if by magic, slipped under the door of the printing house under cover of night. He and the Couranteers discussed her possible identity at length. They believed she was not really a woman, but rather a man "of some Character . . . for Learning & Ingenuity" writing as a woman.[8] Names were proposed and leads were pursued, but to no avail. The truth, of course, was that Silence Dogood was right under their noses, hiding in plain sight.

BENJAMIN FRANKLIN HAD come into his brother's business in 1718 thoroughly demoralized by his removal from school two years earlier, his father having decided that there was no point in shouldering the expense of a prolonged education for a boy who had no inclination to go into the ministry. It's telling of Ben's state of mind after he had been forced to transition from the schoolroom to his father's tallow shop that in due course even Josiah had felt a sense of urgency to find some alternative that would bring him out of his doldrums and restore him to his

lively and curious former self. It's hard to imagine that short of sending him back to school—which Josiah wouldn't consider—he could have
found a more congenial vocation than printer for his youngest son. Ben
might not have been happy to be stuck with a brother he barely knew and
didn't particularly like (in part, it seems, because he recognized James
was as willful as he was), but the intellectually vibrant atmosphere of a
printing house—and, in particular, a printing house run by a man as ambitious as James Franklin—proved a tonic to his mind and his soul. The
constant flow of words and ideas transfused and rejuvenated him, and he
began to emerge from his depression. Within a few months of becoming his brother's "printer's devil," his desire to run away to sea had been
replaced by a determination to give himself the education that had been
taken from him.

One inspiration for that drive was the Franklin printing house library,
a trove of great philosophy, history, commentary, and literature that, by
1722, would contain a *"vast Quantity of Pamphlets"* and more than forty
titles, including Aristotle's *Politicks*, works by Virgil, Milton, and Shake-
speare, comprehensive histories of France and Rome, and books by some
of the European Enlightenment's greatest writers.[9] The other inspiration
was the conversation that filled the small printing house on a daily basis.
James and the friends who visited his shop talked about authors, philoso-
phers, books and pamphlets, politics in general, and the sorry state of liberty in Massachusetts in particular, and they joked about sex, marriage,
and social mores. Head down, attention seemingly focused on the work at
hand, and, as an apprentice, more or less invisible to all present, Benjamin
soaked it all in. Nothing was lost on him.

He would later admit that his desire to join in the discussions and
debates going on around him made him determined to become educated.
Benjamin began his self-education where his formal education had left
off, improving his writing and remediating his mathematical shortcomings. Then he moved on to logic and rhetoric with an eye toward becoming a champion of argument. When a book titled *Logic: or the Art of*

Thinking (popularly known as *The Port Royal Logic*) failed to provide the strategy necessary to best "another Bookish Lad" named John Collins in debates on ethics and public policy, Benjamin abandoned it in favor of the Socratic method.[10] "I was charm'd with it," he wrote, "adopted it, dropped my abrupt Contradiction, and positive Argumentation, and put on the humble Inquirer & Doubter."[11] Aggressive by nature, Benjamin had been on his way to becoming "obnoxiously assertive."[12] Now, though, he had changed course, adopting a deceptively nonconfrontational style that in the decades to come would make him an effective politician and his country's essential diplomat.

His campaign of self-improvement got a boost in 1720 when he moved out of the Franklin family home and began boarding elsewhere at the expense of his master, as was customary for boys once they became apprentices. (Letting Benjamin live at home initially, with his expenses covered by his parents, seems to have been a concession James demanded in exchange for taking him on.) With no parental oversight, Ben began utilizing the empty printing house as a reading room "at Night, after Work or before Work began in the Morning" and on Sundays, when he "contrived" to be there alone, "evading" as much as possible "the common Attendance on publick Worship" that had formerly been an obligation.[13] He read the books in his brother's library and cajoled boys apprenticed to booksellers to make him secret, unauthorized loans from their masters' stock. To buy the books he couldn't borrow, he struck a clever deal with his brother, offering to provide his own meals and save James 50 percent in the process. James gave the food money to Benjamin; and Benjamin, by using only about half that reduced allowance to provide himself with a sparse and meat-free diet, slowly accumulated a fund for books. A side benefit of the plan was yet more time for reading. "My Brother and the rest going from the Printinghouse to their Meals," he later wrote, "I remain'd there alone, and dispatching presently my light Repast, (which often was no more than a Biscuit or a Slice of Bread, a Handful of Raisins or a Tart from the Pastry-Cook's, & a Glass of Water), had the rest of the Time till their Return for Study."[14]

Forsaking meat-heavy New England cooking was easy for Benjamin, who had read a book titled *The Way to Health, Long Life and Happiness; or, A Discourse of Temperance*, and had been convinced by its author, Thomas Tryon, to stop eating animals on moral grounds. (The difficulty of finding meat-free meals for Benjamin was another reason James had been happy to hand off the problem to his brother.) In early eighteenth-century Boston, vegetarianism was considered a radical act; his mother was convinced that he had fallen under the influence of "a mad philosopher."[15] Not long thereafter he had surprised his family again, this time with a conversion that made his rejection of meat insignificant by comparison. As in the case of his vegetarianism, the idea had originated in a book. Right around his fifteenth birthday, Benjamin read John Locke's *Essay Concerning Human Understanding*, which discussed the relationship between reason and religious belief. It argued for skepticism regarding aspects of uncritically accepted dogma. That book, and several others he read after it, impelled Benjamin to renounce his father's Calvinist faith and declare himself a Deist, which, for most Puritans, was tantamount to being a nonbeliever.

Two and a half years into his printer's apprenticeship, Benjamin Franklin had undergone a substantial—and, for his parents, at least, troubling—metamorphosis. Josiah must have held James at least partly responsible—not for converting Benjamin, since James had no use for either of his brother's new enthusiasms, but for allowing the boy exposure to outlandish opinions, both written and spoken. That, in turn, must have notched up the tension between James and his printer's devil, who were already frequently at odds, Benjamin increasingly resentful of James for acting more like a master than a brother and James increasingly impatient with Benjamin for his presumptions and small rebellions, his refusal to play his given role as dutiful apprentice.

When James started publishing the *New-England Courant*, Benjamin studied it with the fanatical attention he had given to Locke and Tryon. He also became a devoted student of its influences, "Cato's Letters" and the *Spectator*. Joseph Addison, in particular, became a model and, vicariously, a teacher. Determined to attain the simple elegance of Addison's masterful prose, Ben went to school on his style, reading one of his essays "over and over," taking notes on it, and then, with only the notes before him, attempting to re-create it in his own words—first in verse, which allowed him to conjure up more expressive language, and then in prose informed by the verse.[16] His elation with the result was still evident fifty years later when, in his *Autobiography*, he remembered that although in some respects Addison's version remained superior, he had managed to improve upon it in certain small but important ways. That realization encouraged him, he wrote, "to think I might possibly in time come to be a tolerable English Writer, of which I was extremely ambitious."[17]

His immediate ambition was to write well enough to earn a place in the *Courant* alongside his brother's "ingenious" friends, whom he had come to admire for their "amused if impatient and relentless skepticism of the old and the habitual" and their talent for questioning authority in a way that was new and youthful.[18] "Hearing their Conversations, and their Accounts of the Approbation their Papers were receiv'd with," he later wrote, "I was excited to try my Hand among them."[19]

The problem was James, who had made it clear that Benjamin was not welcome to contribute, not to the debates at the printing house and not to the *Courant*. Nominally, his objection was to Ben's youth and presumed callowness. Perhaps he had also decided to err on the side of caution as concerned his father's earlier ruling against encouraging his brother's poetic pretensions. Mostly, though, he seems to have been concerned that allowing his apprentice to become a Couranteer would make him even more difficult to control. Understanding that James would reject, as he later put it, "any thing of mine in his Paper if he knew it to be mine," Benjamin had decided to contribute anonymously.[20]

Disguising his handwriting helped mask his true identity. So did assuming the character of a middle-aged widow. But Silence Dogood and her creator were more alike than their obvious differences made it appear. Indeed, when it eventually came to light that Benjamin was Silence, the underlying similarities between the author and his creation would become embarrassingly obvious. Like apprentices, most widows were poor, with negligible legal clout. Silence Dogood had been apprenticed at an early age and deprived of a full and formal education—Benjamin's plight precisely. She had also been determined to remedy that deficiency, "indefatigably studious to gain and treasure up in my Mind all useful and desireable Knowledge, especially such as tends to improve the Mind, and enlarge the Understanding," she explained in letter three, summarizing exactly the mission to which Ben had devoted himself for three years.[21] There were also more subtle similarities. Silence's master and future husband had opened his library to her. If James had proven less generous with his library than the late Reverend Dogood, it was nevertheless the case that one of the Honest Wags, Matthew Adams, had taken an avuncular interest in Benjamin and offered him full access to his personal library, which, although modest, had a particularly good collection of poetry.

At the same time Benjamin sought to fit in, he also wanted to stand apart, to introduce, in the person of Silence, a voice very different from any that the newspaper had featured. He had "seen enough of the boomeranging effect of the somewhat determined iconoclasm of the Couranteers," wrote one biographer, "to realize that one could get nowhere, by way of influencing opinion, by displaying built-in prejudices, and by confusing expressions of heated contempt with dispassionate critical observations."[22] By the time he was finished writing the letters under her pseudonym he would have established a new kind of voice in Boston, "the reformer tempered by wit and a dash of irreverence, whose concern is genuinely benevolent but whose manner is wholly relaxed."[23] It was the public face he would wear for the rest of his life—and the "symbolic role . . . with which he could charm and conquer even Versailles."[24]

Benjamin wanted Silence to be charming; he wanted Boston to embrace her. But like his earlier use of Socratic questions in debates, Silence's charm and sweetness were not ends unto themselves but rather means to an end. He wanted to say bold things about the world around him but in a voice disarming and entertaining enough that readers would hear him out. Even in Silence's first three letters, which were more charm offensive than topical or provocative, there were hints of stronger medicine to come. Indeed, her very first letter contained a remonstrance against the *Courant* itself for its "determined iconoclasm." Careful readers—and certainly the paper's publisher—instantly recognized that Silence's self-introduction approximated John Checkley's in the very first *Courant*, which had been an attempt to imitate Joseph Addison's famous introduction in the *Spectator*. Writing as Silence, Benjamin had proceeded to give Checkley a clinic on the proper way to pay homage to the master and to capture the interest of an audience. Checkley's take had been haughty and even contemptuous; Benjamin's was winning and alluring. Addison-like in obvious ways, this letter and those that would follow were, like the character of Silence herself, something new and unique, "an idiom of provincial New England, more town than country . . . and full of warmth, good humor, and good sense."[25] They marked the introduction of what Walter Isaacson called "the quintessential genre of American folk humor: the wry and self-deprecating homespun character whose feigned innocence and naivete is disarming but whose wicked little insights poke through the pretensions of the elite and the follies of everyday life."[26]

Silence was no less charming in her second appearance. Now, however, she was surprisingly political. "Vice" and "arbitrary Government & unlimited Power," she declared, were her enemies.[27] Indeed, she was so "naturally very jealous for the Rights and Liberties of my Country," she told readers, that "the least appearance of an Incroachment on those invaluable Priviledges, is apt to make my Blood boil exceedingly."[28] If at that moment she sounded more like a sixteen-year-old boy drunk on "Cato's Letters" than a country widow it was because she was.

By letter four Silence had established herself as charming and winning, if also somewhat outspoken and idiosyncratic (not to mention a little macho for a mother of three). But fans were brought up short on May 14 when she launched an all-out attack on one of the colony's sacred cows, Harvard College. She didn't call it Harvard, of course. It was a "Temple of LEARNING" that she claimed to have visited in a dream. But it was patently, undeniably Harvard. Her claim that the students there were "little better than Dunces and Blockheads" who graduated "as great Blockheads as ever, only more proud and self-conceited" was a display of jaw-dropping effrontery, as was her conclusion that the real problem wasn't the students but, rather, their parents, who "consulted their own Purses instead of their Children's Capacities" when deciding to educate them there.[29] The letter was polarizing. Men like James Franklin and nearly all the Honest Wags, who had lacked the financial wherewithal to attend Harvard and were tired of having its graduates lord their superiority over them, were delighted. That approval was equaled if not surpassed by the outrage of the college's faithful, who tended to occupy leading positions in Boston's political, religious, and business communities. Their responses came fast and furious. Some well-read Harvard men informed James that he ought to think twice about allowing Silence Dogood to call Harvard students and alumni plagiarists (yet another of her accusations), since his own contributors had, on more than one occasion, appropriated the words of others without attribution. Another letter from "John Harvard" (probably Mather Byles) mocked Silence for calling Harvard men dumb in one sentence and then using a badly mixed metaphor in another. Understanding that controversy produced sales, James reveled in the uproar. In the May 28 issue he admitted that, from time to time, he had been lax in vetting the ideas expressed in his newspaper. Then on June 4 he penned some verse in support of Silence, hailing the widow for her "sharp Satyrs."[30]

James had found a new contributor who brought him everything he had hoped for since the *Courant*'s second issue, when he had put out a call for members of the public to submit "some short Piece, Serious; Sarcastick, Ludicrous, or otherways amusing."[31] Even Silence's jab at the inaugural *Courant* had pleased him. As his publication of Thomas Walter's *Anti-Courant* had shown, he would print anything that kept debate lively and subscriptions growing. Who Silence Dogood was didn't matter. What mattered was that she keep sending him her inimitable letters.

22

THE ARREST OF JAMES FRANKLIN

One week after Silence Dogood's debut in the *Courant*, the newspaper ran what appeared, at a glance, to be a fishing report from Maine. Datelined "Piscataqua," it read:

> We hear there is no catching Fish at Winter-Harbour without baiting the Hook with a *Gudgeon*: and it happens to be so all along the Eastern Shore, as far as the English Settlements. 'Tis thought by many that the Price of Fish will be very high by Reason the Bait is so very scarce.[1]

Readers not thrown by the incongruousness of the report understood that the *Courant* was offering an editorial comment on what appeared to be the imminent outbreak of war with the Eastern Indians—specifically on the running dispute between the House of Representatives and the governor over how best to deal with acts of Abenaki aggression. Shute and his Council favored continued negotiations aimed at renewing the 1717 treaty of pacification. The House and the *Courant* believed that the governor was trying to bribe the Indians into peace, "baiting the hook" with money and other concessions that Massachusetts could scarcely afford and that would only delay an inevitable military solution.

Having publicly questioned the royal governor's judgment on matters of war and peace, the *Courant* continued to reflect on the government and on Massachusetts politics for the next several weeks. On April 30 Matthew Adams authored an essay condemning wealthy property owners who coerced tenants into voting with them by threatening eviction. On May 7 the newspaper again inveighed against political corruption, this time singling out the governor's supporter Paul Dudley as a culprit. (The paper printed the previous summer's House vote calling for Dudley to be stripped of his position on the Council on the grounds that he had falsified his residency qualifications.) A week later, on the eve of the elections for the General Court, James published his most overtly political issue yet, with four separate commentaries. Under the pseudonym "Elisha Trueman," another *Courant* contributor named Thomas Lane appealed to the voters to not let "Hope of Gain or Fear of Displeasure" cause them to vote for unprincipled candidates who would "become Wax to receive every Impression the Enemies of our Constitution shall think fit to make on them."[2] Next, John Eyre chimed in on a similar if more cynical note, arguing that political corruption in the colony had become "very bad"—so rampant that the time had come when men could "hardly rise to Preferment and be honest; and when honest Men are oblig'd to decline Posts of Honour and Profit, for fear of being reputed Knaves."[3] Captain Taylor, another frequent contributor (and the same man who had threatened to pummel Samuel Shute's nephew for striking Elisha Cooke), quoted a long extract from "Cato's Letters" on natural law. (Cato argued: "The Violation . . . of Law does not constitute a Crime where the Law is bad; but the Violation of what ought to be Law, is a crime even where there is no Law."[4]) James Franklin addressed the upcoming election directly in the last item. "'Tis hoped," he wrote, "the Eyes of the Town will be fix'd on honest Men, and Friends to their Country. *Quaere*. Whether those Gentlemen who held up their

Hands in the House for the Payment of Mr. B[ridge]r's Money, are fit for Representatives?" *Quaere.* Whether one who gives no Account of Money appropriated by Law to purchase Arms and Ammunition for the Town's Use, be fit to serve the Town in that Station?"[5] Press historians credit this final commentary with being the first editorial opinion on an upcoming election published in an American newspaper. But an argument can be made that the issue as a whole marked the first time an American newspaper assumed the role "that the press was destined to fill in the American democracy," namely "to be a third factor in the electoral process, aligned on the side of the voter."[6] In this, observed Tourtellot, James Franklin's newspaper was "far ahead of its time."[7]

On May 21 Philip Musgrave attacked the *Courant* on behalf of the Prerogative Party, calling the newspaper's accusation that the Dudleys had come by their political power unethically "a notorious & positive lye."[8] James and his friends, he charged, were "so many Misfits barking at the Moon."[9] But it was Musgrave, not Franklin, who was treated like a disgruntled misfit a few weeks later. On June 5, six days after the General Court began its new session, the House ordered him "forthwith to appear" and to "give his Reasons why he printed the Election of Councellors made by the General Court of Assembly" in the previous day's issue of his newspaper.[10]

The deputies claimed to be upset because Musgrave had reported government proceedings without their approval. Their real objection, though, was to *how* he had reported them. The *Gazette* had published only the final, approved list of councilors, omitting the names of the two Popular Party members, William Clark and Nathaniel Byfield, who had been chosen but subsequently negatived by the governor. A reader of Musgrave's report would think that Clark and Byfield had never been chosen at all. House members were also upset that Musgrave had credited John Clark's reelection as their speaker to the Court as a whole rather than the House alone, implying that the speaker was serving at the pleasure of the Board and therefore of the royal governor—whose approval, they still insisted (the letter from London be damned), they did not require. Their demand to know why Musgrave had reported the elections in that fashion was disingenuous; it was obvious he had done so to satisfy Samuel Shute's expectations. That question—indeed, the whole interrogation—was merely a pretense for harassing him over his fealty to the royal administration and especially for propagating the impression that the governor had any say in the choice of speaker.

Philip Musgrave made no effort to justify his actions, pleading ignorance as the cause of his error. John Campbell, whose newspaper had published a similarly worded report on the Court elections, was called in next and likewise chastised for "Mistakes made by him in his News-Letter."[11] He, too, apologized. (This was one of the last straws for Campbell. Several months later, after again being attacked in the *Courant* for his newspaper's poor writing, he sold the newspaper to his printer, Bartholomew Green.) Both men were rebuked and then dismissed with instructions not to print any other actions of the General Court except from official reports.

Conspicuously, James Franklin received no summons from the deputies, even though, like Musgrave and Campbell, he had published the results of the Court's internal elections. The reason for this was apparent in the wording of his report, which announced John Clark's election as speaker without specifying who had done the electing, and which noted that William Clark and Byfield had been elected councilors and subsequently negatived by the governor. What might have pleased the House most, though, was that the *Courant* had also declined to publish Samuel Shute's session-opening speech, a presumed obligation for authorized newspapers.

For the moment, James could relax. But his favored treatment by the House made it more likely than ever that the councilors would find an excuse to move against him, if only out of a quid pro quo need to defend the governor's take on the Court elections and to assert its official and ultimate authority in matters of censorship. Indeed, they were determined to do the House one better, making an example of the publisher who had been a thorn in the paw of the governor and the establishment for months.

• • •

THE ITEM THAT got James Franklin thrown in jail appeared at the tail end of the following week's *Courant*, just above the advertisements. It had nothing to do with inoculation, Cotton Mather, or, directly, at least, the newspaper's bold insistence on Whiggish liberties. The subject was piracy. A short dispatch, purportedly originating in Newport, Rhode Island, on June 7, announced that "a Pirate Briganteen, with two Carriage Guns, and four Swivel Guns, and about 40 to 50 Men on Board" had attacked and captured two ships, including one commanded by a Block Island captain.[12] Within hours of receiving the news, the Rhode Island governor had ordered "Drums . . . to be beat about Town for Volunteers to go in quest of the Pirates; and by 3 of Clock the same Day," the *Courant* reported, two large sloops were under sail.[13]

Nothing here was objectionable. The offense was contained in the lines that followed. Having pointed up the urgency with which Rhode Island had responded to the pirate attacks, the dispatch offered a stark contradiction in the lackadaisical reaction by the government of the *Courant*'s home colony:

> We are advised from Boston, that the Government of the Massachusetts are fitting out a Ship to go after the Pirates, to be commanded by Capt. Peter Papillion, and 'tis thought he will sail sometime this Month, if Wind and Weather permit.[14]

Two more short dispatches elaborated on and updated the initial report. The first revealed that the perpetrator of the pirate attacks was Edward "Ned" Low, a former Boston sailor who was beginning a reign of terror that would continue two more years and earn him a reputation as perhaps the most sadistic and bloodthirsty of all of the era's pirates. Low, the *Courant* reported, had severely wounded the captain of one ship and had captured two other ships, one of which had departed Boston a few days earlier. The ship in which he had conducted this attack was another Boston vessel he had previously commandeered. It also noted that several more vessels from Boston's fleet were sailing into harm's way, their courses set to take them past Block Island on their way south to the Leeward Islands. The final dispatch, dated June 11, the day all three appeared consecutively in the *Courant*, reported that two days earlier Massachusetts had stepped up its response, issuing a proclamation calling for volunteers to go after Low and his fellow pirates and securing the enlistments of more than one hundred men who were set to sail that very day.

James wanted to have it both ways: He wanted to mock his home government for its bureaucratic nonchalance in the face of a terrorist threat while indemnifying himself from its wrath by pointing out, in the final update, that the government had done the right thing in sending the ship *Flying-Horse* in pursuit of Low well in advance of its original end-of-the-month deadline. It was a punch thrown and then pulled at the last moment, so as to make the government flinch. But the gag fell flat with both the government and average readers, who found joking about piracy distinctly unfunny. Just a week earlier the *Courant* itself had reported that a large French ship recently arrived in New York had lost 150 of its 200 passengers to an attack by pirates who had also "barbarously abus'd the Women."[15] Among Samuel Shute's several reasons for objecting to the dispatch was that the mere suggestion of foot-dragging in bringing Low to justice opened him up to possible accusations that he was in cahoots with the pirate—that he was allowing him to operate unmolested in return for payoffs, a form of corruption not unheard of in other colonies.

On the morning of June 12, James was ordered to appear before the governor and his Council, who commanded him to divulge the author of the offending dispatch. He refused. A heated exchange ensued, during which the newspaper publisher treated his inquisitors, they later charged, with "Indiscretion & Indecency."[16] James likely pointed out, in a less than respectful manner, that the dispatches were patently bogus, as proven by, among other things, the chronological impossibility of an actual Rhode

Island correspondent knowing the things he claimed to know when he claimed to know them. Whatever the particulars, the gist of his rebuttal seems to have been that a person would have to be pretty stupid to take the dispatches seriously; and that, since he had not meant them to be a serious reflection on the government, it was nobody's business who had written them.

That afternoon the Council voted that the publisher of the *New-England Courant* had affronted the government. Three Council members, Samuel Sewall among them, hand-delivered the vote to the House chamber where, following little if any debate, the deputies voted their concurrence. Shortly thereafter a resolution was issued: "That the Sheriff of the County of *Suffolk*, do forthwith commit to the Gaol [jail] in *Boston*, the Body of *James Franklin* Printer, for the gross Affront offered to this Government, in his Courant of Monday last, there to remain during this Session."[17] James was taken into custody at his printing house, led across the street, and locked up in the stone jail.

After what the House had done to his competitors because of their loyalty to the royal prerogative, James couldn't have been completely shocked that the Council had come after him. Despite his claim that the *Courant* "was never design'd for a Party Paper," he had gone out of his way to stand with the House on most issues, even to the extent of using William Hutchinson's obituary to claim him for the Popular Party, eulogizing him as "ever solicitously careful on all proper Occasions, to assert and defend the just Rights and Liberties of this People," a description that also put his own "Whiggish ideological tendency" on display.[18] It was no coincidence that Christopher Taylor, the man who had threatened to thrash John Yeamans for striking Elisha Cooke, had become a *Courant* contributor. At times the newspaper seemed an organ of Cooke's party, sworn to do its bidding whatever the question.

What probably did surprise James, given all that, was the deputies' failure to block his incarceration. For the past several years the House had reflexively checked the punitive impulses of the Council and the governor when it came to the press, rejecting calls for the arrest or prosecution of offending printers, authors, and publishers in every case except that of John Checkley. James must have assumed the deputies would follow suit here, especially given the special favor they had recently shown him. But he had underestimated the extent to which his newspaper had discomfited not just the governor and his Crown-friendly supporters, but the entire political establishment. The House deputies might nod their heads at his endorsement of their tough stance against the Eastern Indians and his suggestion that Paul Dudley's qualifications for a seat on the Council were bogus. Perhaps they even chuckled over his satirical treatment of Shute's defender and apologist Cotton Mather. But they took umbrage at his broad-brush condemnation of "Massachusetts" for its inadequate response to the pirate threat. In failing to specify exactly who in the government it held responsible for that failure, the newspaper seemed to be suggesting that both the governor *and* the House deserved a share of the blame. Nor was this the first time the *Courant* had come uncomfortably close to reflecting on them. Its suggestion that wealthy officeholders ought to be voted out in favor of men of modest means, although seemingly directed at Dudley and other affluent supporters of the governor and the status quo, could also be read as a reflection on the many well-off members of the House and the Popular Party. In any case it was a little more democracy and egalitarianism than most of them were comfortable with. They narrowed their eyes at the very idea that a newspaper would presume to judge their performance as public officials, an expansion of the role of the press no other publisher had dared. And like many establishment readers they "tsk-tsked" at the paper's coarse, colloquial language, its sexual indiscretion, and its bad form in mocking religious and social conventions. James, many of them believed, was a loose cannon that might fire in any direction.

One thing is certain: The reaction to James's ill-advised joke about the pirate attack was out of scale with the relative triviality of his offense in that matter. Benjamin Franklin's inability several decades later to remember how the government had justified jailing his brother (he called it "some political Point which I have now forgotten") has a ready explanation, namely that the government had never bothered to offer a justification.[19] James was jailed without being charged with a specific offense and would remain uncharged but incarcerated for the balance of the General Court session. Even for its time this was extraordinary, "the kind of exercise of 'parliamentary privilege' that had long been held repugnant to British principles and inconsistent with the restraints imposed by Magna Charta," whose thirty-ninth article declared: "No free man shall be taken or imprisoned . . . except by the legal judgment of his peers or by the law of the land."[20] Jailing James without formally charging him also violated the spirit of the Massachusetts Body of Liberties, which in 1641 had declared that "no mans person shall be arested [sic]" unless it be by "some expresse law of the Country warranting the same."[21] Three decades had passed since a Massachusetts author or publisher had been incarcerated in this manner. Then it had been Governor Edmund Andros putting a man behind bars for distributing an English newspaper reporting the landing of forces led by future monarch William of Orange, whose coronation would set in motion the governor's forced retirement. Now James had been imprisoned by authorities reflexively, and simply because they were fed up with his newspaper and wanted him silenced. No one in or out of power raised an objection.

Dark, hot, dank, and putrid, James Franklin's windowless cell was no place for a man with a naturally weak constitution compromised by overwork, the stress of his collision with the censors, and possibly too much drink. By his second day in confinement he was ill. His friends and family went to the House of Representatives with a petition "acknowledging his Offence, and praying that he may be allowed the Liberty of the Yard" so that he could breathe fresh, healthful air.[22] The House tabled the request for three days. Finally on the afternoon of June 18 it voted to let him spend some time each day in the prison yard providing that he put up security "for his faithful abiding there."[23] The vote was sent up for concurrence, but two more days elapsed before the Council took it up and voted to grant his request.

The General Court's decision to show leniency was probably influenced by a statement James (or someone writing for him) had submitted with the request. It declared that he was "Truely Sensible & Heartily Sorry" for "his Inadvertency & Folly therein in affronting the government."[24] But the deciding factor was almost certainly a note from Zabdiel Boylston. The doctor, who had been attacked directly and indirectly by James Franklin's newspaper for most of its history, vouched for the publisher's compromised health and urged authorities to give him access to the yard.

Whoever convinced Boylston to examine James in jail—perhaps Josiah Franklin—doubtless paid a sizable fee for the doctor's visit, since even under the best circumstances his services did not come cheap. And the doctor surely understood that examining James would pay off in a way that went beyond the fee—that nothing he or his supporters could write would do more to negate the effects of William Douglass's continuing pamphlet attacks on his character and professional ability than word that James Franklin, the publisher of the newspaper in which Douglass had branded him a quack, had summoned him for his personal medical care, choosing him over Douglass and every other Boston practitioner.

But Boylston could easily have taken the other route, passing up the money and the good publicity for the satisfaction of vengeance. Refusing to help James—letting him molder in jail—would be the perfect way to strike back at the *New-England Courant* publisher for the damage the newspaper had done to his practice and his reputation and for the frenzy of dangerous hatred it had helped whip up against him. If the doctor had considered that response at all, he had ultimately dismissed it. Possibly his resentment toward James had softened as a result of the *Courant*'s recent turn toward a more equitable treatment of inoculation in its coverage of the successful trial going on in London. In the final analysis, though, his decision to take James on as a patient, which had come as quickly and decisively as the decision to attempt inoculation nearly a year earlier, was essentially an act of magnanimity. It would not be the last time a member of the Franklin family benefited from the doctor's essential decency. Several years later, Benjamin Franklin would find himself stranded and penniless in London. Discovering that Boylston was also in the city as a guest of the Royal Society, Ben would seek him out and ask him for assistance. Once again, Boylston would provide it.

23

THE PRINTER AND
HIS DEVIL

Benjamin Franklin had been keeping two secrets from his brother. One was that he was the mysterious author of the Silence Dogood letters. The other was that he had been meticulously annotating and archiving the *New-England Courant* since its inception. On many of the first forty-three issues, in the spaces above major letters and essays by the likes of Ichabod Henroost and Zerubbabel Tindal, he had scribbled the author's actual identity. It's thanks to these annotated copies (whose existence was unknown for nearly two hundred years, until the historian Worthington Chauncey Ford stumbled upon them in a file at the British Museum) that today we can be certain that the real identity of Henroost and Tindal (as well as "Jethro Sham, Advisor General," "Ben Treackle," and "Hortensius," among others) was "Mr. Gardner." Likewise, Ben had scribbled "Mr. James Franklin" at the top of letters from "Lucilius" and "Timothy Turnstone," among others. His notations revealed all the major *Courant* writers, including "Mr. John Eyre" and "Dr. Douglass." Above the second Silence Dogood letter he had placed the initials "B.F." A boon to posterity, the annotated copies were, at the time, a reckless undertaking. Discovered by the wrong persons, they could be used to fine or prosecute the Honest Wags, whose true identities James had implicitly promised to protect. Had James discovered the file, he would certainly have destroyed it and perhaps beaten his apprentice for good measure. To his credit, Benjamin was not oblivious of the dangers posed by the secret collection. The final annotated *Courant* in his file is dated March 28, 1722, two weeks before his brother's arrest. It might have been that he sensed trouble with the censors was imminent and acted preemptively to protect the publication's contributors. It's more likely, though, that he continued to annotate the newspaper up through the issue containing the Rhode Island piracy dispatches, destroying both that issue and the previous one, which contained the report on the House elections, shortly after James was ordered to the Town House for questioning or when Ben learned that his brother had refused to cooperate and the councilors sent for him.

Benjamin Franklin had never seen the inside of the Council chamber—not, at least, while that body was in session. Presently he found himself in front of a scowling assemblage of the most powerful and intimidating men in the province. He had no legal counsel and, as an apprentice, only a little more personhood than a slave. No record of his interrogation exists, but there can be little doubt that he was led to believe—if not told outright—that his refusal to cooperate would land him in jail alongside James. The prudent course of action was to do as his brother's friend Thomas Fleet and others had done and accommodate the censors. Certainly he had little reason to sacrifice his liberty for a master who treated him condescendingly and sometimes raised a hand against him. But Benjamin's resentment for James paled in comparison with his resentment against the men who had had him arrested. Like James, he had inherited the DNA of their feisty maternal grandfather, Peter Folger, a "perpetual champion of the underdog" who had repeatedly stood up to authority, going so far as to argue for the Indian side in King Philip's War.[1] Genetically predisposed to chafe at government overreach, Ben's close study of "Cato's Letters" had inculcated him with a firm belief in justice and the importance of political liberty. Now, when he was "taken up & examin'd before the Council," he refused to "give them any Satisfaction."[2] Instead of jailing him, the councilors admonished him and dismissed him. He conjectured that it was his status as an apprentice "who was bound to keep his Master's Secrets" that prevented them from taking further action.[3]

Sent back to the printing house, he found himself in charge. He was highly proficient at every aspect of composing and printing the *Courant*, which had been one of his primary responsibilities. Editorial decisions were another matter. James had allowed him no say whatsoever in those. But the apprentice's close study of his master's newspaper and its influences had given him a better sense of what kind of content belonged in it than anyone knew.

On June 18 the *Courant* came out on schedule and under the supervision of its sixteen-year-old stand-in publisher. Tamer certainly than some recent issues, it nevertheless dared to post a short update on the continued treachery of Low the pirate, a pointed reminder that, a week after the government had jailed James for criticizing its inept response to the pirate's treachery, he was still out there terrorizing New England ships. A week later Benjamin published the seventh Silence Dogood letter, which, in purporting to celebrate the traditional New England elegy, actually ridiculed the form's triteness and gratuitous moroseness by offering a do-it-yourself recipe for creating an elegy from scratch. Among his suggestions were picking someone who "went away suddenly, being Kill'd, Drown'd or Froze to Death," and borrowing "Virtues, Excellencies, &C." from other persons if the deceased lacked "a sufficient Quantity" of his own.[4] After mixing those with "last Words, dying Expressions, &c. if they are to be had," and straining well, the mixture was to be seasoned with "Melancholly Expressions, such as, *Dreadful, Deadly, cruel cold Death, unhappy Fate, weeping Eyes,* &c."[5] The highly amusing letter was conclusive proof that Josiah Franklin had been correct in believing its author lacked the piety required to become a minister.

The *Courant* Benjamin published on July 2 contained the newspaper's first direct reference to its publisher's incarceration three weeks earlier. Under the heading "To the Readers of the New-England Courant," the letter, apparently written by James in jail and smuggled to his apprentice, began by claiming success for the *Courant*, which had "met with a general Entertainment and Acceptance," even if it could not "boast of pleasing all Men."[6] Its "great Design" was "to promote Virtue and real Goodness." The Couranteers, he wrote, were not

> Ignorant of the vile abuse and Invidious Calumnies of Licencious Tongues: However, the Words *Saucy*, *Impudent*, (and others too vile for us to mention) in no wise move us; for we can easily soar above the little Vulgar, and look down on those who reproach us, with Pity and Contempt.[7]

The Governor's Council was not happy with the newspaper's swaggering self-defense. Back in mid-June, when James had taken ill in jail and had appealed for freedom of the yard, his tone had been apologetic. Now that he was recovering and close to the presumed completion of his sentence, he was retracting his earlier admission of guilt and, by his own admission, looking down on his jailers "with Pity and Contempt."[8] Three days after this defiant letter appeared, the Council resolved that every issue of the *Courant* from that point forward would have to be approved by the secretary of the province. They further stipulated that James provide £1,000 in security for his "good Behaviour to the end of the next Fall Sessions of this Court."[9]

The Council sent its resolution to the House for its concurrence. On the morning of July 6 the deputies took it up for consideration. Neither Elisha Cooke nor John Clark could have relished the prospect of allowing a newspaper that had cast aspersions on their commitment to fighting piracy and had called them (or at least the majority of their fellow Harvard college men) "Blockheads . . . only more proud and conceited" to remain untethered, free to print whatever unflattering reflection it saw fit. At the same time, they and their fellow deputies understood that in granting the Council the power to suppress the *Courant* they would be establishing a precedent for its pre-publication censorship power over them as well. The Council's resolve was nonconcurred. The next day, after an unsuccessful attempt to put it to another vote, the governor prorogued the Great and General Court, and James Franklin was freed. He had served nearly a month in jail.

THE ENTIRE FRONT page of the *Courant* that appeared two days later was devoted to a new letter from Silence Dogood. But except for a brief preface, Silence yielded the floor to Thomas Gordon, offering an extended excerpt from a "Cato's Letters" essay he had penned in February of the previous year. Gordon began:

> WITHOUT Freedom of Thought, there can be no such Thing as Wisdom; and no such Thing as publick Liberty, without Freedom of Speech; which is the Right of every Man, as far as by it, he does not hurt or controul the Right of another: And this is the only Check it ought to suffer, and the only Bounds it ought to know.[10]

After asserting that "Whoever would overthrow the Liberty of a Nation, must begin by subduing the Freeness of Speech; a *Thing* terrible to Publick Traytors," he continued:

> That Men ought to speak well of *their Governours* is true, while *their Governours* deserve to be well spoken of; but to do publick Mischief, without hearing of it, is only the Prerogative and Felicity of Tyranny: A free People will be shewing that they are *so*, by their Freedom of Speech.[11]

Gordon wrote that public measures, "when they are honest," should be publicly commended. But when they were "knavish or pernicious," he added, "they ought to be publickly exposed, in order to be publickly detested."[12]

The letter's timing left no question that Silence was rebuking the government officials who had first jailed James and then tried to impose pre-publication censorship against him. Quoting chapter and verse from Cato now, with James fresh out of jail, was a remarkable display of indignation and defiance—a boy scolding the most powerful men in the colony and lecturing them on liberty of expression and dissent. Back in his second letter, Benjamin had warned readers that something like this might be in the offing. Silence had described herself as "a mortal Enemy to arbitrary Government and unlimited Power," whose blood would "boil exceedingly" at "the least appearance of an Incroachment" on the "Rights and Liberties" of her country.[13] She was, she had said, "courteous and affable, good humor'd (unless I am first provok'd)."[14] Now Boston was seeing just how out of humor she could get.

Ben's anger was part philosophical indignation, part guilt. He understood that he was culpable in provoking the authorities to the point where they had arrested James and attempted to impose pre-publication censorship on the *Courant*. Indeed, the councilors had said as much; in calling for a clampdown on the newspaper they had cited the publication's *"many Passages . . . boldly reflecting on His Majesty's Government and on the Administration of it in this Province, the Ministry, Churches and College"*—an unmistakable indictment of Silence Dogood's mockery of Harvard and funeral elegies and her pointed citing of "Cato's Letters."[15]

In his *Autobiography*, Benjamin would boast that as the stand-in editor of his brother's newspaper he had "made bold to give our Rulers some Rubs in it" and that James had taken those efforts "very kindly."[16] Now that both brothers had vented their outrage, the prudent thing would have been to move on. But neither had exhausted his indignation. In the very next *Courant* James addressed his enemies directly, sarcastically entreating them to "bear with Patience the unwelcome News" of his release from jail.[17] He quoted from a letter purportedly written by one of those enemies, who suggested that James and other members of his "Factious Brood" ought to be hanged rather than imprisoned. And he complained about having been jailed without due process, asking whether "an Englishman may have Liberty to answer for himself before the Legislative Power."[18] Meanwhile, Benjamin, in what a biographer called "probably the most serious piece of literature" that he ever wrote, zeroed in on the man or men he believed had spearheaded the actions against James and the newspaper.[19] Although he was still, technically, writing as Silence Dogood, this letter, like the one previous, all but dropped the façade of the character so that its author could vent his anger. Without so much as a hint of humor or the least attempt to charm, Ben wrote that "hypocritical Pretenders to Religion" were a greater threat to society than were "the openly Profane," particularly if the hypocrite held a position in government.[20] The "most dangerous Hypocrite in a Common-Wealth" was

> one who *leaves the Gospel for the sake of the Law*. . . . And here the Clergy are in great Danger of being deceiv'd, and the People of being deceiv'd by the Clergy, until the Monster arrives to such Power and Wealth, that he is out of the reach of both, and can oppress the People without their own blind Assistance.[21]

Benjamin didn't drop any additional hints about whom he had come to see as that "Monster." But his father's onetime friend and social mentor Samuel Sewall, one of the Council members who had led the action against James, fit the description exactly. As a former divinity student who had abandoned his pursuit of ordination to become a judge, Sewall was the literal embodiment of someone who had left the Gospel for the law. With his prayer meetings, obsessive funeral attendance, and critiques of the shortcomings of the piety exhibited by the town, the province, and even, on occasion, the ministers, he was also the most ostentatiously religious layman in Boston. Portrayed by himself and others as a paragon of Christian righteousness throughout Benjamin's childhood, Sewall had betrayed Josiah Franklin twice: first, in failing to support Josiah's bid for a deaconship in the Old South Church several years earlier; and now by enthusiastically spearheading the movement to jail his son without due process and to saddle that son's newspaper with a burden that would give it a crippling disadvantage in its competition with the town's other papers. Sewall, Benjamin believed, had used his holier-than-thou persona to bamboozle the town and the colony into giving him "blind Assistance" in the same way he had bamboozled Josiah—and a young, impressionable Benjamin Franklin. It was a corruption all the more monstrous because it lurked beneath a façade of piety. "*Corruptio optimi est pessima*" read the superscription atop Benjamin's Silence letter.[22] *The corruption of the best is the worst.*

THE ABENAKI HAD launched an attack along the eastern frontier at about the same time James had been hauled off to jail. Near the middle of June, word reached Boston that sixty Indians in canoes had taken nine families prisoner at Merrymeeting Bay in Maine, releasing most but not all of the captives thereafter. Indians had also attacked the crew of an Ipswich fishing vessel, which had managed to fight them off, killing two or three of the attackers. On June 18 Samuel Shute wrote to London informing Secretary Popple of the Board of Trade and Plantations that "the Indians have burnt a house, pulled down a mill, killed ten oxen, and taken five Englishmen captives, so that I'm afraid there will be no avoiding a war with them."[23]

The House moved quickly to gain control over the colony's military response. Shute resisted. The near standoff dragged on through the rest of June and into July. The only significant agreement achieved during that period was to bolster the colony's relationship with the Five Nations—the Mohawk, Oneida, Onondaga, Cayuga, and Seneca tribes that comprised the colony's Indian allies—by offering them a "Present" of one thousand pounds. On July 7, the final day of the General Court session, the Council proposed the formation of a joint committee that would continue meeting during the recess in order to determine how, exactly, the present would be dispensed. The House gave its approval with the proviso that Elisha Cooke serve as a provincial representative to the Five Nations. But Shute, who was feeling particularly uncooperative after the House had once again voted him a substandard £500 salary (and no pay whatsoever for Lieutenant Governor Dummer), rejected the condition. He would not have Cooke in a position where he could force his own agenda with allies or foes.

It was in that spirit of obstinacy and gridlock, and with the threat of war growing by the day, that the governor prorogued the Court until early August. One week later came the full-scale attack everyone had been expecting for months. Approximately five hundred Indians descended on Fort George at Thomaston. Although they failed to take the fort, their twelve-day siege cost the lives of five Englishmen and several times as many of their own men. In other attacks, a sawmill, several houses, and an English sailing vessel were burned and cattle were killed. The Indians closed out their campaign by burning the village of Brunswick for a second time.

Philip Musgrave's *Gazette* offered the most detailed and graphic account of the hostilities, perhaps because, as postmaster, he had the best access to information from the front. On July 23 he reported that, upon learning of the attack, a captain named Harmon had gone in pursuit of the Indians, eventually locating one of their encampments, where he and his men observed them "Dancing & Rejoycing" over having "shed blood."[24] Sometime after two in the morning, when the last of the Abenaki had gone to sleep, Harmon and his men had descended upon the camp, killing eighteen or twenty Indians. Musgrave reported that a subsequent search of the area revealed "the Hand of a White Man laid upon a Stump, & the Body to which it belonged hard by, which the Indians had most barbarously murther'd, by cutting his Tongue out & cutting off his Nose & private Parts; besides having given him innumerable Stabs & Wounds all over his Body."[25]

The *Courant* offered a similar report. What distinguished its coverage, though, was the addition of an editorial comment, a call for a declaration of war. It came indirectly, by the strategic placement, immediately prior to the report, of a letter supposedly written before the news of the attack had reached town. In the letter, an anonymous correspondent argued that it was premature to declare war on the Indians because, for all their threats and their vandalism against property and cattle, they had yet to kill anyone. Probably James or one of the Couranteers had written the letter *after* the news of the deadly attacks had arrived and inserted it before the report in order to make the *Courant*'s argument for a declaration of war. Two days later, on advice from his Council, Samuel Shute issued that declaration.

But even a matter as serious as war proved only a momentary distraction from the *Courant*'s preoccupation with its publisher's mistreatment by the government. On July 30, the *Gazette* and *News-Letter* both ran Governor Shute's declaration of war as their leads. James, though, ignored the declaration completely and devoted almost his entire newspaper to a diatribe arguing that he had been incarcerated in violation of English law. He suggested that those who had imprisoned him knew "little or nothing" of "the happy Constitution of an *English* Government" and were guilty of "Stupidity."[26] He then proceeded to educate them by reprinting both the twenty-ninth chapter of the Magna Charta and a brief excerpt from the Massachusetts Charter of 1691, which appeared to guarantee that "ALL MANNER OF CRIMES" would be heard, tried, and determined by the court system in an approximation of what today we would call due process.[27] The following week, when he reported on a case of political bribery in London, it seemed mostly an excuse to comment parenthetically that at least in England the dubious propriety of gifts of that kind was acknowledged, and the press not threatened with censorship for making the people aware of them.

All through August and well into September, James and the newspaper continued to accuse the government of corruption and hypocrisy. On September 17 the *Courant* ran a long, allegorical poem about the injustice of its publisher's imprisonment. The verse harkened back to "News from the Moon," the Defoe essay James had printed early the previous year. Now, instead of a tailor accused by many men of slandering them because the coat he had fashioned for fools and knaves happened to fit them perfectly, the protagonist was a painter whose brushes expertly captured the faces of knavish men. It concluded with a decree from the "Senate" ordering that the painter be jailed until the end of its session—a sentence identical to the one James had received. If this and the other essays and letters the newspaper had published on its theme hadn't already made it clear that James had come to see nearly everything through the lens of his victimization, the new colophon at the bottom of the newspaper's back page surely did the trick. Whereas previously it had read: "BOSTON: Printed and Sold by J. Franklin in Queen-Street, over against Mr. Sheaf's [later "Mr. Mills's"] School . . . " it now read: "BOSTON: Printed and sold by J. Franklin, at his Printing-House in Queen-Street, *near the Prison* [my emphasis]."[28]

In the two months since James and been released from jail, his anger had festered. Now he latched on to any and every opportunity to denigrate the government that had jailed him and to embarrass or undermine those who had orchestrated or supported that incarceration. In September he was the first—and, for a time, the only—newspaper publisher to report on the scandalous defection of the Congregationalist minister Timothy Cutler, Yale's president, to the Church of England. Cutler's defection devastated Puritan Boston, which regarded the Connecticut college as a second bastion, after Harvard, of Puritan theology and education in New England. For the religious establishment, especially enemies of the *Courant* like Cotton Mather and Samuel Sewall, the "Yale Apostasy," as it became known, was both deeply embarrassing (evidence that the formerly all-powerful Puritan theocracy had lost control over its own institutions) and genuinely worrisome, a major encroachment on Puritan control of New England and a significant defeat in the cold war that the Puritans and Anglicans had been fighting for decades. The news was so traumatic, indeed, that neither the *News-Letter* nor the *Gazette* would print a word about it for three weeks. James not only reported on the defection of Cutler and six other men—essentially the school's entire leadership—as soon as the news reached Boston but also gleefully revisited the scandal one week later, when he ran three items clearly intended to exacerbate Puritan embarrassment while poking fun at fears of a larger and more insidious plot to overthrow Puritan control of New England. In a series of "updates," James reported that at least two new Anglican churches were in the works: one in Providence, Rhode Island, and the other in Stratford, Connecticut. He also reported an alleged rumor that Cotton Mather was being recruited to take over the presidency of Yale, a snide reference to another long-standing rumor that, almost since Yale's founding, the minister had been secretly scheming for it to replace Harvard, which he believed had become too secularized and which he resented for having dismissed his father as its president. For James, the apostasy constituted, among other things, a fitting and glorious comeuppance for the minister. He was giddy over the opportunity to rub it in Mather's face while sending fanatical Puritans like Sewall into fits of apoplexy. On October 29 a Couranteer facetiously asked whether Cutler's renunciation of his Congregational ordination meant that the couples he had joined in marriage were not really married after all and therefore free "to separate one from the other."[29] If that was true, it followed logically that persons he had baptized were not really baptized. Both notions struck men like Cotton Mather and Samuel Sewall as abhorrent—all the more so because of the glibness with which the *Courant* voiced them.

James was once again "steering a hazardous course."[30] In December the *Courant* combined two of its favorite themes, its contempt for flatterers and suspicion of the ministry, calling ministers who flattered the governor, among other things, *"Wolves* in Sheps' Cloathing."[31] A more prudent man would have tempered the pace and ferocity of his attacks and removed "near the Prison" from his colophon. But it was still there as the end of the year approached, and with it a development that would shock everyone in Massachusetts and trigger a response from the *Courant* even more outlandish than anything it had previously published.

By EARLY AUGUST, Benjamin Franklin had decided to end Silence Dogood's campaign against his brother's enemies. James's July 30 screed on the Magna Charta had made it clear that his rage had not abated; Ben realized that by continuing to feed it with the kind of rhetoric he had employed in his eighth and ninth Dogood letters he would probably land both of them in jail. When the country widow reappeared on August 13 it was to advocate the establishment of *"An Office of Ensurance for Widows"*— a government department that would oversee a fund for women rendered indigent by the death of their husbands.[32] Benjamin's observation that the country was "ripe for many such *Friendly Societies*, whereby every Man might help another, without any Disservice to himself," was his first public expression of enthusiasm for what would become a hallmark of his life: the creation of organizations and initiatives based on mutual benefit and with the purpose of furthering the civic good.[33] But even this letter seems to have struck its author as too somber and self-serious—too much like what Silence had been doing of late. Eager to return her to her earlier, irreverent self, he quickly penned a new letter, which appeared the very next week and offered a tongue-in-cheek proposal to establish another fund, similar to the one for widows but in this case intended to aid accidental spinsters, women whose vanity had caused them to reject every possible suitor until, having reached a certain age, they found themselves no longer marriageable. Women who qualified for the program would receive £500 cash—hardly enough, Silence conceded, to cover the £50 per year that some of them required for cosmetics. Then on September 10 Ben took another step away from his erstwhile sobriety (literally, this time) when he had Silence ruminate on the subject of drunkenness. His inspiration was Joseph Addison's July 1714 letter on the same subject. But he quickly deviated from the Englishman's moralistic approach and took a wry perspective. At the letter's close, he had Silence reel off nineteen euphemisms for "intoxication." Ostensibly the point of this torrent of slang was to illustrate both the scope of the problem and how its wickedness had been trivialized. But its actual effect was hilarious. While the clergy and prigs like Samuel Sewall cringed, other readers smiled or laughed. Indeed, the essay was so successful that Benjamin would repurpose the gag fifteen years later in his own newspaper, the *Pennsylvania Gazette*.

Silence Dogood's thirteenth letter, which appeared on September 24 at the head of the issue in which James "scooped" his competitors by reporting the Yale Apostasy, upped the ante again, poking fun at Boston's most shameful secret—its sex trade. Like the essay on drunkenness, this subject had been appropriated from the *Spectator*. But whereas that publication had addressed the socioeconomics of prostitution, arguing that the blame ought to be placed on the pimps and the patrons, not just the women who traded sex for money, Benjamin's letter was the epitome of frothiness. Silence was seemingly—and improbably—ignorant of the women's purpose in walking the streets at night, which she declared a boon to shoemakers because they "exceedingly" promoted "the Consumption of their Ware."[34] Even more scandalously, she referred to the streetwalkers as "a Set of People, who contribute very much to the Health and Satisfaction of those who have been fatigu'd with Business or Study."[35] Needless to say, the letter mortified the clergymen and social conservatives still shaking their heads over Silence's cavalier treatment of drunkenness. But Benjamin had given them and the rest of Boston something to talk about other than the *Courant*'s egregiously bad form in broadcasting the embarrassment of the Yale Apostasy.

Indeed, if Benjamin's primary reasons for writing about drunkenness and prostitution were to have fun scandalizing the town and to delight the Honest Wags so that he could bask, albeit vicariously, in their praise, he also seems to have been trying—perhaps without quite realizing it—to create a diversion that would draw people's attention away from his brother's increasingly worrisome inflammatory rhetoric. When James continued to make sport of the Yale Apostasy, however, Ben realized that, having exploited the community's biggest taboos, there was nowhere left to go with that diversionary approach. Silence Dogood's fourteenth letter eschewed scandalous humor and political proselytizing and counterbalanced the *Courant*'s malicious glibness with thoughtfulness and circumspection, addressing the Yale Apostasy directly. Empathizing with the deceived Puritans, Silence asked why, if Timothy Cutler was so certain his life as a Congregationalist minister had been a fraud, he did not repent his former wickedness. Ben's real purpose, though, was to condemn not only Cutler but all religious extremists. "All I would endeavour to shew is, That an indiscreet Zeal for spreading an Opinion, hurts the Cause of the Zealot," he wrote. "There are too many blind Zealots among every Denomination of Christians; and he that propagates the Gospel among *Rakes* and *Beaus* without reforming them in their Morals, is every whit as ridiculous and impolitick as a Statesman who makes Tools of Ideots and Tale-Bearers."[36] That statement, written at age sixteen, would stand as a fair representation of Ben Franklin's attitude toward religion for the rest of his life.

SILENCE DOGOOD'S FANS were disappointed when she failed to return with a new letter two weeks later. But they were unconcerned; she had failed to keep to her normal every-other-week schedule before. When several more weeks passed without a letter, the Honest Wags began to speculate about what had become of her. Finally, after eight weeks, the *Courant* publicly acknowledged that it had lost touch with the widow. An unnamed correspondent asked why, with "Whoring, Drinking, Swearing, Lying, Gaming, Cheating and Oppression, and many other Sins" still flourishing in Boston, she had gone silent.[37] In a note immediately following, James asked for help making contact with Mrs. Dogood. But the widow was gone forever.

Many years later, Benjamin Franklin would explain his decision to abandon the Silence Dogood persona at the height of its popularity as a simple matter of having "pretty well exhausted" his "small Fund of Sense for such Performances."[38] He seems to have been referring, in part, at least, to the impossibility of continuing to outdo himself. It's also probably true that, after fourteen letters, "the exquisite Pleasure" of basking in the "Approbation" of the Couranteers had worn off.[39] Mostly, though, he seems to have realized that, as Perry Miller wrote, he was "playing for high stakes"—that in going to great lengths to have fun at the expense of the establishment and draw its attention away from James he had actually increased the danger that the censors would come after the *Courant*.[40]

It's not clear when Benjamin revealed he was Silence. Probably the announcement came shortly after the December 3 issue in which James had asked for information about the missing Widow Dogood. What we know for certain is that James did not take the revelation well. (Benjamin's recollection that his news "did not quite please" his brother might be the biggest understatement in the *Autobiography*, a work with no shortage of examples of that literary device.)[41] Being duped by one's own apprentice— the person whose every waking move was supposed to be under one's control—was embarrassing. But it was more complicated than that. The revelation that Benjamin Franklin was Silence Dogood played havoc with the balance of power between master and apprentice. Overnight, Benjamin had ceased to be just another indentured servant. The Couranteers, who with the exception of Matthew Adams had for years mostly ignored Benjamin, now celebrated him, clapping him on the back and marveling aloud at his wit and wisdom and the cleverness with which he had fooled them and his own brother. In addition to the difficulties of grappling with his enemies and the authorities, James now had a younger brother and apprentice who had become, as Albert Furtwangler put it, "a celebrity and rival under his own roof."[42] Benjamin, too, saw himself in a new way. Having earned the plaudits he had dreamed of and worked toward for years, he had no intention of quietly sinking back into simple servitude and anonymity.

It was ironic that the beginning of the end of the Franklin brothers' partnership came at what was, in many respects, the high point in their collaboration. Their shared indignation over James's unjust treatment by the government had provided common ground, and Benjamin's brave refusal to cooperate when hauled before the censors had proved his loyalty to his master. Although Ben's Silence Dogood revelation was an embarrassment for James, it was also true that Benjamin had now revealed himself to be his brother's most eloquent and passionate defender. And the character of Silence had benefited both brothers significantly, giving Benjamin an opportunity to try out his public voice for the first time and James a popular correspondent who had helped him sell more newspapers.

But neither brother saw it that way. Deeply resentful of each other, they were more at odds than ever. In retrospect, Ben would admit that his sudden prominence made him "too vain."[43] But he could not countenance his brother's determination to ignore what had changed in their relationship and keep him down. "Saucy and provoking," the apprentice found himself on the receiving end of more beatings.[44] Soon, and for reasons that went beyond the violence, he would decide he had had enough.

24

THREE EXITS

"Foreign wars," Thomas Hutchinson wrote in 1767, "often delivered Greece and Rome from their intestine broils and animosities."[1] An optimist could hope that the onset of war with the Eastern Indians would do likewise for Massachusetts, healing the political divisions that had all but paralyzed the government for several years. But that was not to be the case. War with the Eastern Indians, Hutchinson wrote, simply "furnished a new subject for contention" between the governor and the House of Representatives.[2]

At the start of the August General Court session, Samuel Shute had tried to preempt the House's intrusion into the war effort with a warning couched in a diplomatic-sounding appeal to patriotism. "One thing I must Particularly Remark to You," he told the deputies, "is, that if my Hands and the Councils be not left at a much greater Liberty than of late they have been, I fear our Affairs will be carried on with little or no Spirit."[3] To no one's surprise, the appeal had fallen on deaf ears. For the next several weeks the House had done everything in its authority—and, arguably, a few things outside of that authority—to usurp powers related to the conduct of the war, culminating in its call for the governor to remove the commander of the eastern forces for incompetence and dereliction of duty. When Shute pushed back, refusing to fire the commander and insisting that to do so without giving him a fair hearing was "contrary to the Liberty of an English Man" (a claim to the right of due process that James Franklin must have found bitterly ironic), the House simply voted to stop paying the officer's salary.[4] Shute's attempt to halt the meddling by proroguing the Court until November was no more successful; despite being recessed, the deputies dispatched a committee to investigate charges of *Repeated Abuses and Mismanagements among the [military] Forces now in pay.*"[5] A few days after they resumed business, the deputies dictated a re-allocation of troops, something, Hutchinson wrote, that "had not been the practice in former wars" but that Shute found himself compelled to allow for fear of leaving the frontiers defenseless.[6]

By late November 1722 the House of Representatives had become "a full partner in the conduct of the war."[7] Realizing they had the governor on his heels, its membership pressed him again, demanding to know why he had reneged on launching an expedition against the Indians at Penobscot after they had authorized and funded it. When Shute defended the cancellation by saying he had been advised to do so by his best field commander, Shadrach Walton, the House demanded that Walton be summoned to Boston for questioning. Shute's attempt to stonewall that demand resulted in a threat by the deputies to cut off nearly all funding for the war unless he produced the colonel. This was followed by a campaign of harassment—committees were sent repeatedly to the governor's residence demanding action on Walton. When Shute finally appeared it was to tell the committee members "he would not be spoke to by any body."[8] He capitulated three days later.

During the second half of 1721 Samuel Shute had tried to exploit fear of smallpox to force the House into compliance with his agenda. Now the deputies were using the war—or, more specifically, the threat that they would sabotage Shute's management of it and ruin his standing in London, where there was zero tolerance for losing territory and natural resources to the Indians and the French—to extort concessions from him. Their insistence on creating a joint committee that would give them a direct hand in running the war constituted a claim of what Thomas Hutchinson tactfully described as "unprecedented" powers.[9] The deputies were co-opting authority that clearly and unequivocally belonged to the royal governor. It was a power grab, plain and simple.

COLONEL SHADRACH WALTON arrived in Boston as ordered on December 18. A fight immediately broke out over who should have first dibs on questioning him. The House wanted him to meet with its membership. The governor refused to allow it, insisting that Walton meet with him and then with the General Court as a whole. While the House pondered its retaliation, which would eventually take the form of another and more explicit threat to cut off military funding unless Walton—or, at minimum, his journal—was made available to its membership, another and more sensitive dispute broke out, this time between Shute and his Council, a relationship that had generally been amicable.

As a meeting of the "board" (the Council and the governor) was ending, Samuel Shute buttonholed Judge Samuel Sewall and drew him over to the southeast end of the Council chamber for a private chat. Standing at the window that overlooked King Street and, in the distance, Long Wharf and the harbor, the governor dropped a bombshell: He wanted Sewall to help him secure the Council's approval for a Christmas adjournment of the General Court. The judge was stunned. As Shute well knew, the noncelebration of Christmas remained one of the most conspicuous and immutable symbols of Puritan Boston's rejection of what it considered the Church of England's corruption. Not even the tyrannical Edmund Andros, who had commandeered the Town House to celebrate Christmas in 1686, had been able to force the general populace to recognize the holiday. Considered sacrilege under the best of circumstances, it was especially unthinkable now, with the sting of the Yale Apostasy still fresh. News that the Court had shut down on Christmas would effectively hand the Church of England its second symbolic victory in New England in just over three months.

Too much the loyal subject to voice his deep offense or categorically refuse the request, Sewall promised to consider it. He knew, however, that there was no chance his fellow councilors would condone such a recess. The next day he sought out Cotton Mather, the one man who could be counted on both to oppose the recess and know whether his friend Shute could be talked out of it. Sensing that the governor was acting out of frustration with the belligerence of the House and therefore would not be reasoned with, the minister suggested that Sewall offer to put the question before the entire General Court. When the overwhelmingly Puritan and refractory membership of the House rejected the Christmas recess, Sewall could push the blame off on that body's unreasonableness. But before the judge could act, Shute once again asked for a word in private, drawing him to the same window in the Council chamber and pressing him for an answer on the Christmas adjournment. Backed against the wall, both figuratively and literally, Sewall admitted that he opposed the idea but would comply with the wishes of a vote by the General Court. He added that he hoped the governor would do the same. Shute, though, had no intention of waiting out a vote he knew would go against him. He gathered a quorum of councilors and ordered them to endorse the Christmas adjournment. Sewall became indignant. He and his fellow Congregationalists had come "a great way for their Liberties and now the Church [of England] had theirs," he told the governor, "yet they [the Anglicans] could not be contented, except they might Tread all others down."[10] To this accusation that the Anglicans were oppressors, Shute offered a curt reminder that although he had been born a Puritan, he himself now belonged to the Church of England. Late the following morning, without any formal endorsement from the Council or the House, he adjourned the General Court through Christmas Day.

The fear that Bostonians would capitulate to the will of the governor and commemorate the holiday en masse caused Puritan stalwarts like Sewall and Mather to lose sleep on the nights leading up to December 25. James Franklin, on the other hand, was thrilled. Just as he had exploited Puritan anxiety over the Yale Apostasy, he now made hay of the governor's scandalous directive, publishing, in the December 24 *Courant*, a debate on the pros and cons of celebrating Christmas. When December 25 proved more or less just another Tuesday, Puritan Boston rejoiced. "The Shops were open, and Carts came to Town with Wood, Hoop-poles, Hay &c. as at other Times; Being a pleasant day, the street was fill'd with Carts and Horses," an exuberant and relieved Sewall noted in his diary.[11]

The Council and the governor resumed business the next day, and the matter of the forced adjournment went unmentioned. That evening, in what the councilors must have believed was an attempt to smooth ruffled feathers, Shute invited them to dine with him. The governor's friend Thomas Durrell, the captain of the HMS *Seahorse*, was also present. Perhaps because he found the captain's inclusion curious, Sewall made a note of it in his diary. Two days later he would look back on Durrell's involvement in the dinner and see it for what it had been: an inside joke between the governor and the captain, made at the expense of everyone else in attendance.

Sewall had become suspicious enough of Shute by this point that he also made special note of the governor's absence from that week's Thursday religious lecture. But he was as unprepared as the rest of Boston for what transpired the next day. The judge was in session with his fellow councilors when Lieutenant Governor William Dummer appeared unexpectedly and announced that Samuel Shute had left Massachusetts. As Sewall later recorded, the lieutenant governor "produc'd a Letter from the Govr to him declaring that he was gone on board the Sea-Horse, Capt. Durell Comander, at Nantasket, intended to return early in the Fall."[12] The letter was dated the previous day. Shute hadn't said why he was leaving. Nor, as a perturbed Sewall noted, did he "salute the Council," as was customary of governors taking leave.[13] Eventually it would come to light that two years earlier, under the pretense of needing "to settle some private affairs," the governor had secured permission to come back to England at his convenience.[14] Now a thoroughly fed up Shute had put that escape plan into action, keeping his departure secret from everyone except the captain of the *Seahorse* and "two or three of his domesticks."[15] The men of the Council and even the lieutenant governor had been left in the dark.

Shute's forced adjournment for Christmas had constituted "a final act of defiance of a body that had constantly defied him."[16] It was a sign of how effectively the men of the General Court had undermined his power that by the end he had been able to do little more than spite them.

The suddenness and secretiveness of the governor's departure were indefensible. But he could hardly be blamed for leaving. The political situation had deteriorated to a point where "all hope of amicable relations" with the leadership of the House of Representatives "seemed to be at an end, at least until the questions which had arisen between them should be settled by an authority superior to both."[17] Embraced by his constituency when he had arrived in Boston six years earlier, Shute had fallen so far in the estimation of the people that, according to Hutchinson, an attempt had been made on his life. "It was known to his friends," the historian and future governor wrote, "that as he [Shute] sat in one of the chambers of his house, the window and door of a closet being opened, a bullet entered, through the window and door passages, and passed very near him."[18] He had enough "virulent enemies," Hutchinson insisted, that "suspicion of a wicked design" appeared more than warranted.[19] Shute had two choices: He could either remain in Boston until he was shot by a constituent or recalled to England by superiors exasperated with his ineffectiveness; or he could proactively return to London and put forward an alternative narrative, casting himself as an exemplary governor up against a treasonous mob. For a man who cared about his life, his reputation, and his future prospects, the latter was the only real option.

Shute had hoped to be well on his way to England via Barbados by the time his letter was delivered. But winds as uncooperative as the Massachusetts House had stranded the *Seahorse* just south of Boston Harbor. For two days the ship foundered off the coast of Nantasket, waiting for the breezes to shift. Finally, on the third day, an impatient Shute transferred from the warship to the ship *Ann*, a merchant vessel bound directly for England. Shortly before sunrise on January 1 there was an eleven-gun salute from the *Seahorse,* followed by a twenty-one-gun salute from the fort on Castle Island. A few hours later, Samuel Shute was gone.

BACK IN 1689, when Bostonians had arrested and deported Governor Edmund Andros, prodding him aboard a ship to England at the business end of a musket, they had gone out of their way to make sure the Crown understood they were rebelling against a tyrant who had abused his power, not against the authority he represented. It was the governor they abhorred, not the governance. All they asked was that England appoint a man who was not a scoundrel. Now, three decades later, the colony had dispatched a governor who was vindictive, impatient, inflexible, obtuse (a trait one historian would ascribe to his "natural imbecility"), and breathtakingly petty.[20] For all his faults, however, Samuel Shute fell well short of being a scoundrel on the order of Andros. That the people of Massachusetts had forced him into exile anyhow indicates that something fundamental had changed in the relationship between the colony and the Crown. Now it was the governance—and not merely the governor—that they were rebelling against. It's hard to imagine that a man more amenable and politic but equally committed to carrying out the instructions he had received from London would have fared much better than the unlikable Shute. Nor, as it turned out, would any of the governors who succeeded him. Among those men, the ones most bent on following Shute's lead in imposing the Crown's prerogative would find themselves similarly banished—not by men armed with muskets, as in the case of Andros, but rather by the same highly developed and disciplined political organization that had sent Samuel Shute running.

Shute's departure marked the beginning of a new era in colonial American politics. For the first time, Americans had both the strategy and the infrastructure necessary to wage an ongoing and highly effective political resistance against the mandates of the Crown. The political machine invented by Elisha Cooke would continue to frustrate royal governors and undermine their attempts to bring Massachusetts into compliance with London's demands for the next five decades. Ultimately it would prove the mechanism by which a revolution was launched. Not incidentally, one of the leaders of that revolution would be a direct political descendant of the Popular Party founder, the son of Cooke's right-hand man during the 1730s. His name was Samuel Adams Jr.

DUTIFUL AS ALWAYS, the *Gazette* and the *News-Letter* published the official government statement concerning the governor's departure. Shute, the *News-Letter* reported, had "been pleased to Communicate to the Honourable the Lieutenant Governour, His Majesty's Leave of Absence." According to that newspaper, he had also left detailed instructions for the management of the province with Dummer and the Council prior to going to Nantasket and boarding the *Seahorse* and was "designing (by GOD's Permission) to return . . . early the next Fall."[21]

In the final *New-England Courant* of 1722, published four days after the governor's disappearance, James Franklin made clear what the other newspapers had discreetly sidestepped: that Shute had never met with his lieutenant governor and Council to inform them of his intentions but had merely written them a letter—and only *after* boarding the *Seahorse*. The publisher or one of his correspondents wrote:

> On Friday last we were surpriz'd with the News of his Excellency our Governour's Design to go for England. He went privately on board his

Majesty's Ship Sea-Horse (bound to Barbadoes) on Thursday in the Afternoon, and wrote a Letter to the Hon. William Dummer Esq., our Lieutenant Governour, desiring him to take his Place in the Government, and acquaint the Council that he had taken his Passage for Barbadoes, in order to go from thence to London, and intended to return hither in the Fall. The Reasons of his Excellency's sudden Departure (at this Juncture) are variously guess'd at; but it being our Business to relate Matters of Fact, we shall purposely omit mentioning the different Surmises of People.

Then, sarcastically, he closed:

However, it is certain that he has hereby depriv'd the Town of an Opportunity of showing those public Marks of Respect, which are undoubtedly due to him for his WISE and JUST Administration among us.[22]

Two weeks after Shute's disappearance, and a week after the *Courant* revealed that he had left on the *Ann* rather than the *Seahorse*, James published an issue as taunting and belligerent as any that had preceded it. The lead essay was a full frontal assault on religious hypocrisy. Of all the "Knaves and Villains" in the world, the essayist wrote, the worst were religious knaves, who were "cry'd up by their neighbors for Eminent Saints" and thought to be honest in every affair; but for whom religion was "nothing but a *cunningly devised Fable*, a Trick of State, Invented to keep Mankind in awe." Even *"Publicans & Harlots,"* the writer asserted, would *"enter into the Kingdom of Heaven"* before men of that ilk.[23] If that piece seemed pointed directly at Samuel Sewall, the next was a completely undisguised dig at Cotton Mather. It reminded Bostonians how, in his 1720 pamphlet "News from Robinson Cruso's Island," the minister had lavishly praised Samuel Shute, who, two weeks gone from Boston, was now widely resented and suspected of bad intentions toward the colony. The effect was to make Mather appear both unctuous and a dupe, and even culpable for the situation in which Massachusetts now found itself.

Between that piece, which implied the governor was anything but the great man his biggest ministerial supporter had claimed, and the earlier week's sarcastic reference to the loss of his "WISE and JUST Administration," the *Courant* had made its low opinion of Samuel Shute abundantly clear. Now, though, it proceeded to declare him an enemy of the people. One of the Honest Wags, probably James himself, authored a short editorial urging the General Court to send two representatives after Shute so that when the governor bad-mouthed Massachusetts to his superiors in London his charges could be rebutted before they gained currency.

The underlying premise of this call to action—that the governor was determined to have his revenge on the colony—was a belief shared by most Bostonians and an idea that had been whispered about in every corner of the town. But its publication in a newspaper was a shock and a scandal. Worse still was the public call for the government to pursue Shute, who, whatever the people might think of him, was still very much the governor and not an escaped fugitive. The most egregious offense of all, though, came in the form of a question that served as a postscript to the editorial:

> *Quare*, Whether (pursuant to the Charter) the *Ministers* of this Province, ought now to pray for *Samuel Shute*, Esq.; as our immediate Governour, and at the same time pray for the Lieut. Governour as Commander in Chief? Or, Whether their praying for his *Success* in his Voyage, if he designs to hurt the Province (as some suppose) be not in Effect to pray for our Destruction?[24]

Since his release from jail six months earlier, James had been ratcheting up the rhetoric, testing the limits of official tolerance and daring the authorities to stop him. In December his newspaper had called the ministers of Boston (or at least "many of them") "Tygers and Wolves in Sheps Cloathing" who had made the world suffer "extreamly by their blind and furious Conduct."[25] Now he was suggesting that Massachusetts would be better off if the ship carrying its governor was lost at sea. A violation of decency and propriety, the comment was certain to fall into the hands of the governor after he arrived safely in London, hardening his hatred for the province and his resolve to have revenge on his constituents. It would also support his claim that the people of Massachusetts were disloyal, if not traitorous.

The government's response was nearly instantaneous. The *Courant* had been out on the street for only a few hours when the Council issued a resolve:

> Whereas the Paper call'd the *New-England Courant*, of this day's date contains many passages in which the Holy Scriptures are perverted, and the Civil Government, Ministers and People of the Province highly reflected on: Ordered, That *William Tailer*, *Samuel Sewall*, and *Penn Townsend*, Esqrs; with such as the Honourable House of Representatives shall joyn, be a Committee to consider and report what is proper for this Court to do thereon.[26]

The makeup of the committee did not bode well for James. Sewall and Townsend had already shown themselves only too happy to jail him. The House deputies chosen to join them were conservative–leaning Puritans from outside of Boston who had close personal ties to Sewall. Indeed, the committee needed only part of a single day to settle on a recommendation. Inasmuch as the *Courant*'s tendency was to "mock Religion and bring it into Contempt," to "Prophanely" abuse the holy scriptures, "injuriously" reflect upon the ministers, affront "His Majesty's Government," and disturb the peace, James should be "strictly forbidden" from printing the newspaper or any other paper or pamphlet without the supervision of the province secretary.[27] The order passed the full Council easily. Then it went to the House.

With Samuel Shute in the governor's chair, the House deputies had been unified against pre-publication censorship, determined that he should not be allowed to muzzle them along with troublemakers like

James Franklin. But now that Shute was headed to England and that threat was no longer imminent, the nearly unanimous opposition to licensing crumbled. When the House took up the order for consideration on January 16 it passed by a narrow margin—by just a single vote, James would later claim.

From a business standpoint the verdict was ruinous. The censor would have free reign over the *Courant*, the power to excise anything he considered disrespectful of the government, irreligious, or immoral—essentially everything that made that newspaper different and popular. Out of malice or sheer laziness he could delay its publication long enough to make its content old news and worthless. And since the censorship applied to other materials James printed, any and every work that came out of his shop could be similarly gutted or delayed at the censor's pleasure.

Late Sunday night, four days later, someone threw a "virulent Libel" into the entryway of Samuel Sewall's home.[28] The judge was mum about its exact nature. But he believed that the person responsible was connected to the *New-England Courant*. Benjamin Franklin biographer J. A. Leo Lemay took Sewall's hunch a step further, speculating that Ben was the perpetrator.[29] On the one hand, the gesture seems out of character for the apprentice, who by this point had seen the consequences of recklessly lashing out and had committed himself to emotional discipline. On the other hand, he was barely seventeen years old and, as his run-ins with James demonstrated, still vulnerable to the rash impulses of youth. And if there was one man Benjamin resented so deeply that his passions would overwhelm his better instincts it was Samuel Sewall.

For his part, James simply ignored the ruling. On January 21 he published the next issue of the *Courant* in exactly the manner he wished and without submitting it to the official censor, secretary of the province Josiah Willard (the son of Sewall's friend the Reverend Samuel Willard). Readers picking up the newspaper and expecting a polite, reformed version of its formerly audacious self were shocked to discover that the first two items attacked the very men who had ordered it censored. Both were psalms of

David as interpreted by the hymnwriter Isaac Watts. The first, titled "De-liverance from oppression and falsehood," was directed generally at the government officials who had meted out what James considered arbitrary and unfair punishment against him and his paper. The second psalm zeroed in on judges. Titled "Warning to Magistrates," it had been employed—as James likely knew—by the Reverend Ebenezer Pemberton to chastise Sam-uel Sewall a little more than ten years earlier.[30] Its second stanza read:

> *Have ye forgot, or never knew*
> *That God will judge the judges, too?*
> *High in the heav'ns his Justice reigns;*
> *Yet you invade the Rights of God,*
> *And send your bold Decrees abroad,*
> *To bind the Conscience in your Chains.*[31]

James went on to print the latest government proceedings against him in their entirety, including the Council's initial resolution to investigate his alleged abuses, the committee's order for pre-publication scrutiny, and the House's passage of that order. And in a final expression of contempt, this time for his dull and obsequious journalistic competitors Campbell and Musgrave, neither of whom had uttered a supportive word at any point in his battle with the censors, he wrote that he was certain the *News-Letter* and the *Gazette* would print the government's censorship order against him—not once, but "Three Weeks successively."[32]

Samuel Sewall's diary entry for that day consisted of six words: "The Courant comes out very impudently."[33]

Prorogued two days earlier, and not scheduled to meet again until March, the General Court as a whole was in no position to respond to the flouting of its order. The Council, however, remained on call to handle any needs or emergencies that arose during the recess. It took three days for Sewall to convene his colleagues. Once gathered, they immediately voted to ask for a warrant for James Franklin's arrest.

On January 28 Undersheriff John Darrell came to the Franklin printing house to apprehend James but found only his apprentice. If Benjamin knew where his brother had gone he didn't say. Neither did anyone else.

Darrell assembled a posse and dispatched its members to every corner of the town with instructions to find and apprehend the printer. By the end of the day he was obliged to report that his team had come up empty. Meanwhile, a second *Courant* had been published without government approval. Its lead essay, written by James prior to his disappearance, purported to be a reader's advice to the besieged newspaper. It took the form of a series of rules "which if duly observ'd will render your Paper not only inoffensive, but pleasant and agreeable."[34] These amounted to steering clear of every conceivable possibility for offending, and not appearing to usurp the proper role of the ministers by sermonizing or editorializing. In essence, the only way for the paper to avoid offensiveness was to be as dull and obedient as the *News-Letter* and *Gazette*.

With James in hiding, Benjamin once again found himself in charge. This time, though, James managed the paper's editorial content from a secret location. The lead item of the February 4 issue, written by someone who called himself "Juba," offered another scathing condemnation of judges. "I FIND it was a heinous Crime in old King *Alfred's* Days," he began, "not only to condemn a Man without *Action* or *Answer*, but also to punish him *against Law*, or where there was *no Law* provided." Juba went on to give a specific example from Andrew Horn's fourteenth-century legal fable, *The Mirror of Justices*: "King *Alfred* caused Forty Four Judges in one Year, to be hanged as *Murderers* for their *false Judgments*."[35] Having established the theme—that in more just times corrupt judges were *hanged*—Juba presented a letter he claimed to have found in the street, which was addressed to a "Sir" who, it quickly became obvious, was Judge Samuel Sewall. Reminding Sewall that "it cannot be long before you must appear at *Christ's* enlightened Tribunal, where every Man's work shall be tried," the letter writer "humbly" beseeched him to consider whether "the late Extraordinary procedure against *F—n* the Printer" was in accordance with *"the strict Rules of Justice and Enquiry."* If men could be punished for laws made after the fact, "Farewell *Magna Charta*, and *English Liberties*," he wrote. And he reminded Sewall of his "Error" as a Salem judge, arguing that his mistakes then ought to have made him "the more Cautious & Circumspect" in his actions against others forever after.[36]

JAMES HAD BEEN gone about two weeks when his friends and contributors gathered at the printing house for what Benjamin later called a "Consultation."[37] The men brainstormed about how to free the paper from the pre-publication censorship mandate. Someone suggested changing its name, since the censors had identified the *"New-England Courant"* as the paper that required inspection. From hiding, James rejected that idea as both too inconvenient and unlikely to solve the problem, inasmuch as the censorship was directed primarily at him and not his publication. The best and only real chance of continuing the *Courant* without pre-publication licensing was to replace him as its publisher. But since James had no intention of giving up the newspaper, the trick was to make it *appear* he had ceded control.

That "change of ownership" had been put into effect by the time the next *Courant* hit the streets. At the top of the first column of issue number eighty, published on February 11, 1723, a notice informed readers that the "late Publisher" had abandoned his efforts, having decided that the "many Inconveniencies" of publishing a newspaper requiring government approval made it unprofitable. It went on to promise that what followed would offer an accurate picture of the *Courant* under its new regime. From this point forward, its "main Design" would be to "entertain the Town with the most comical and diverting Incidents of Humane Life," which were plentiful in Boston. There would also be "a grateful Interspersion of more serious Morals, which may be drawn from the most ludicrous and odd Parts of Life." The guiding spirit of the paper would be a personage known as "old Janus . . . a Man of such remarkable *Opticks*, as to look two ways at once." At the bottom on the back page, the paper's colophon now read: "BOSTON: Printed and sold by BENJAMIN FRANKLIN in Queen Street, where Advertisements are taken in."[38] The words "near the prison" had been removed.

No longer in violation of publishing a newspaper without official approval, James surfaced at the printing house the next day. He was arrested for his earlier violations of the prior restraint order but was released soon thereafter when two close acquaintances, the baker James Davenport (the husband of his sister Sarah) and printer Thomas Fleet each posted £50 as surety for his good behavior for the next twelve months. No one seems to have objected when a grand jury declined to indict him. Josiah Franklin must have been relieved. One day after the warrant had been issued for his son's arrest, Josiah had mortgaged his house to Hannah Clarke for £220, quite possibly fearing that he would have to pay dearly to spare his frail son another extended stay in jail, this time in the middle of winter.

For the rest of 1723, the *New-England Courant* "prospered under its discreeter policy, increased its circulation, and raised its price," wrote the historian and biographer Carl Van Doren.[39] The newspaper had not *entirely* reformed. On March 4 it ridiculed a *News-Letter* author, possibly Cotton Mather, who attributed a dramatically high tide that had destroyed houses, washed ships out to sea, and, by one exaggerated account, caused as much damage as the great fire of 1711 (and which, in reality, might have been a small tsunami), to the proliferation of giant wharfs in seaport towns. The *Courant* scoffed that, by such logic, Noah's flood had been caused by "the Antediluvians . . . running too many Great Wharffs out into their Harbours."[40] James also continued to mock his competition, especially the ongoing inability of the *News-Letter* to deliver news that was either timely or interesting. On May 6, one day before he was formally acquitted and discharged from his recognizance, he tempted fate by publishing an argument that he should never have been charged and arrested in the first place. For the most part, however, he steered clear of the kind of provocative material that had formerly defined the paper. The absence of the extreme political partisanship that had been the norm with Samuel Shute present helped him reign in his impulses to be controversial. So, apparently, did his decision to propose marriage to Ann Smith, a woman too practical to become the wife of a man incapable of staying out of jail. How successfully he reconciled himself to publishing this kinder, gentler *Courant* is another question. The temptation to push harder and to be more provocative must have nagged at him, especially after Philadelphia's *American Weekly Mercury* came fulsomely to his defense in late February, asserting that he had had "a severe Sentence pass'd upon him, even to the taking away Part of his Livelihood, without being call'd to make Answer," and branding the men of the Massachusetts General Court "Oppressors and Bigots."[41] And it must have been deeply frustrating for him to see that the *Courant* "seemed to have lost the spark and spirit that animated its pages before his latest brush with the legislature and courts."[42] If he felt any contentment with the new normal—or at least relief over not to having to worry constantly about fines and jail time—it didn't manifest itself in an improved relationship with his apprentice. Indeed, in the months following his return from fugitive exile, things went from bad to worse.

Decades later Benjamin Franklin called his designation as publisher of the *Courant* "a very flimsy Scheme."[43] It succeeded, enabling the newspaper to continue without pre-publication government approval, mainly because early issues put out under his name offered toned down, acceptable content and because government officials were preoccupied with more pressing threats from the Abenaki and the colony's estranged and vengefully inclined governor. No one, it seems, objected to the claim that a seventeen-year-old boy was in charge of the newspaper but the boy himself. Benjamin deeply resented his forced participation in the charade. More than that, he resented the machinations necessary to make it appear legitimate, particularly the "Contrivance" of his supposed release from his apprenticeship.[44] Since an apprentice could not legally own his master's business, James had been obliged to sign the back of Benjamin's indenture contract, discharging him from its obligations and rendering him a free man. What the government did not know was that James had secretly forced his brother to sign another indenture continuing his apprenticeship "for the Remainder of the Term."[45] As much as Ben disliked being indentured to James, being forced to pretend he was a free man was worse. That juxtaposition of freedom and servitude might have inspired what some Franklin scholars believe was Benjamin's final contribution to the *Courant*. On July 15, 1723, a letter purportedly dictated by "an aged Negro Man (and a Slave to a Gentleman in this Town)" named "Dingo" appeared in the newspaper.[46] Dingo explained that he had been unjustly fined for misbehavior, denied counsel and a fair hearing because of his race and lowly social status, and then betrayed by his master, who refused to post the bond necessary to keep him out of jail. The letter marked another first in American journalism—the first time a newspaper printed the words of a black man (or at least a man who purported to be black). Benjamin's conceit here—that his plight was like that of an African slave—was, to put it mildly, a stretch, since a white man with a finite end to an unhappy indenture was far better off than an African enslaved for life. Still, the letter was extraordinary and unprecedented for its empathy—its author's willingness to attempt to see the unfairness of a black slave's life through his eyes.

Sometime in late July or August, a "fresh Difference" arose between the brothers, and Benjamin let on that he intended to leverage his supposed status as a free man to take his talents to another printer in town.[47] What he didn't count on was that James would undermine the defection "by going round & speaking to every Master, who," Ben later wrote, "accordingly refus'd to give me Work."[48] That was the last straw. Benjamin had already begun to wonder whether he had a future in Boston, having made himself "a little obnoxious to the governing Party" and having, through his "indiscreet Disputations about Religion," found himself "pointed at with Horror by good People, as an Infidel or Atheist."[49] Feeling as trapped as a slave, and with no prospect of success in his hometown, Ben decided to do what a slave would do and run.

On September 16 the *New-England Courant* noted the arrival from New

York of the sloop *Speedwell*. That issue, the 111th published by James Franklin with the assistance of his brother, was the last saved in Benjamin's personal file. Soon after the ship's arrival, Ben sent his friend John Collins to
its captain with a story about a friend needing to escape Boston because he
had gotten a "naughty" girl pregnant (Ben would later dress up the claim to
read: "had an intrigue with a girl of bad character") and enough money to
purchase that friend's secret passage out of town.[50] The money came from
selling a number of the books he had accumulated with his food savings.

On September 24, Ben appeared at his brother's printing house as
usual and did a full day's work. At the end of the day he took off his
printer's apron and left the shop for the last time. Either that evening or
early the next morning, he snuck aboard the *Speedwell*. By dusk on the following day, a "soft September night," the sloop had left the harbor.[51]

James must have been furious when the hours passed without any
trace of Benjamin and he realized that his brother had skipped out on him.
The default reaction of many masters faced with such circumstances was
to have their apprentice hunted down and returned for a reward—just as
with slaves. In this case, though, the situation was problematical for James,
since, insofar as the rest of Boston knew, Benjamin was a free man, not an
indentured servant. By the time the next *Courant* came out on September
30, five days after Benjamin's disappearance, James had resigned himself
to the desertion. At the conclusion of that issue's advertisements he ran a
short, succinct notice: "James Franklin, Printer in Queen-Street, wants a
likely lad for an Apprentice."[52] With that, the partnership of the brothers
Franklin was over.

JAMES MARRIED ANN SMITH on his twenty-seventh birthday. By
the time they had been married a year his business had fallen off, partly because of the limitations intense government scrutiny had placed on what
he was able to print, partly because he had been blackballed by elements of
the government and the clergy, and partly, it seems, because Boston had

grown tired of the drama surrounding the *Courant*. By midway through 1726 he concluded, like his younger brother before him, that he had no future in Boston. Now that his wife had given birth to their first child, a son, he began to look elsewhere for a fresh start. Sometime late that year or early the next he stopped publishing his newspaper (whose colophon, right up to the end, listed the long-absent Benjamin Franklin as its publisher), closed his printing house, and relocated to Newport, Rhode Island, which was growing quickly but still lacked a printer. The knowledge that his tallow chandler brother was established there was one draw. The colony's reputation for religious and political tolerance was another.

Boston was rid of its least favorite son. But he did not go quietly. Late in 1726 he committed a final act of defiance, publishing, perhaps on the day he left town for good, a seven-page poem that was both a biting condemnation of those who had opposed the *Courant* and a cocky claim for the paper's lasting significance. In "The Life and Death of Old Father Janus, the vile Author of the late Wicked Courant. A Satyr," James wrote that although the *Courant* had been "deem'd a Publick Pest," it had given a "Smart" to vice.[53] He castigated Boston for undermining the *Courant*'s crusade against hypocrisy, knavery, dishonesty, and flatterers and for failing to support its fight for liberty and virtue. He took one last swing at Harvard College, boasting that he had outwitted its highly educated alumni and faculty and suggesting that their embarrassment had fueled their determination to see him silenced. And he gloated over his success in protecting the identities of the paper's authors.

With the *Courant* gone, he warned, Boston had lost its champion for truth and virtue, not to mention its last bastion against dullness. Now, like "Rats and Mice once the Light's withdrawn: / The Golden Days of Ignorance return, / And *Wit*, like Janus, meet with gen'rous Scorn."[54]

James Franklin's battle with the Boston establishment had produced a new and distinctly American form of journalism. Even more important, he had given his country both its first taste of a free press and its first argument for that freedom as an essential liberty. It was fitting that despite his opponents' repeated attempts to silence him, he had gotten the last word.

EPILOGUE

The Revolution was effected before the war commenced. The Revolution was in the minds and hearts of the people; a change in their religious sentiments of their duties and obligations. . . . *This radical change in the principles, opinions, sentiments, and affections of the people, was the real American Revolution.*

—John Adams, letter to Hezekiah Niles, 1818

God offer'd to the Jews Salvation;
And 'twas refus'd by half the Nation:
Thus, (tho, 'tis Life's great Preservation)
Many oppose *Inoculation.*
We're told by one of the black Robe
The Devil inoculated Job:
Suppose 'tis true, what he does tell;
Pray, Neighbours, *Did not Job do well?*

—Benjamin Franklin, *Poor Richard's Almanack,* 1737

BOYLSTON'S FAME, WASHINGTON'S GAMBLE,
AND THE END OF SMALLPOX

As Bostonians had discovered four months into the inoculation controversy, a similar experiment was under way in England. The heroine of the
London inoculation trial was the "unconventional and forward" Lady Mary
Wortley Montagu.[1] While living briefly with her diplomat husband in Constantinople in 1717 she had permitted an "inoculatrix" of the kind described
by Pylarini and mocked by William Douglass to inoculate her three-year-
old son. When smallpox began spreading though London in April 1721, she
decided to have the procedure performed on her second child, a daughter.
(The physician who performed it, Charles Maitland, had been in Constantinople with the Montagu family and had assisted in their son's procedure.)
Once it was clear that both five-year-old Mary Alice Montagu and a second
subject, the child of an observing physician, would recover from their inoculations without consequences, Lady Mary's friend, Princess Caroline, and
several royal physicians appealed to the king to sanction a further explora-
tion of the procedure's merits. The Newgate Prison experiment reported
in the Boston newspapers began shortly thereafter. Finally, on April 17,
1722, five days after a letter from Cotton Mather touting Boylston's success
with inoculation in Boston was presented to the Royal Society, Princess
Caroline permitted two of her daughters, aged eleven and nine, to be inoculated by the king's surgeon. The princess's children fared well, although
another child and a footman inoculated at the same time died, adding fuel
to an anti-inoculation movement similar to the one in America. Boston
pamphlets and letters on both sides of the issue factored into the ensuing English debate. Medical historians Raymond Stearns and George Pasti
wrote that the published pro-inoculation testimonies from Cotton Mather
and others arrived "just in time to stiffen and sustain the wavering case for
inoculation." They contended that the procedure might not have become
established in England but for "the timely, well-authenticated reports of a
wider, successful experience in New England."[2]

The pro-inoculation testimony from New England piqued English interest in the Boston physician who had single-handedly performed the operation on six times as many persons as had been inoculated in the London experiments. Invited to speak to the Royal Society, Zabdiel Boylston sailed from Boston in December 1724 and addressed the organization's members in February of the following year. While in London he declined repeated requests to perform inoculations, concerned that it would make him appear mercenary. Another request he initially resisted was to turn his records of the inoculation experiment into a book. But his attempt to beg off by claiming that writing was "a Talent which, of all things, I never made any Pretensions to" proved no match for the persistence of Hans Sloane, president of the Royal College of Physicians, and the persuasiveness of Princess Caroline, to whom he dedicated the finished volume.[3] *An Historical Account of the Small-Pox Inoculated in New England* featured a patient-by-patient account of the Boston trial and a fifteen-step guide for bringing patients through inoculation. It drew medical conclusions based on statistics seventy-five years before the word "statisticks" first appeared in an American dictionary. Gerald Mager said it was "one of the first times quantitative analysis was applied to a medical problem."[4] The book was also ahead of its time in its discussion of contagion. Boylston, Mather, and Benjamin Colman had all speculated on the existence of microscopic creatures that entered the body "through food and drink, through respiration, and even through the skin."[5] Although none of them was entirely correct either about the nature of infection or about the mechanism of immunity, they were closer to the truth than most theorists would get for many decades to come. Indeed, another century and a half would pass before "germ theory" took hold as the dominant explanation for communicable disease.

Boylston was voted a Fellow of the Royal Society in July 1726, becoming the eighth New Englander and first full-time American physician to gain membership. It was a stunning achievement for a man who, prior to the 1721 epidemic, had been dismissed as second rate by American standards, which, even at their best, were considered inferior to standards in England

and Europe. But success did not heal the wounds he had received from the attacks of inoculation's opponents. In his book, written well after the small-pox epidemic was over and in the glow of his acclaim by English medical authorities and royalty, Boylston sounded a surprisingly intense note of bit-terness toward Douglass, Lawrence Dalhonde, and unnamed others, com-plaining that he had been "basely us'd and treated" and been made to "incur the Displeasure" of many of his "best Friends" as a consequence of inocu-lation.[6] What Gerald Mager called Boylston's "persecution complex" con-tinued for well over a decade.[7] Sixteen years after the fact he still described the opposition to his experiment as "a Clamour as never was made there [in Boston] before or since."[8] For many of those years he suffered from a "Convulsive Asthma" he blamed on the stress of the controversy.[9] In a letter to Hans Sloane he complained of "such a Catarrhal Distillation upon My Whole Breast, that I have not had ye last twelve Years, twelve hours ease in twenty four."[10] Unconventional his whole life, Boylston by age fifty-seven had become conspicuously eccentric. His efforts to bolster his resistance to his mysterious affliction included the following compulsive ritual:

> I Shave my Whole Head 3 times a Week, Wash it, brush, & do every-thing to harden it even ye Cold Bath, which We have exceeding Cold, & us'd all ye Means, that I could Read or Hear of, as my Constitution Wou'd bear, but all to little purport ye Disease Increases, & My Strength abates & Age Creeps on so yet My Prospect as to this World is very Melancholly.[11]

Over time he regained his strength and energy. He went on working part-time as a physician through his seventies. A lifelong horse enthu-siast, he was spotted breaking a colt when he was eighty-two years old. Although by that point he had long since stopped corresponding with the Royal Society, he continued collecting samples from nature and conduct-ing experiments, some of which were aimed at finding an antidote for rattlesnake bites.

Given up for dead in his early twenties, and afflicted with debilitating infirmities throughout the 1730s, Boylston came within a week of reaching his eighty-seventh birthday. He died on March 1, 1766, and was buried in the Walnut Street Cemetery near Brookline. Today, the epitaph on his raised, flat tombstone is cracked and badly faded but still legible. It identifies him as "Zabdiel Boylston Esqr. Physician and F.R.S. who first introduced the practice of Innoculation [*sic*] into America."

ALTHOUGH INOCULATION WOULD come to be considered "the chief *medical* contribution of the Enlightenment, at least in the opinion of the age itself," Europe was slow to adopt the practice.[12] It was virtually nonexistent in Holland until 1749 and in Germany until 1750. It was 1755 before it got a foothold in France. Fifteen more years elapsed before it was taken up in Spain. In Great Britain, though, the procedure continued to gain ground in the years following Lady Mary's introduction. In 1754 the Royal College of Physicians gave it their endorsement. By 1771 the inaugural edition of the *Encyclopaedia Britannica*, published in Edinburgh, included a long passage on smallpox, noting that inoculation "is now so well known and so generally practiced, that a particular detail of it in this place is unnecessary."[13]

In America, the practice of inoculation became widespread, but remained controversial. In 1738 a Charleston physician named John Kirkpatrick and a naval surgeon named Arthur Mowbray inoculated eight hundred persons, only eight of whom died. Notwithstanding their success, however, the South Carolina Assembly passed a law banning inoculation in or near Charleston and levying a fine of £500 to anyone performing or receiving an inoculation. The impetus behind that fine—fear that inoculation would spread smallpox faster and more widely than would otherwise be the case—prompted New York to pass a prohibition against it in 1747. Newport, Rhode Island, repeatedly wavered on inoculation, approving it and then barring it. When an epidemic arrived in 1771, the town was split down the middle on the question of whether to allow the operation. Thousands of successes were sometimes undermined by a single, conspicuous failure. Perhaps no death had a more chilling effect on the movement toward acceptance than that of the revivalist preacher Jonathan Edwards, an outspoken inoculation advocate who died in 1758, shortly after undergoing the procedure. By the eve of the American Revolution, inoculation had also become, in some quarters, a political wedge issue. Those wealthy enough to afford the procedure also tended to be (or at least were seen as being) loyal to the Crown. Attacks on inoculation hospitals in Marblehead and Salem in 1774 were as much about opposing British influence in America as about the fear of the procedure itself.

Contrary to the image of inoculation as some kind of loyalist conspiracy, its proponents included a number of the men who would become America's Founding Fathers. Some of them arrived for the Continental Congress in Philadelphia in September 1774 already inoculated—a fortunate thing, since smallpox had recently broken out there. John Adams, whose support for inoculation might have had something to do with his lineage—Zabdiel Boylston was his great-uncle on his mother's side—had undergone the procedure in 1764. (One of Adams's physicians was Joseph Warren, a future compatriot in the Revolutionary cause.) Adams would quip that the only reason he had been chosen to represent Massachusetts in Congress was that he was immune to smallpox. Thomas Jefferson also arrived inoculated. Unable to undergo the operation in Virginia, where it was illegal, he had traveled to Philadelphia in 1766 expressly to be inoculated. (His doctor there, William Shippen Jr., would later become head physician for the Continental Army.) Josiah Bartlett, John Hancock, and Patrick Henry all were inoculated by their fellow delegate Dr. Benjamin Rush during the Second Continental Congress. By that point a ban placed on inoculation during the First Continental Congress, largely at the request of smallpox-vulnerable delegates afraid that the procedure would expose them to greater danger, had been lifted due to the persistence of the epidemic. But not every vulnerable delegate was persuaded to submit to

the procedure. Early in 1776 the chairman of the Congress's secret committee, Rhode Island delegate Samuel Ward, died of smallpox after refusing the appeals of John Adams and others to undergo inoculation.

In 1775, Philadelphia was just a small part of a much larger outbreak—
North America's first continental smallpox epidemic. Its onset and dura-
tion tracked almost exactly with the American Revolution. The influx of
English, German, and French combatants, and the movement throughout
the theaters of operation of those men and the Americans assembled from
the various colonies, spread and perpetuated the disease in a way unprecedented in America. Many prospective American soldiers were scared off
from enlistment not by the possibility that they would be killed in battle
but for fear that living in close quarters with men infected by the deadly
disease would kill them before the British did. Those fears were not
misplaced: The war would claim an estimated 25,000 lives; meanwhile,
approximately 130,000 Americans would die of smallpox during the same
period. Elizabeth Fenn placed the two events in context. "While the American Revolution may have defined the era for history," she wrote, "epidemic smallpox nevertheless defined it for many of the Americans who
lived and died in that time."[14]

Even leaders of the war effort were, especially early on, more worried
about smallpox than about the British. In July 1775 George Washington
pledged to John Hancock that he would exercise "the utmost Vigilence
against this most dangerous Enemy."[15] Several months later the danger was
brought home in dramatic fashion when the sickness of approximately 900
of the 2,500 Americans involved in the invasion of Quebec doomed that
expedition, prompting John Adams to call smallpox "the King of Terrors
to America this year" and "ten times more terrible than the British, Cana-
dians and Indians together."[16] Benedict Arnold, wounded in the fighting,
worried that smallpox would cause "the entire ruin of the army."[17]

By February 1777 that possibility appeared ominous enough that
Washington, who had suffered naturally acquired smallpox as a young
man but had argued for the legalization of inoculation in Virginia and

recommended it to his stepson, John Parke Custis, ordered the inoculation of troops already in service and new recruits as they came into the army in Philadelphia. Later that year he ordered the pace dramatically accelerated. His army went from over 14,000 troops in December 1777 to about half that size in March of the following year, as healthy men left active duty to be inoculated and were confined for several weeks thereafter. As a result, General Horatio Gates, no fan of Washington in most respects, could declare smallpox "perfectly removed from the Army."[18] Historian Joseph Ellis wrote that Washington's daring preemptive attack against smallpox, pulled off without the knowledge of the British, was perhaps "the most important strategic decision of his military career."[19] A major outbreak of the disease in the American ranks would almost certainly have finished off an army already overmatched and struggling, dooming the American Revolution.

There is a link between the 1721 Boston experiment and Washington's bold decision to inoculate. His name is Benjamin Franklin. Both of the men who served as chief physician of the Continental Army leading up to the mass inoculation, John Morgan and William Shippen Jr., were from Philadelphia, the most inoculation-friendly town in America thanks significantly to Franklin, who had been converted to the procedure by Boylston's success during the Boston inoculation trial. Nine years after that experiment, when smallpox appeared in Franklin's adopted hometown, he enthusiastically urged the procedure on his fellow Philadelphians. From 1730 forward he was regarded as one of his country's foremost inoculation evangelists. His contributions to the cause included arranging for a young Morgan and Shippen to meet some of the most prominent, pro-inoculation physicians in London. Thanks to Boylston's early inoculation experiment, George Washington could justify his confidence in the procedure by citing a record of its success that extended back more than fifty years. Thanks at least partly to Franklin, the general had the support of Morgan, who in 1776 wrote a pamphlet recommending inoculation for both the general public and the military, and his successor, Shippen, who, although apprehensive about aspects of the mass inoculation plan, was a firm believer in the procedure itself (he most likely inoculated Washington's wife, Martha) and oversaw its successful implementation.

THERE WERE THREE problems with inoculation. Although considerably safer than a naturally acquired case of smallpox, it still involved transplanting the actual disease, producing a sickness that was often severe and sometimes fatal. Second, it sometimes left, in those more severe cases, considerable scarring. Last but not least it was contagious; a person with inoculated smallpox could spread it as easily as a person with a naturally acquired case. Vaccination remedied those defects.

In May 1796, in the town of Berkeley in Gloucestershire, England, Edward Jenner made two shallow cuts in the arms of a healthy eight-year-old boy named James Phipps and inoculated him with fluid he had harvested from a cowpox pustule on the hand of a local dairymaid. Cowpox was an infection of the cow udder that was transmitted during milking. It was common knowledge among country folk that milkmaids who had had cowpox, which produced little more than a light, fleeting rash, didn't get smallpox. Following his cowpox inoculation, young Phipps developed a rash at the incision points, as well as swollen joints, fever, and pain in the groin. Shortly thereafter, though, his symptoms disappeared. Months later and on two separate occasions Jenner inoculated him with the smallpox virus to test his immunity. Both times the boy exhibited no signs of infection. In Jenner's 1798 paper on his experiment he referred to the cowpox agent as "Variolae vaccinae," from the Latin word for "cow," *vacca*. Within a few years the procedure became known as "vaccination." (The use of the term "vaccination" generically—that is, in reference to immunizations for diseases other than smallpox—is thanks largely to Louis Pasteur. In 1881 Pasteur developed an immunization against anthrax and referred to it as a vaccination in tribute to Jenner.) Vaccination was safer than inoculation with smallpox and produced no communicable disease.

Vaccination came to America in 1800, introduced once again by a

Boston doctor, Benjamin Waterhouse. Like Boylston before him, Waterhouse included his own young son among his first subjects. About a year later, President Thomas Jefferson arranged for the vaccination of eighteen members of his family, a group of neighbors, and some of the last surviving members of the Mohican tribe, who were visiting him at the time. He then arranged for cowpox to be secured from England (the disease didn't exist in America) and distributed to physicians in Philadelphia and in several towns in the South. Thanks largely to Jefferson's advocacy, vaccination was being practiced throughout the United States within five years of its introduction. Indeed, it was Jefferson who predicted that smallpox vaccination "would finally extirpate the disease from the earth."[20]

The last major smallpox scare in the United States took place in New York in 1947. In about three weeks, more than 6 million persons were vaccinated and the outbreak was confined to twelve persons. But the near disappearance of the disease in America was the exception. As Michael B. A. Oldstone has pointed out, the nearly 300 million persons who died of smallpox in the twentieth century amount to three times the number killed in two world wars and smaller armed conflicts combined.[21]

In 1966 the World Health Organization (WHO) committed itself to eradicating smallpox. When the effort began the following year, the disease was still rampant in thirty-three countries and its annual toll remained devastating: approximately 15 million persons afflicted and about 2 million killed. Just eight years later the last natural case of lethal smallpox occurred in Bangladesh. In 1979 the WHO officially declared the world smallpox-free. This marked the first time in history that science had eradicated a deadly, epidemic disease.

COTTON MATHER, SAMMY MATHER, AND HAWTHORNE'S DILEMMA

Cotton Mather was haunted by John Checkley's claim that he had fabricated his membership in the Royal Society. By May 1723 he was so desperate to refute the aspersions that he wrote to James Jurin of the Society, appealing for exoneration and offering to "lay aside my pretensions to be at all related unto that illustrious body" if it turned out that his claim of membership was in error.[22] As it happened, the satisfaction Mather so desperately wanted was on its way to him at the time he wrote the letter. In April his friend John Woodward had taken his case to the Society, and, after demonstrating that the minister had indeed been proposed and approved for membership a decade earlier—slated for election but never actually elected—a new vote was taken and Cotton Mather was formally added to the roll of Royal Society members. Nearly two years after Checkley had written to Edmond Halley questioning the validity of Mather's claim to membership, that membership was finally a matter of record.

In April 1724 Mather experienced the financial crisis he had feared—and cried wolf about—for years. "I must either be lodg'd in the Prison or forc'd into a private Withdraw," he wrote.[23] Informed that this time their pastor really was in the direst of straits, wealthy members of his congregation covered his most pressing debts. In July, learning that Mather faced another potentially ruinous financial deadline, the congregation once again came to his rescue.

August 1724 was a terrible month for Mather. Shortly after he was passed over for the presidency of Harvard (for the second time that year), his wife left him. He blamed her angry departure from the Ship Street house on "a prodigious Return of her Pangs upon her; that seemed little short of a proper Satanical Possession."[24] Clearly, though, Lydia was fed up, exasperated by her husband's failure to get the Harvard presidency—which she probably (and correctly) saw as his own fault for having schemed against the college in his support for Yale—and deeply embarrassed over his need to accept charity from his congregation.

Seven days after Lydia moved out, Mather learned that his son Cresy was lost at sea and presumed dead. Right up until the end, Mather had clung to the faintest of hopes that Increase Jr. would redeem himself. (Not so with Increase Sr., who had cut his namesake grandson out of his will.)

The boy had sailed from Boston in late February or early March 1724, right around the time his father, probably not coincidentally, had discovered £6 missing from his study. In late July, Mather had had an intuition that something terrible had happened to Cresy. ("My Son *Increase*! My Son, my Son!" he had written in his diary.[25]) Now his premonition had been proven correct and he was again forced to deal with the loss of a child. Cresy became the twelfth to precede him in death. Two years later he would lose yet another, his daughter Elizabeth.

A few days after Cresy's loss became public knowledge, Lydia returned to the family home to support her bereaved husband. Mather wrote that she came to him "entreating that there might be an eternal Oblivion of every thing that has been out of Joint, and an eternal Harmony in our future Conversation."[26] Eternal harmony was probably too much to expect of any marriage, let alone one as combustible as theirs. But the four years following their reconciliation, the last of Mather's life, were domestically quiet. No doubt it helped that by October 1724 the remaining suits against the Howell estate were settled. Although Mather would never recover financially—his biographer Kenneth Silverman recorded that outside of his enormous library his possessions at the time of his death were "dingy and mean: pie plates, lumber, a crosscut saw, three old rugs . . . broken chairs, broken pewter, broken spoons"—he no longer lived in constant fear of public embarrassment and debtors' prison.[27]

Early in 1727 his health began to fail. On October 29 of that year, a Sunday, a major earthquake struck Boston and all of New England. It began in the nighttime darkness, just before eleven o'clock. Mather described it as a "horrid rumbling like the Noise of many Coaches together, driving on the paved Stones with the utmost Rapidity."[28] Silverman wrote that "Bostonians assembled in the churches throughout the night and day, the *Gazette* reported, in a state of 'great and Just Terror and Dread.' "[29] The approach of what might be "the Great Day of the Son of man's appearing in the clouds of heaven" energized Mather.[30] The next day he took to the pulpit, proclaiming the quake a sign of the need to repent and reform. Fear of what the quake might portend, kept alive by the aftershocks that continued throughout much of 1728, proved beneficial to his church. So did the general rehabilitation of his reputation, thanks partly to the demise of the *New-England Courant*, but mostly to a general perception that his advocacy of inoculation had put him on the right side of that issue. The result was the addition of seventy-one persons to the North Church in 1727. It was the biggest single jump in membership in its history.

He preached for the final time on December 24, 1727. His subject was the death of the controversial minister Peter Thacher, whose acceptance into Boston he and his father had first promoted and then opposed. After so many jeremiads, Mather ended on a note of hope. "He did not threaten or warn," noted Silverman. "Instead he offered a comforting certainty, that the troubled body which goes to the cold chamber where the sun shines not, shall be reborn at rest in paradise, envisioning God."[31] Confined to his bed for the last month and a half of his life, Mather endured a final family tragedy. In mid-January, Lydia's grandsons George and Nathan Howell, the two young boys Mather had taken in after the death of their father, drowned after falling through thin ice while skating.

Cotton Mather died on the morning of February 13, 1728, one day after turning sixty-five. His final word was said to be "Grace!"[32] He was buried with his father and other family members in a tomb on Copp's Hill. Of Mather's fifteen children only Sammy and the severely burned Hannah survived him. Mather's surrogate son, the African ex-slave Onesimus, continued to live in Boston for at least another decade and a half after the smallpox epidemic of 1721. The last time his name appeared in the town's public records, noted Jennifer Lee Carrell, was 1738, when he was drafted to a street-cleaning detail "pursuant to the Act for the Regulating of Free Negroes."[33]

Disappointed by life in many ways, Mather died knowing that his longest held and dearest ambition, to produce a son who would honorably continue the family's ministerial legacy, had been fulfilled. By that point Sammy was serving as chaplain at Castle William. In 1731 he became a minister of his father's church. Eleven years later he founded his own church, the Tenth Congregational Society, where he continued to preach until his death in 1785.

Appraising Cotton Mather was a challenge while he was alive and remains one more than two centuries later. In his 1840 book *Grandfather's Chair*, Nathaniel Hawthorne wrote: "It is difficult . . . to make you understand such a character as Cotton Mather's, in whom there was so much good, yet so many failings and frailties."[34] Posterity has tilted decisively toward understanding Mather as a failed if not malevolent figure. The image of him as a Salem witch hunter seething with hatred has been bolstered by popular culture, including several appearances as a *Spider-Man* comic book villain in 1976. (Adolf Hitler was another Marvel Comics nemesis.) Biographers, historians, and even Mather's contemporaries have tried to provide a fuller and more balanced perspective. Shortly after his death, a number of Boston eulogists began to see past his excesses and the more irritating and difficult aspects of his personality and to take on what Silverman described as an "apologetic air . . . of trying to do justice in limited space to someone gargantuan and perplexing."[35] But two of his most endearing tributes came from Ben Franklin, who four decades after leaving Boston struck up a brief correspondence with Sammy Mather. In a 1784 letter reminiscing about their Boston childhoods, Franklin recalled a visit he had made to the Mather home in the spring of 1724, during his first, brief return to Boston following his escape from his apprenticeship. Benjamin didn't say why he made a special point of seeing the man his brother's newspaper had attacked relentlessly. But as his anecdote makes clear, the minister accepted the overture with graciousness and even a touch of paternal affection. Benjamin wrote:

> He [Cotton Mather] receiv'd me in his Library, and on my taking Leave
> show'd me a shorter way out of the House thro' a narrow Passage which
> was cross'd by a Beam overhead. We were still talking as I withdrew, he
> accompanying me behind, and I turning partly toward him, when he

said hastily, Stoop, Stoop! I did not understand him till I felt my Head hit against the Beam. He was a Man that never miss'd any Occasion of giving Instruction, and upon this he said to me, *You are young, and have the World before you; Stoop as you go through it, and you will miss many hard Thumps.* This Advice, thus beat into my head has frequently been of use to me, and I often think of it when I see Pride mortified, and Misfortunes brought upon People by their carrying their Heads too high.[36]

In the same letter, the last extant in the correspondence between the two men, Franklin also revealed a personal debt he owed Cotton Mather:

When I was a Boy, I met with a Book intitled *Essays to do Good*, which I think was written by your Father. It had been so little regarded by a former Possessor, that several Leaves of it were torn out: But the Remainder gave me such a Turn of Thinking as to have an Influence on my Conduct thro' Life; for I have always set a greater Value on the Character of a *Doer of Good*, than on any other kind of Reputation; and if I have been, as you seem to think, a useful Citizen, the Publick owes the Advantage of it to that Book.[37]

Benjamin Franklin was, by this point, a world-famous figure, widely regarded as a genius yet still covetous of the credit for even his most modest accomplishment. His voluntary admission of Mather's influence on a life as consequential as his own was an act of largess, a gift to the devoted son of a man who had meant well but not always done well, and who had suffered disproportionately not only in life but also in his posthumous reputation.

JAMES FRANKLIN, BEN FRANKLIN, AND FREEDOM OF THE PRESS

In Newport, James Franklin set up his printing shop in the basement of the town schoolhouse, which was located at Tillinghast's Wharf. Initially he printed legal and financial forms including powers of attorney, bills, and bonds. To supplement his income he imported and sold books and pamphlets from London and Boston. He also sold paper by the ream, tea and coffee, and snuff. Business improved in 1730, when he was chosen to print the acts and laws of the Rhode Island Assembly, an assignment that had previously been farmed out to Boston printers. After two years his salary for the printing was set at a respectable £20 a year. After two more years he was designated the official printer for the Assembly.

Having successfully established himself in Newport, James launched Rhode Island's first newspaper, the *Rhode-Island Gazette*. Cast in the image of the *Courant*, it lasted only five months. James might have found it impossible to gain traction without the big controversies and deeply ingrained antipathies the *Courant* had exploited. He also had to be careful about creating newsworthy controversy given his status as the official printer of the Assembly and his need to provide for a family that now included Ann, James Jr. ("Jemmy"), and three daughters. In the final analysis, though, Newport in 1732 was probably still too small and provincial to provide a regular readership for a weekly newspaper.

Never entirely hale, James became seriously ill soon after his *Gazette* folded. His deterioration was rapid enough that, in late September or early October 1732, Benjamin made a detour to Newport on his way back to Philadelphia from a visit to family and friends in Boston. By that point there had been a tentative rapprochement between the brothers after seven years without any contact whatsoever. His biographer Lemay reported that notations in Benjamin Franklin's accounts for October 30, 1731, indicate that they "had established business relations."[38] A little less than two months later, Benjamin's *Pennsylvania Gazette* contained an advertisement for a book printed and published by James in 1729. But the two had not been face-to-face since late April or early May 1724, when Benjamin materialized in Boston for the first time since running off from his apprenticeship. His bumptious deportment during that brief visit—dressed in a conspicuously new suit (the traditional gift an apprentice received upon fulfilling his indenture), he jingled the money in his pocket and boasted to the men working in his brother's shop about his success in Philadelphia— "extremely" offended James, who vowed to "never forget or forgive it."[39] Now, however, the brothers put aside their resentments. As Ben movingly wrote about the reunion:

> Our former Differences were forgotten, and our Meeting was very cordial and affectionate. He was fast declining in his Health, and requested of me that, in case of his Death, which he apprehended not far distant, I would take home his Son, then but 10 Years of Age, and bring him up to the Printing Business.[40]

James Franklin died sixteen months later, on February 4, 1735. It was his thirty-eighth birthday and his eleventh wedding anniversary. Reactivated tuberculosis and a constitution weakened by years of drinking might have been responsible. In Boston, news of his death barely earned a mention from the town's newspapers. No one eulogized him; there was no acknowledgment of the liveliness and intelligence he had injected into Boston publishing, not even from his contemporary Samuel Kneeland, who not long after the *Courant* folded had appropriated its format of publishing essays, letters, and verses in his *Weekly Journal*, thereby creating a more genteel version of the newspaper James had published.

Ann Franklin took over her husband's business, becoming one of the first women in America to run her own printing house. She was assisted by her son and daughters. She also received help from afar courtesy of her husband's former colleague Thomas Fleet. After posting bond for James in 1723, Fleet had remained his most faithful and enduring friend, loyal even after James was awarded some of the Rhode Island printing formerly farmed out to Fleet in Boston. Prior to James's death, Fleet had sold copies of his friend's almanac in his Boston shop and printed advertisements for the short-lived *Rhode-Island Gazette* in his own newspaper, the *Boston Evening Post*. Afterward, Fleet continued to sell and advertise the *Rhode-Island*

Almanack in support of his friend's widow. (He also sold *Poor Richard's* for Benjamin Franklin.) Unlike most of his fellow Honest Wags—who never again wrote for publication after the *Courant* had run its course—Fleet continued on in the spirit of his dead friend's journalistic mission. His *Evening Post*, which he published until his death in 1758, earned a reputation as one of the best-written newspapers in America. Because of his willingness to publish "unorthodox opinions," Fleet was, in the opinion of at least one historian, the "boldest" publisher since James Franklin.[41] He was threatened with legal action several times, once for publishing "a scandalous and libelous reflection upon His Majesty's Administration."[42] All attempts to punish him were unsuccessful.

Benjamin Franklin also supported his brother's family financially. In 1737 he took James Franklin Jr. into his family as promised. After a time, Jemmy became his uncle's apprentice. The relationship between Benjamin and his nephew proved nearly as dysfunctional as the one between James and Benjamin. Like the younger Benjamin, Jemmy resented being treated like a common apprentice. Benjamin described him as "always dissatisfied and grumbling," words James Sr. might have used to describe young Benjamin.[43] When Jemmy's apprenticeship ended in 1748 his uncle offered to set him up in New Haven, a branch of his expanding network of printers and booksellers. But either out of resentment or a desire to assist his mother and sisters, Jemmy declined the offer and returned to Newport where, ten years later, he launched the *Newport Mercury*, the first attempt at a Rhode Island newspaper since his mother had tried without success to resurrect his father's *Rhode-Island Gazette*. (His uncle supported the venture, H. P. Smith wrote, by providing him with "a font of type for the purpose."[44]) Despite Jemmy's fickle relationship with responsibility, the *Mercury* survived. By 1761 it had become solidly established, proof that its publisher had inherited his father's knack for putting out a readable newspaper. He had also inherited his father's nose for controversy and his itch for challenging authority. Early in 1762 he printed a pamphlet that attacked the Rhode Island governor. In the war of printed words that followed, he took both sides, exploiting controversy to drum up readership. That pamphlet war was winding down when, on April 21, 1762, he died. He was in his midthirties. With her daughters now also deceased, sixty-six-year-old Ann Franklin had no choice but to resume full management of the printing house and the *Newport Mercury*.

Almost a year to the day after she lost her son, Ann died. She was buried in the Common Ground on Farewell Street (now Island Cemetery) beside her husband. Forced into the printing business by adversity, she had become just the third woman printer in America, the third to edit and publish her own newspaper without the assistance of her husband, and the first to write and publish her own almanac. An argument can be made that she was America's first complete woman printer and publisher, its first female "jack of all trades," as her husband had described himself at the birth of the *Courant*.

Under new hands, the *Mercury* continued to distinguish itself. In 1767 it published the first surviving work of the African-American poet Phillis Wheatley. The next year its new publisher Solomon Southwick, an outspoken Whig, gave it a patriot motto: "Undaunted by TYRANTS—we'll DIE or be FREE!" By 1776 the newspaper had become such a nuisance to the Crown that both it and Southwick were strategic targets of the British army. On December 2, as General Clinton's forces approached Newport to begin their occupation of the town, Southwick dismantled his press— the same one James Franklin had used to print his newspaper—and buried the pieces in a garden before fleeing. The printer escaped the redcoats, but a Tory sympathizer divulged the press's location. The British dug it up, reassembled it, and put it to work printing a Tory newspaper. After the British evacuated Newport in 1780 Southwick returned and began publishing the *Mercury* again. James Franklin's press was finally taken out of commission in the early 1820s, more than a century after it had printed the first issue of the *New-England Courant*. (It is on display at the Museum of Newport History.) The *Mercury* went on publishing under that name until 1928, when it merged with the *Weekly News*. In 2005 the newspaper changed format, becoming a free alternative weekly newspaper and reverting to its original name. As of this writing the paper continues to be published in Newport. Had its publication not been interrupted during the British occupation it would be America's oldest newspaper in continuous circulation.

MANY YEARS AFTER the fact, Benjamin Franklin would characterize his apprenticeship as "very tedious" and James as physically abusive, exploitative, envious of his talent and fame, and not as clever as the "ingenious" friends who contributed to his newspaper.[45] He would also minimize the advantage of having worked for his brother rather than in his father's tallow shop, reducing it to a matter of access to "better books."[46] That scorn and dismissiveness might be understandable as a reflection of his lingering resentment over the mistreatment he had received from the "passionate" James.[47] But it did a disservice both to James and to the truth. The record leaves little question that Ben's years as his brother's apprentice were the most formative of his life. Dismissed in the *Autobiography* as a bully and a boor, James was actually "the powerful liberating force in his brother's life."[48] Simply by familiarizing Benjamin with the *Spectator*, whose central idea was that one could and ought to improve oneself and become a better and more highly esteemed member of society, James helped lead his brother to a philosophy that would become the essence of his character and of his writing, in everything from *Poor Richard's Almanack* to the *Autobiography*. In addition to introducing him to "the world of words, of books, of ideas," James, through his battles with the government, gave his brother—who would one day "defy the rule of the Penns, the sovereignty of the king, and the terror of lightning"—what Claude-Anne Lopez and Eugenia W. Herbert called "his first heady taste of challenging authority."[49] (Thanks to James, Ben also got what would prove a valuable early lesson in staying cool under pressure. His 1774 interrogation by the Privy Council in the "Cockpit"—his finest public moment—was in some respects a repeat of his 1722 interrogation by the Massachusetts Governor's Council.) The opinions of the mature Benjamin Franklin about politics, press freedom, religion, medicine, and diplomacy—and his mettle as man and a rebel—all had their origins in his early years with James.

The older brother's fingerprints are equally recognizable on Benjamin's hugely successful career as a printer, author, and publisher—beginning at the beginning, with Ben's very James-like decision to start a printing house in Philadelphia even though no one except he and his partner Hugh Meredith believed the town could support a third printer. That business would struggle until, like James before him, Ben began creating content in the form of a newspaper. Especially during the early years of that publication, he frequently reached back to the *New-England Courant* for themes and ideas. Precisely as his brother's paper had done, Ben's *Pennsylvania Gazette* printed titillating letters about sexual impropriety and covered the war between the sexes from both the male and female perspectives. He also borrowed and half-borrowed *Courant* characters. A decade after James Franklin invented "Abigail Afterwit," Benjamin invented characters named "Abigail Twitterfield" and "Anthony Afterwit." In his complaints about a too-extravagant wife, Ben's Afterwit bears a striking resemblance to an earlier *Courant* character invented by James named "Anthony Fallshort." Ben's enemies accused his paper of some of the same crimes the *Courant* had supposedly committed, including indecency and an "abundant Malice against Religion and the Clergy."[50] Like James, he eloquently (if more tactfully) argued for his right to publish pieces that discomfited and angered some readers.

In 1732 Ben Franklin launched one of his most famous and lucrative ventures, *Poor Richard's Almanack*. Among the models he consulted in creating it was the then four-year-old *Rhode-Island Almanack*, whose author was the similarly named "Poor Robin," a sobriquet for James Franklin, who had already revolutionized the traditional almanac form. The antiquarian Clarence Brigham noted that, unlike the publishers of the other "dull" almanacs available at that point, James "tried to give his almanacs a literary and readable flavor."[51] What truly differentiated Poor Robin from the competition, though, was the addition of "proverbs, sayings and jests in the midst of the calendar information wherever there was a blank space that could be filled in."[52] Benjamin would famously exploit a similar approach to maximum effect. Having been inspired by James to add proverbs and aphorisms to his almanac, he also seems to have mined his collection of *Courant* issues for musings that could be converted to epigrams. It's likely, for example, that Benjamin took Nathaniel Gardner's assertion that "he is not the Happy man, who has abundance but he who is contented in the Enjoyment of what he has" and turned it into one of his most celebrated sayings, the much pithier "Who is rich? He that is content."[53]

If James had done nothing more for his brother than teach him his trade, Benjamin would still have owed him a debt of gratitude. James Franklin had been the most technically proficient, artistic, literary, and innovative printer in America. Part of Ben's genius was in recognizing that. Long after he left his brother's printing house and claimed to have put all thoughts of the abusive master behind him, he continued to keep a close eye on what James was doing in Rhode Island, always ready and willing to borrow a good idea and make it his own.

ON THE DAY James Franklin died, another printer and publisher sat in a New York jail awaiting prosecution. John Peter Zenger had been arrested two months earlier for offenses much like those that had landed James in jail in 1722. "Unlike Benjamin Franklin (but much like James Franklin)," wrote Franklin biographer Joyce Chaplin, "Zenger had, in his *New-York Weekly Journal*, attacked members of his colony's government."[54] He and his authors—men who had formed a "popular party" similar to the one in Massachusetts—had launched the *Journal* to counteract the propaganda campaign of Governor William Cosby, a man so arbitrary and vengeful in his exercise of power that Samuel Shute's imperiousness paled by comparison. In November 1734, a year after the paper's debut, Cosby had Zenger arrested and charged with printing "seditious libels."

His trial began on August 4, 1735. One of his lawyers was Andrew Hamilton, a prominent Philadelphian who eleven years earlier, upon discovering he could not use the ship's quarters he had reserved for a passage to England, had generously offered them to a young stranger named Benjamin Franklin. In the intervening years, the two men had become close acquaintances. Inasmuch as James Franklin's earlier legal difficulties with the Massachusetts censors constituted the nearest thing to an American precedent for Zenger's case, Hamilton had undoubtedly familiarized himself with the particulars. It's nearly inconceivable that he would not have requested and received a firsthand account from Benjamin, who followed the Zenger trial very closely from Philadelphia, reporting on the proceedings and printing the court transcripts in his newspaper. Directionally, at the very least, James Franklin's published arguments for press freedom in the *New-England Courant* appear to have influenced Hamilton's defense. Like James, Hamilton cited Trenchard and Gordon's "Cato's Letters." The *Courant* had emphasized Cato number 32 on the difference between true and false libels. The heart of Hamilton's defense of Zenger was based on Cato number 100, "Discourse on Libels," a letter that expanded upon the ideas of number 32 and might well have been cited or quoted in defense of James had it been published earlier. (It appeared in October 1722, three months after James was released from jail.)

Although Hamilton didn't specifically cite the Couranteers' own arguments in defense of liberty of expression, he might well have read the December 1721 essays in which the newspaper had expressed what Perry Miller called the "utterly novel doctrine" that governmental errors and misdeeds "should be published rather than suppressed, because they less endanger the state when exposed than when circulated without opposition in private conversation."[55] That idea, combined with James's assertion that it was wicked to "anathematize" a printer for publishing an opposition

opinion, constituted an early version of the truth-as-a-defense appeal
Hamilton presented to the Zenger jurors.

Even if he had never read a word of the *New-England Courant*, Hamilton must have recognized something significant and useful in the fact that
neither of James Franklin's arrests had resulted in a prosecution: namely,
that although Americans believed impudence needed to be addressed,
they were reluctant to give government too much power to quash dissent.
When Hamilton's truth-as-a-defense argument against libel was rebuffed,
he was still able to win the jury by convincing its members that the issue
went beyond Zenger—that they were charged with protecting the idea of
free expression against the overreach of the government.

Zenger's acquittal six months and one day after James Franklin's death
was a landmark not because it changed the definition of libel to allow for
truth as a defense—it didn't—but because it disabused the royal government of the belief that the threat of prosecution for seditious libel was an
effective tool for limiting dissent. As the law professor Doug Linder has
pointed out, the belief that those tried on seditious libel charges would
benefit from "jury nullification"—juries acting in defiance of the stated
instructions of the judge in pursuit of a higher principle—"discouraged
prosecutions, and press freedom in America began to blossom."[56] From the
Zenger verdict forward until the Revolution, no court in America would
successfully prosecute a printer or publisher for seditious libel. "The trial
of Zenger in 1735 was the germ of American freedom, the morning star of
that liberty which subsequently revolutionized America," wrote Gouver-
neur Morris, great-grandson of Lewis Morris, one of the New York Popular Party leaders and a contributor to Zenger's newspaper.[57] But before
there was Zenger there was James Franklin. And before there was Andrew
Hamilton making his eloquent plea to the jurors of New York there was
the *New-England Courant* making its own eloquent arguments for press
freedom to the people of Massachusetts—arguments substantively similar not only to those employed in the Zenger case, but also to those that
would eventually secure freedom of the press in America.

ELISHA COOKE, SAMUEL ADAMS, AND
THE AMERICAN REVOLUTION

Samuel Shute never returned to Massachusetts. He did, however, nearly succeed in causing the province to lose its charter. When Shute filed a formal complaint against the Massachusetts House in 1723 he found a receptive audience among the many members of the English government who had been insisting since the rise of Elisha Cooke that Massachusetts was scheming to achieve independence from the Crown.

Realizing that his home colony was about to be stripped of its cherished liberties and perhaps come under martial law, Jeremiah Dummer, the colony's former agent in London, worked behind the scenes to strike a bargain with the Crown. The result was the "Explanatory Charter" of 1726. It explicitly stated that the royal governor possessed most of the powers that had been under dispute, including the power to manage military affairs, negative the House speaker, and protect England's rights to the valuable timber harvested in Maine. Those concessions overshadowed an important victory: Dummer preserved his colony's right to its own semi-autonomous government, something it had been in imminent danger of losing to those in England who wanted all of New England brought under much tighter and more centralized British control.

Despite the near certainty that rejecting the Explanatory Charter would cost Massachusetts its existing charter and bring severe punitive ramifications, the vote in the General Court was close. In a House session minimally attended because many members preferred to stay home rather than go on record one way or the other, there were 48 votes for acceptance and 38 votes against. The entire Boston contingent voted against accepting the charter, consequences be damned. Even Thomas Hutchinson later offered grudging admiration for the chutzpah of deputies who were "still resolute to risque all" by voting against a charter that, as George Ellis pointed out, was "calm and moderate, even if decisive in its terms," a fairly balanced response to a province that had been "not only indocile, but stiffly self-willed, refractory, and in fact rebellious."[58]

The periods immediately preceding and following the ratification of the Explanatory Charter saw a dip in the power and influence of the Popular Party. With Cooke away in London as part of an unsuccessful effort to argue the colony's case against Shute's charges, and with many voters and politicians unnerved by the prospect of British retaliation, the House of Representatives swung conservative, electing William Dudley as its speaker—the first time in more than a decade that the leadership position had gone to a man aligned with the Court Party. (Dudley reiterated that allegiance to the Crown by voting "Yay" on the Explanatory Charter.) In 1727, Samuel Kneeland's royalist-friendly *New-England Weekly Journal* declared Elisha Cooke's political career finished, dubbing him "Christopher Careless" and accusing him of being "a drunken, hot-tempered casuist who wasted his influence."[59] But neither Cooke nor his party was anywhere near finished. John Clark had retired from politics, but William Clark, Ezekiel Lewis, and Thomas Cushing were all still in the House. Each would be reelected annually for the next several years. Meanwhile, a new generation was being groomed for leadership. With Cooke's support, Samuel Adams Sr., later known as "the deacon," was elevated to Boston selectman in 1729. The two men sometimes talked strategy at the Adams house on Purchase Street, where Sam Adams Jr., seven years old at the time his father became a selectman, watched enthralled.

The Explanatory Charter was only a stopgap solution, a way to stave off a more devastating judgment against Massachusetts. No one understood that better than the man who had proposed it. In a letter written a year after the vote of acceptance, Jeremiah Dummer, who at that point still expected Samuel Shute to return to the colony as he had promised, expressed doubts the Assembly would "come into his [Shute's] demands," new charter or not.[60] Shute's Crown-appointed successor, William Burnet, quickly discovered that the people of Massachusetts had already recovered from their chastened state. If anything, Perry Miller wrote, the

House deputies under Cooke's leadership "behaved even more arrogantly toward Burnet than they had against Shute."[61] It didn't help that shortly after assuming the governorship in 1728 Burnet demanded an established salary of at least £1,000 and threatened action against the new charter if he didn't get it. Despite that threat and Burnet's attempt to sever the Popular Party from its power base by moving the General Court from Boston to Salem, Cooke was able to rally the House to defeat the salary demand. By late December 1729 the House was again on the attack, threatening to send agents to London to lodge a formal complaint against their still-new governor. Burnet retaliated by writing to England to accuse Cooke of being "a professed enemy to the king's lawful authority."[62] The fighting would have continued had Burnet not suffered a mortal accident, dying after being thrown from his carriage into some frigid water and taking sick with a fever. Many people were of the opinion that exasperation, not the accident or the subsequent sickness, had done him in.

Burnet's successor, the Boston native Jonathan Belcher, tried to flatter Cooke into submission by offering him a spot in his administration. When that failed he switched to demeaning and dismissing him, dubbing him "the late (now abandon'd) head of the scum."[63] But Belcher's mounting frustration with Cooke's opposition belied his claim that Cooke was a has-been. By 1734 he was complaining that the Popular Party leader "endeavoured, to poyson the Minds of His Countreymen, with his republican notions, in order to assert the Independency of New England"—almost the same accusation that the former royal surveyor Jonathan Bridger had leveled at Cooke fifteen years earlier.[64]

Cooke died in August 1737 at age fifty-nine; Thomas Hutchinson wrote that he was "worn out with service" to his cause.[65] His funeral was the "greatest" ever given a Bostonian who was neither a governor nor a Congregational minister. "Every church bell tolled solemnly, cannon boomed mournfully, the colors of every ship in the harbor flew at half-staff," wrote a chronicler of the city, G. B. Warden.[66] It didn't matter to most Bostonians that Cooke was "an unlikely hero," a man who drank to excess, recklessly pursued personal vendettas, and was a persona non grata with the king, not to mention someone who had used his power and position to feather his own nest.[67] Despite his substantial wealth—his estate included a dozen houses, several warehouses, thousands of acres of timberland that he owned personally, and a partner's stake in the Muscongus Company, which held the title to over thirty square miles of Maine wilderness—he had remained the people's champion, as the outpouring of grief from rank-and-file Bostonians demonstrated.

In the first elections after Cooke's death, the House again swung conservative. Even the Boston contingent included three representatives who "had the character of friends to government."[68] But that trend was short-lived. In 1739 the town replaced two of its Crown-friendly representatives with men who were "professedly disaffected to the governor and [were] promoters of popular measures."[69] Belcher complained that the "Common People" had "grown so Brassy, & hardy, as to be now combining in a Body to raise a Rebellion."[70] But his complaining annoyed the Crown, as did his failure to preemptively quash a new Massachusetts attempt to launch a private land bank. His general inability to tame the colony, together with an orchestrated Popular Party campaign to undermine his standing in England by way of "forged and anonymous letters" and "unscrupulous falsehoods," resulted in his dismissal in 1741.[71]

In 1746 Samuel Adams Sr. was elected to the Massachusetts House for the first time. He died two years later, but by that point his son and namesake had also entered the fray. A few days after the Impressment Riots of 1747, Samuel Adams Jr. published his first pamphlet, which maintained that the people had a "natural right" to band together and which criticized the wealthy for supporting the British officer who had ordered the impressment.[72] The younger Adams, wrote Gary B. Nash, was part of a growing group that opposed the new governor, William Shirley, and was "attempting to revive the populistic politics of the Elisha Cooke era."[73]

In January 1748 Adams expanded his populist campaign and stepped up the battle against the royal governor with a new newspaper, the

Independent Advertiser. Like James Franklin's *Courant*, the *Advertiser* re-printed "Cato's Letters" on liberty; it even counted among its contributors former Couranteer William Douglass, whose research on scarlet fever had finally earned him a small measure of the fame he had coveted. (It had not however, lessened his envy of Zabdiel Boylston, whom he contin-ued to despise and disparage even as he himself took up the practice of inoculation in subsequent epidemics.) By December 1749 the *Independent Advertiser* was defunct, but it had made its impact. In publicizing Shirley's failures and misdeeds, the newspaper had helped force him to sail to En-gland to defend himself. Another royal governor had been evicted.

The arrival of Governor Francis Bernard, who took over after the brief tenure of Thomas Pownall, perhaps the best liked of the Massachusetts royal governors, initiated the rise of Samuel Adams Jr. and his fellow pa-triot James Otis. When England imposed the Stamp Act in 1765, Adams was propelled into the House of Representatives on the strength of a pub-lic indignation that, as historian Richard Bushman wrote, reconstituted "a popular party as large and implacable as the bloc that backed Cooke against Shute."[74]

The comparison was not gratuitous. As a young boy, Adams had been indoctrinated into Whig politics literally at the feet of Elisha Cooke. By nature or by calculation he had adopted the public persona of his father's mentor, affecting the dress and bearing of a common man to a degree that his cousin John Adams found excessive and unseemly. His cultiva-tion and consolidation of supporters outside of the political class proved crucial, though, when, from the Stamp Act forward, the Crown stopped trying to force intransigent colonial governments into compliance and began disabling and circumventing them. Elisha Cooke had been the first politician in America to realize that "the people" could be a force in poli-tics. Now Sam Adams gave Cooke's notion teeth by empowering political organizations that operated outside of elected government and harnessed the power—and the threat—of public anger over British policy. The Sons of Liberty, so named by Adams, became the chief vehicle for that effort.

Simultaneously, he built popular support for the patriot cause among prospective Sons of Liberty members and others by helping to launch a second radical newspaper, the revamped *Boston Gazette*, which Benjamin Edes and John Gill had purchased from James Franklin's old adversary Samuel Kneeland in 1755.[75]

Following the repeal of the Stamp Act in March 1766, Adams was reelected to the House with more votes than any of his fellow Boston representatives, at long last achieving a Cooke-like prestige. Bernard tried to reassert control by negativing the charismatic James Otis as speaker; but he quickly discovered that Massachusetts had never made peace with the Explanatory Charter's assertion that the governor had a legal right to veto a speaker. Adams, his party, and their supporters "rose to a man at this 'signal to battle' and screamed for vengeance upon Bernard."[76] When the General Court met in the spring of 1769, the governor tried to intimidate its members by stationing British soldiers outside the Town House and pointing two cannon at its doors. His heavy hand and vengeful inclination made him, like Samuel Shute before him, "an easy target for attacks."[77] Adams and his friends hounded him, first by obtaining and publishing copies of his letters to London and then by sending the king a seventeen-point argument for his removal as governor "forever."[78] All the governor could do was shut down the Court again, this time until January 1770. By that point King George III had come to the conclusion that Bernard was no match for the Americans and ordered him replaced.

Thomas Hutchinson, the final civilian royal governor of Massachusetts, had advantages over most of his predecessors: a lifetime spent in Boston, an insider's knowledge of every aspect of provincial politics, and a record as a political moderate. As a historian, Hutchinson had made a close examination of his predecessors' administrations and was in a position to avoid their mistakes. He also had the benefit of a brief, earlier stint as interim governor before Bernard's arrival in 1760. But just as he had found himself "embroiled in argument with the opposition from almost the first day of his acting governorship," he now foolishly tried to take the spine out of the General Court by moving it away from Boston.[79] The ploy failed. After the Boston Massacre in March 1770, Samuel Adams and others forced him to withdraw both regiments of British soldiers from Boston. But it was Parliament's 1772 decision to pay Hutchinson and other royal governors a fixed salary directly—thereby depriving the colonial assemblies of their long-standing ability to check a governor's exercise of the royal prerogative by threatening to reduce or delay his compensation— that heralded the downfall of his administration. Decades earlier, Elisha Cooke's stubborn refusal to grant Samuel Shute a fixed salary had seemed to some persons gratuitously contentious and even disloyal, suggesting as it did that a royal governor was, by nature and definition, his colony's adversary. But now that England had circumvented the charter, which stipulated that the Americans, through their home government, should pay the governor, the people viewed Thomas Hutchison's fixed salary as a dire and immediate threat to their liberty. Led by Samuel Adams, they condemned the governor for accepting his compensation from England. The *Boston Gazette* declared that "a governor independent of the people for his *support*, as well as his *political being*, is in fact a MASTER and . . . soon will be a TYRANT."[80] The colony's impassioned opposition to the Tea Act—culminating in the Boston Tea Party of December 1773—was less about "taxation without representation" than its outrage over the Crown's utilization of the revenue from the tax on tea to fund the direct payment of Hutchinson's salary. Shortly after the Tea Party destroyed approximately £9,000 worth of cargo, Hutchinson decided to leave the colony. He retreated to his country house in Milton, where he awaited the arrival of his replacement, General Thomas Gage. On June 1, 1774, Hutchinson boarded the ship *Minerva* for England, leaving behind him what he called the "most perverse set of men upon earth."[81] He also left behind "a province in open rebellion."[82]

The political machine that Elisha Cooke had begun building in 1719 and had perfected by late 1721 had forced Shute, Belcher, Shirley, Bernard, and Hutchinson out of Massachusetts. Over the decades it had grown and evolved, so that by the eve of the American Revolution the original Caucus Club had become three caucuses and spawned not only the Sons of Liberty, but also the Long Room Club and the Committee of Correspondence. (Arguably, the *Boston Gazette*, a direct spiritual descendant of James Franklin's 1721 newspaper, was part of the machine as well.) Yet, for all that, it remained fundamentally the same mechanism that Cooke had introduced decades earlier. Indeed, at least one pre-Revolutionary victim of its effectiveness saw the visage of Cooke himself in the faces of the Patriot opposition. In a letter to the Earl of Shelburne just eight years before the start of the American Revolution, Governor Francis Bernard wrote that "the faction against him was the same that attacked his distant relative" Samuel Shute.[83]

Throughout Elisha Cooke's career his enemies had repeatedly accused him of scheming for independence from England. Now, as revolution and independence drew near, the royal governor had seen fit to lump him in with the men who would foment it. He was with the patriots, where he had always belonged.

ACKNOWLEDGMENTS

I n researching this book I consulted hundreds of primary sources including newspapers, pamphlets, broadsides, records of governmental proceedings in Boston and in London, letters, diaries, and maps. For access to digitized and microfilm copies of those materials, and to the scores of books and academic journals I also needed to construct this narrative, I would like to thank the staffs of the Memorial Library at the University of Wisconsin–Madison and the Wisconsin Historical Society.

My research took me to Boston and Rhode Island. At the Massachusetts Historical Society I had the great privilege of viewing original copies of the *New-England Courant*. At the Rhode Island Historical Society in Providence I found a wealth of information about James Franklin and his family post-Boston. The Newport Historical Society assisted me in locating the gravestones of James and Ann Franklin in the Common Burying Ground beside Island Cemetery. I also visited the Museum of Newport History, where the printing press James and Benjamin Franklin used to print the *Courant* is on display. After spending so much time reading and writing about the Franklin brothers it was a thrill to see their printing press "in the flesh." My thanks to each of those fine institutions.

There is no single history of anything. Our best chance at understanding important events and persons is by way of a rigorous study of the known facts together with a kind of triangulation of complementary and disparate interpretations of those facts. For valuable perspectives on the political and social forces at work during the colonial and Revolutionary periods I am indebted to Perry Miller, Bernard Bailyn, G. B. Warden, Gary B. Nash, Gordon S. Wood, Alan Taylor, Clinton Rossiter, and John Gorham Palfrey, among others. Before Thomas Hutchinson became the final civilian royal governor of Massachusetts he wrote the first part of a perceptive and illuminating history of that colony. To read his take on the politics of the early eighteenth century is to understand the consternation with which American loyalists regarded what would prove the beginning of the end of British rule in America.

I gained much of my understanding of Western medicine in the early eighteenth century, and of the menace of infectious diseases in general and of smallpox in particular, from medical historians and biographers including John Duffy, Richard H. Shryock, Otho T. Beall Jr., Reginald M. Fitz, Whitfield J. Bell, Elizabeth A. Fenn, Henry R. Viets, and Donald R. Hopkins. Similarly, press historians Isaiah Thomas, Charles E. Clark, Clyde Augustus Duniway, William David Sloan, Julie Hedgepeth Williams, Joseph Fireoved, and Frank Luther Mott, among others, provided me with the context necessary to understand the significance of James Franklin's *Courant*. Among the many excellent Benjamin Franklin biographies that informed this work were those by J. A. Leo Lemay, Carl Van Doren, Joyce E. Chaplin, H. W. Brands, David Waldstreicher, Claude-Anne Lopez, Eugenia W. Herbert, Albert Furtwangler, and Walter Isaacson. Arthur Bernon Tourtellot's *Benjamin Franklin: The Shaping of Genius, the Boston Years*, offered the most detailed account of Ben Franklin's apprenticeship with James and proved invaluable. Nian-Sheng Huang's biography of Josiah Franklin offered a fascinating perspective on the family. And I am no less indebted to Cotton Mather's biographers, especially Kenneth Silverman and David Levin, who managed to throw light on a man so complicated even Nathaniel Hawthorne struggled to understand him. Gerald Marvin Mager's doctoral dissertation on Zabdiel Boylston remains the essential starting point for any discussion of that daring physician.

I am not the first author to address the Boston inoculation experiment of 1721. I learned from all of my predecessors, including Jennifer Lee Carrell, John B. Blake, Carolyn Garrett Cline, Ola Elizabeth Winslow, Margot Minardi, Tony Williams, and the aforementioned Gerald Mager.

Several scholars, authors, and scientists were kind enough to answer my questions by email or letter. I'm grateful to the late Leo LeMay and to H. W. Brands, Elizabeth Fenn, Nian-Sheng Huang, Stephen Pemberton, Ronald L. Numbers, and D. A. Henderson, the man who led the international effort to eradicate smallpox.

Thanks to my editor, Alice Mayhew, who told me with conviction and passion what was wrong with my manuscript and what was right with it, and was correct on both counts. To say it's an honor to be edited by her would be an understatement. The same goes for being published by Jonathan Karp. Eight years ago Jon was heading up another imprint when he purchased the proposal for my at-that-point unwritten book. When he left that position to become the publisher of Simon & Schuster I feared the book had lost its champion. But one day about two years later he sent me an email expressing his interest in possibly obtaining the rights to the book for S&S. I have never been more grateful for an email. Thanks, also, to assistant editor Stuart Roberts, who guided me through the process of first-time authorship; to copy editor Bob Castillo, who brought an impressive command of the material to his work; to Jackie Seow, who oversaw the jacket design; and to the rest of the publication team at Simon & Schuster.

I never would have had the temerity to begin this book without the coaxing of my good friend and fellow author James Campbell. Jim and I were having a drink at a Madison, Wisconsin, bar one evening some eight years ago when I told him I'd written a rough draft of a screenplay about a smallpox epidemic in colonial America and the first widespread use of inoculation in Western medicine. He asked me to tell him more, and by the time the evening was over he was insisting that I expand the idea into a nonfiction book. Write up a short synopsis, he said. I'll pass it along to my agent. If he likes the idea, you can decide what you want to do. A few months (and a lot of work) later I had an agent and a book contract. Since then, through the several ups and downs of the journey to publication, Jim has remained the book's most stalwart supporter.

I'd like to thank my agent, David McCormick, who has been with me from inception of this book. David recognized something in those first few pages I sent him at Jim Campbell's urging, helped and encouraged me in the writing of my proposal, and remained a partner as this book evolved, at one point providing me with a detailed vision for reshaping the narrative.

I wrote this book in many locations, but if there's one that deserves a special shout-out, it's the Ground Zero coffee shop in Madison, Wisconsin.

I am grateful for the love and support I received before and during the writing of this book from my mother, Mary Coss, my late father, James Coss, and my in-laws, the late Garrett and Dee Fleming.

My biggest debt is to my wife, Judy, who over the course of the long and sometimes painful gestation of this book kept our lives functioning while, day after day, night after night, and weekend after weekend, I disappeared (literally and figuratively) to research, write, and revise. I want her and our four sons, Dylan, Kevin, Brett, and Stephen, to know how much I appreciate their patience. It's not easy for the author to explain why his book is taking so long to finish. It's a far more thankless and tedious job for his family to have to do that for him. Now that this book is published I can relieve them of that burden. My hope is that everyone who wondered why it was so long in the making will find a satisfying and compelling answer in these pages.

NOTES

Abbreviations used in Notes:

BNL   *Boston News-Letter*
BG   *Boston Gazette*
NEC   *New-England Courant*
Autobiography   *The Autobiography of Benjamin Franklin*

PROLOGUE

1. Thomas Robie, *A Letter to a Certain Gentleman Desiring a Particular Account May be Given of a Wonderful Meteor that Appeared in New-England, on December 11, 1719, In The Evening* (Boston: J Franklin for D. Henchman, 1719), 3.

2. Ibid., 4.

3. Ibid., 8.

4. Increase Mather, *Heaven's Alarm to the World. Or a Sermon Wherein is Shewed, that Fearful Sights and Signs in Heaven are the Presages of great Calamities at hand*, 2nd ed. (Boston: printed for Samuel Sewall and sold by Joseph Browning, 1682) (preached at a lecture, Boston in New-England, January 20, 1680).

5. Increase Mather, *Burnings bewailed: in a sermon, occasioned by the lamentable fire*

which was in Boston, October 2d. 1711. In which the sins which provoke the Lord to kindle fires, are enquired into (Boston: Printed and sold by Timothy Green, 1712).

6. Robie, *A Letter*, 8.

7. John Colman, *The distressed state of the town of Boston, &c. considered. In a letter from a gentleman in the town, to his friend in the countrey* [*sic*] (Boston: Printed for Nicholas Boone, Benjamin Gray, and John Edwards, 1720), 1–4.

8. John Gordon Palfrey, *A Compendious History of New England from the Discovery by Europeans to the First General Congress of the Anglo-American Colonies,* vol. 3 (Boston: H. C. Shepard, 1873), 376.

9. Ann-Eliza H. Lewis, ed., *Highway to the Past: The Archaeology of Boston's Big Dig* (Boston: William Francis Galvin, 2001), 12.

10. *BNL*, December 12, 1720, no. 874.

11. *BNL*, December 26, 1720, no. 876.

12. Charles Kittredge True, *Shawmut: Or, The Settlement of Boston by the Puritan Pilgrims* (Boston: Charles Waite, 1847), 117.

CHAPTER 1: IDOL OF THE MOB

1. Perry Miller, *The New England Mind: From Colony to Province*, vol. 2 (Boston: Beacon Press, 1961), 311.

2. *BNL*, October 8, 1716, no. 651.

3. J. A. Leo Lemay, *The Life of Benjamin Franklin,* vol. 1: *Journalist 1706–1730* (Philadelphia: University of Pennsylvania Press, 2006), 80.

4. John Eliot, *A Biographical Dictionary Containing A Brief Account of the First Settlers, and Other Eminent Characters Among the Magistrates, Ministers, Literary and Worthy Men in New-England* (Salem: Cushing and Appleton, 1809), 126.

5. Ibid.

6. Zachariah G. Whitman, *History of the Ancient and Honorable Artillery Company (Revised and Enlarged) from its Formation in 1637 and Charter in 1638, To The Present Time; Comprising the Biographies of the Distinguished Civil, Literary, Religious, and Military Men of the Colony, Province, and Commonwealth*, 2nd ed. (Boston: Printed by John H. Eastburn, 1842), 236.

7. Everett Kimball, *The Public Life of Joseph Dudley: A Study of the Colonial Policy of the Stuarts in New England 1600–1715* (New York: Longmans, Green and Co., 1911), 179.

8. Whitman, *History*, 236.

9. Gary B. Nash, *The Urban Crucible: The Northern Seaports and the Origins of*

the American Revolution, abridged ed. (Cambridge: Harvard University Press, 1998), 49.

10. [Elisha Cooke?], *My son, fear thou the Lord* (second pamphlet in opposition to the incorporation of Boston), Publications of The Colonial Society of Massachusetts, vol. 10, Transactions 1904–1906 (Boston: Published by the Society, 1907), 352.

11. [Elisha Cooke?], *A Dialogue Between a Boston Man and a Country Man* (first pamphlet in opposition to the incorporation of Boston), ibid., 345.

12. Nash, *Urban Crucible*, 52.

13. Ibid., 83.

14. *Diary of Samuel Sewall: 1674–1729*, Collections of the Massachusetts Historical Society, vol. 7, 5th series (Boston: Published by the Society, 1882), 105.

15. *BNL*, October 8, 1716, no. 651.

16. Miller, *New England Mind*, 276. (The letter from Dudley to a "Kinsman" and dated Boston, January 12, 1704, was first reproduced in Sir Henry Ashurst's pamphlet *The Deplorable State of New England* (London: n.p., 1708), 9.)

17. *Diary of Samuel Sewall*, 106.

18. George E. Ellis, "The Royal Governors," in *The Memorial History of Boston, Including Suffolk County, Massachusetts, 1630–1880*, ed. Justin Winsor, vol. 2 (Boston: Ticknor and Company, 1881), 52.

19. Timothy Pitkin, *A Political and Civil History of the United States of America from the Year 1763*, vol. 1 (New Haven: Hezekiah Howe and Durrie & Peck, 1828), 127.

20. *Diary of Samuel Sewall*, 211.

21. Thomas Hutchinson, *The History of the Province of Massachusetts-Bay: From the Charter of King William and Queen Mary in 1691, Until the Year 1750*, vol. 2 (Boston: printed by Thomas & John Fleet, 1767), 224.

22. Thomas Lechmere to [John Winthrop?], Boston, May 4, 1719, in Collections of the Massachusetts Historical Society, 6th series, vol. 5 (Boston: The Society, 1892), 388n. (Lechmere wrote: "At the Election this week for Deputys they have chosen Dr. Cooke, Dr. Noyes, W. Clarke, Deacon Joy, all by a considerable majority, notwithstanding all endeavours used to the contrary.")

23. David W. Conroy, *In Public Houses: Drink & the Revolution of Authority in Colonial Massachusetts* (Chapel Hill: University of North Carolina Press, 1995), 170.

24. Nash, *Urban Crucible*, 53.

25. G. B. Warden, *Boston, 1689–1776* (Boston: Little, Brown and Co., 1970), 93.

26. Henry Flanders, *The Lives and Times of the Chief Justices of the Supreme Court of the United States*, vol. 1 (Philadelphia: J. B. Lippincott and Co., 1874), 620n.

27. Hutchinson, *History*, 224.

28. Mr. Secretary Craggs to Governor Shute, London, July 16, 1719, in *Calendar of*

State Papers, Colonial Series, America and the West Indies, vol. 31, 1719–1720, ed. Cecil Headlam (London: His Majesty's Stationery Office, 1933), 160. Also at: http://www.british-history.ac.uk/cal-state-papers/colonial/america-west-indies/vol31/pp159-172 (accessed February 2, 2015).

29. Mr. Bridger to Mr. Popple, Boston, July 17, 1719, ibid.

30. Mr. Bridger to [Mr. Popple?], Boston, May 1, 1720, in *Calendar of State Papers, Colonial Series, America and the West Indies*, vol. 32, 1720–1721, ed. Cecil Headlam (London: His Majesty's Stationery Office, 1933), 37. Also at: http://www.british-history.ac.uk/cal-state-papers/colonial/america-west-indies/vol32/pp36-44 (accessed February 2, 2015).

31. *BNL*, June 6, 1720, no. 846. (Transcript of speech to the General Court by Governor Shute. The full quote reads: "That when it shall please GOD that we Meet again in a General Assembly (which shall be as soon as possible) that you will not let this Province Suffer by the Perverse temper of a particular Person, but that you will choose One for a Speaker that has no other view, but that of the Publick Good; One that Fears GOD and Honours the KING.")

32. Elisha Cooke, *Mr. Cooke's Just and Seasonable Vindication respecting some affairs transacted in the late General Assembly at Boston* (Boston: Printed by B. Green, 1720), 14.

33. Hutchinson, *History*, 238–239.

34. *Journals of the House of Representatives of Massachusetts, 1718–1720*, vol. 2 (Cambridge: Massachusetts Historical Society, 1921), 359 (March 15, 1721).

35. Hutchinson, *History*, 245.

36. *Diary of Samuel Sewall*, 286 (entry from March 31, 1721); *BG*, April 3, 1721, no. 68 (Samuel Shute speech to the House of Representatives).

37. Conroy, *In Public Houses*, introduction, 1. ("Damn [Yeamans]," Taylor cried, "why don't he come out to me, I wish I could see the dog come out—'a God I would have some of his blood." From *Court of General Sessions of the Peace, Suffolk, Record Book, 1719–1725*, April 4, 1721 (80–81).)

38. The South Sea Company, a trading behemoth that had received favored status from the British government, had suddenly and unexpectedly gone bankrupt in September 1720, collapsing the English financial markets and ruining thousands of investors who had gone all-in on what they had been led to believe was a sure thing.

CHAPTER 2: JAMES AND BENJAMIN

1. Cotton Mather to John Winthrop (nephew of Connecticut Governor Fitz-John Winthrop), Boston, December 27, 1707, in Abijah Perkins Marvin, *The Life and*

Times of Cotton Mather: Or a Boston Minister of Two Centuries: 1663–1728 (Boston: Congregational Sunday-School and Publishing Society, 1892), 346.

2. Arthur Bernon Tourtellot, *Benjamin Franklin: The Shaping of Genius; The Boston Years* (Garden City, NY: Doubleday and Co., 1977), 205.

3. Walter M. Whitehill and Sinclair H. Hitchings, eds., *Boston Prints and Printmakers, 1670–1775*, Publications of the Colonial Society of Massachusetts, vol. 46 (Boston: The Society, 1973), ix.

4. Kevin Williams, *Read All About It!: A History of the British Newspaper* (Abingdon, Oxfordshire: Routledge, 2010), 33.

5. *BNL*, November 10, 1718, no. 760 ("On Monday last the 3d Currant an awful and Lamentable Providence fell out here . . . so that they were Drowned, and all found and Interred except George Cutler").

6. Benjamin Franklin, *The Autobiography and Other Writings*, ed. Kenneth Silverman (New York: Penguin Books, 1986), 14.

7. *BNL*, March 2, 1719, no. 776.

8. *The Diary of Cotton Mather*, vol. 2, 1709–1724 (New York: Frederick Ungar, [1957?]), 566–567 (entry for November 10, 1718).

9. *Autobiography*, 14.

10. Ibid., 23.

11. Alan Taylor, *American Colonies: The Settling of North America* (New York: Penguin Group, 2001), 304.

12. William David Sloan and Julie Hedgepeth Williams, *The Early American Press: 1690–1783* (Westport, CT: Greenwood Press, 1994), 18.

13. *BG*, April 25, 1720, no. 19.

14. *BG*, August 22, 1720, no. 36. (Sometime between August 1 and this date, James Franklin was fired and Kneeland was contracted as the *Gazette*'s printer.)

15. *Autobiography*, 11.

16. *NEC*, January 15, 1722, no. 24.

17. Charles E. Clark, *The Public Prints: The Newspaper in Anglo-American Culture, 1665–1740* (New York: Oxford University Press, 1994), 104.

18. Nian-Sheng Huang, *Franklin's Father Josiah: Life of a Colonial Boston Tallow Chandler, 1657–1745* (Philadelphia: American Philosophical Society, 2000), 75. (Huang wrote that after helping set James up in business, Josiah signed two bonds with him "to secure money and help the business. Both were dated June 7, 1720, totaling almost £250.")

19. *A Letter to an Eminent Clergyman in the Massachusetts Bay: Containing Some Just Remarks, and necessary Cautions, relating to Public Affairs in that Province* (Boston: Benjamin Gray, 1721), 9–11. (The imminent publication of this uncredited pamphlet

was announced in an advertisement by Benjamin Gray in the February 27 *Boston Gazette*.)

20. Massachusetts Council order from J. Willard, Secretary, in *Colonial Currency Reprints,* ed. Andrew McFarland Davis, vol. 2, 1682–1751 (Boston: The Prince Society, 1911), 244. ("A Pamphlet Entituled [*sic*], A Letter to an Eminent Clergy-Man in the Massachusetts-Bay . . . contains in it many Vile, Scandalous and very Abusive Expressions which greatly Reflect on His Majesty's Government and People of this Province, and tend to disturb the Public Peace. At the same time Benj. Gray of Boston Book-seller . . . Acknowledged that he had caused the same to be Printed . . . Advised, That the Attorney-General be directed to Prosecute in the Law the said Benj. Gray, or any other Person that may have been concerned in the making or Publishing the said Pamphlet." February 28, 1721.)

21. Defoe's 1710 essay "News From the Moon" was published by Benjamin Gray on March 13, 1721. The great English satirist took public officials to task for attempting to punish their critics. The alleged offender in his story is a tailor who, according to the customs of the strange "Lunar World" he inhabits, is one of society's designated "Satyrs." His job is to fashion an extremely unflattering "Character Coat" for those found guilty of knavishness, cowardice, drunkenness, or viciousness. When a number of prominent and esteemed men try on a coat he has sewn and decide that it fits perfectly—so well that each is convinced it was intended specifically for him—the tailor is dragged into court and charged with defamation.

22. The advertisement appeared in the March 13, 1721, *Boston Gazette* and read: "Just Published, The Mount Hope Packet: And News from the Moon, both to be Sold by Benjamin Gray Bookseller, at his Shop Opposite to the Brick Church, where all Gentlemen, Trades-men and others may be supply'd by Wholesail or Retail at reasonable rates, with *all the Letters, Postscripts, News, Dialogues, and other Pamphlets, which come out from Time to Time*" (emphasis mine).

23. *Journals of the House,* vol. 2: 359. (Shute said: "I must observe to you, that we have been so unhappy of late, as to have many Factious and Scandalous Papers, Printed and publickly Sold at Boston, highly reflecting upon the Government, and tending to disquiet the minds of His Majesties good Subjects: I therefore make no doubt, that whosoever is a lover of the Privileges, Peace & good Order of this Province, will be very desirous to have a Law made, to prevent this pernicious and dangerous practice for the time to come, and more especially since it is the King my Master's positive Commands, that no book or Paper shall be printed without my License first obtained.")

24. See Carolyn Garrett Cline, *The Hell-Fire Club: A Study of the Men Who Founded the*

New England Courant and the Inoculation Dispute They Fathered (MA thesis, Indiana University, Bloomington, 1976), 78–79. (Cline compared the output of the town printers and calculated that Bartholomew Green printed 24 imprints, Kneeland 13, Fleet 7, James Franklin 4, Nicholas Boone 2, John Allen 2. Together, Kneeland and Green claimed 71 percent of the town's printing.)

25. See Clyde Augustus Duniway, *The Development of Freedom of the Press in Massachusetts*, in Harvard Historical Studies, vol. 11 (New York: Longmans, Green, and Co., 1906), 94. (In the May 2, 1721, *Records of Superior Court of Judicature, 1719–1721* (p. 356), the court declared that it would not prosecute Benjamin Gray for "Letter to an Eminent Clergyman" because he had "declared to the Court, that he had no design in Publishing & Printing the s[ai]d Advertise[ment] & Pamphlet, to Affront the Hono[rable] Council; and likewise expressed his Sorrow for what he had done amiss; & humbly moving that he might be discharged from s[ai]d Recognizance, he was thereupon Discharged from the same by Proclamation.")

CHAPTER 3: THE FALLEN ANGEL

1. Cotton Mather to Thomas Prince, Boston, February 12, 1721, in *Diary of Cotton Mather*, vol. 2: 681. See also Kenneth Silverman, *The Life and Times of Cotton Mather* (New York: Harper & Row, 1984), 319. (Mather confessed to Prince that he performed "pitifully." "This last bout," he wrote, "has been the most Shocking, that I have had these twenty years." Silverman observed that Mather's reference to his sudden disability points to a return of a stutter that had disabled him several times since adolescence. The minister's singsong cadence of speaking, which is also reflected in his writing, seems to have been a means of staving off his stammer.)

2. *Diary of Cotton Mather*, vol. 2: 613.; Cotton Mather, *The Lord of Hosts Adored; and the King of Glory Proclaimed* (Boston: Robert Starkey, 1721), 37.

3. Silverman, *Life and Times*, 14.

4. David Levin, *Cotton Mather: The Young Life of the Lord's Remembrancer 1663–1703* (Cambridge: Harvard University Press, 1978), 147.

5. Ibid., 152.

6. "Spectral evidence" refers to a claim by an alleged victim of witchcraft that he or she had been assaulted by an incorporeal form of the person accused—a specter that had appeared in a vision or a dream, which was therefore invisible to others. Impossible to corroborate, it was also impossible to refute.

7. Levin, *Cotton Mather*, 120.

8. Ibid., 274.

9. Ibid., 286–287.

10. Silverman, *Life and Times*, 221.

11. Levin, *Cotton Mather*, 75.

12. Cotton Mather, *Bonifacius, An Essay upon the Good*, ed. David Levin (Cambridge: The Belknap Press, 1966), 82. (Mather reminded readers that the "priests of old" frequently served the physical as well as spiritual needs of their flock. He wrote that it was "an angelical conjunction, when the ministers who do the pleasure of CHRIST, shall also be physicians and Raphaels unto their people!")

13. Silverman, *Life and Times*, 254.

14. *Diary of Cotton Mather*, vol. 2: 245–246.

15. Silverman, *Life and Times*, 270. (Caulfield, as quoted by Silverman, was referring to a pamphlet, *Letter About a Good Management under the Distemper of the Measles*. It was written in plain, practical language and advised those who could not afford physicians on caring for patients. Unlike some of Mather's earlier medical works it did not describe illness as punishment from Heaven.)

16. *Diary of Cotton Mather*, vol. 2: 282. (February 5, 1714)

17. *Journals of the House of Representatives of Massachusetts, 1715–1717*, vol. 1 (Boston: Massachusetts Historical Society, 1919), 175–177.

18. Cotton Mather to [William Ashurst?], in *Diary of Cotton Mather*, vol. 2: 420.

19. Cotton Mather to Oliver Noyes, Boston, November (?), 1716, in *Diary of Cotton Mather*, vol. 2: 417.

20. James B. Bell, *A War of Religion: Dissenters, Anglicans, and the American Revolution* (New York: Palgrave Macmillan, 2008), 8.

21. Cotton Mather, *Concio ad populum: A Distressed People Entertained with Proposals for the Relief of Their Distresses* (Boston: Green for B. Eliot, 1719), 20, 24, 25. (Mather delivered this sermon on March 12, 1719.)

22. *Diary of Samuel Sewall*, 214.

23. Ibid., 222. (On July 13, 1719, Sewall wrote: "As I was at Din[n]er, Mr. Cooke sent me Dr. Cotton Mather's high praises of the Governour, printed from the Flying Post, May, 16.")

24. [Cotton Mather] to Samuel Sewall, Boston, April 13, 1720, Collections of the Massachusetts Historical Society, 4th series, vol. 2 (Boston: Crosby, Nichols, and Co., 1854), 122.

25. Ibid., 123.

26. Virginia Bernhard, "Cotton Mather's 'Most Unhappy Wife': Reflections on the Uses of Historical Evidence," *New England Quarterly* 60, no. 3 (September 1987), 342.

27. Levin, *Cotton Mather*, 282.

28. *Selected Letters of Cotton Mather*, ed. Kenneth Silverman (Baton Rouge: Louisiana State University Press, 1971), 198.

29. [Cotton Mather], *News from Robinson Cruso's Island: with an Appendix Relating to Mr. Cook's Late Pamphlet* (Boston: [Printed by J. Franklin?], 1720), 1–4.

30. Silverman, *Life and Times*, 325.

31. *New News from Robinson Cruso's Island,* in *Colonial Currency Reprints*, 133.

32. Silverman, *Life and Times*, 326.

33. *Diary of Cotton Mather*, vol. 2: 607 (March 16, 1721); Silverman, *Life and Times*, 316.

34. *Diary of Cotton Mather*, vol. 2: 609 (March 24, 1721).

35. Ibid., 611 (April 4, 1721).

36. Ibid., 616 (May 1, 1721).

37. Cotton Mather, *The Lord of Hosts Adored* (Boston: printed for Robert Starkey, 1721), 21, 37, 42–43.

CHAPTER 4: THE MOST TERRIBLE MINISTER OF DEATH

1. *Academic American Encyclopedia*, vol. 17, s.v. "smallpox," 365.

2. Michael B. A. Oldstone, *Viruses, Plagues and History: Past, Present and Future* (New York: Oxford University Press, 2010), 74.

3. Ibid., 63.

4. Alfred Jay Bollet, *Plagues and Poxes: The Impact of Human History on Epidemic Disease* (New York: Demos Medical Publishing, 2004), 79; Elizabeth A. Fenn, *Pox Americana: The Great Smallpox Epidemic of 1775–82* (New York: Hill & Wang, 2001), 23.

5. R. S. Bray, *Armies of Pestilence: The Impact of Disease on History* (Cambridge: James Clarke & Co., 1996), 129.

6. Jim Vrabel, *When in Boston, A Time Line & Almanac* (Boston: Northeastern University Press, 2014), 2.

7. *Bradford's History "Of Plimoth Plantation": From the Original Manuscript (With a Report of the Proceeding Incident to the Return of the Manuscript to Massachusetts)* (Carlisle, MA: Applewood Books, 2010), 387–388.

8. Levin, *Cotton Mather*, 67; Cotton Mather to John Cotton, Boston, November 1678, Collections of the Massachusetts Historical Society, 4th series, vol. 8 (Boston: Wiggin & Lunt, 1868), 383–84.

9. *Public Occurrences Both Foreign and Domestick*, September 25, 1690, no.1; *Diary of Cotton Mather, 1681–1708,* Collections of the Massachusetts Historical Society,

7th series, vol. 7 (Boston: The Society, 1911), 451 (Mather wrote: "More than fourscore people, were in this black Month of *December*, carried from this Town to their long Home."); Samuel Bayard Woodward, "The Story of Smallpox in Massachusetts," *New England Journal of Medicine* 206, no. 23 (June 9, 1932): 1183.

CHAPTER 5: HIS MAJESTY'S SHIP *SEAHORSE*

1. Marcus Rediker, "The Pirate and the Gallows: An Atlantic Theater of Terror and Resistance," the American Historical Association, http://webdoc.sub.gwdg .de/ebook/p/2005/history_cooperative/www.historycooperative.org/proceedings /seascapes/rediker.html (accessed February 4, 2015); Marcus Rediker, *Villains of all Nations: Atlantic Pirates in the Golden Age* (Boston: Beacon Press, 2004), 9.
2. Rediker, "Pirate and Gallows."
3. *BG*, November 28, 1720, no. 50.
4. Jennifer Lee Carrell, *The Speckled Monster: A Historical Tale of Battling Smallpox* (New York: Penguin Group, 2004), 138–139.
5. Ibid., 139.
6. Ibid.
7. *BG*, April 3, 1721, no. 68.
8. *BG*, January 16, 1721, no. 57; *BG*, February 6, 1721, no. 60; *BG*, January 16, 1721, no. 57.
9. *BNL*, April 13, 1721, no. 892.
10. *BNL*, April 17, 1721, no. 893. (Although the *News-Letter* was a weekly, it sometimes appeared twice in one week, apparently in an attempt to catch up on the news and disprove its reputation for chronic tardiness.)
11. Carrell, *Speckled Monster*, 139.

CHAPTER 6: PESTILENCE AND POLITICS

1. *BG*, May 8, 1721, no. 74.
2. *A Report of the Record Commissioners of the City of Boston: Containing the Records of Boston Selectmen, 1716 to 1736* (Boston: Rockwell & Churchill, 1885), 81.
3. Hutchinson, *History*, 249.
4. Warden, *Boston*, 97.
5. *Record Commissioners . . . Selectmen*, 82.
6. *A Report of the Record Commissioners of the City of Boston: Containing the Boston Records from 1700 to 1728*, vol. 8 (Boston: Rockwell and Churchill, 1883), 154.
7. Carrell, *Speckled Monster*, 417.

8. *Diary of Samuel Sewall*, 339.

9. *BNL,* May 22, 1721, no. 898.

10. *Record Commissioners . . . Boston Records*, 155; *Journals of the House of Representatives*, vol. 3, 1721–1722 (Boston: Massachusetts Historical Society, 1922), 39 (this is from the House's June 22 response to Shute's speech at the end of the March session, in which he called for a "loyal and peaceable" behavior); *Record Commissioners . . . Boston Records*, 155.

11. *Record Commissioners . . . Selectmen*, 82.

12. Jacob E. Cooke, et al., eds., *Encyclopedia of the North American Colonies*, vol. 3 (New York: Charles Scribner's Sons, 1993), 207.

13. *BG,* May 29, 1721, no. 77.

14. *Journals of the House*, vol. 3: 5.

15. Hutchinson, *History*, 250.

16. *Journals of the House*, vol. 3: 6.

17. Ibid., 7.

18. Stanley M. Aronson and Lucille Newman, "God have mercy on this house: Being a Brief Chronicle of Smallpox in Colonial New England," for *Smallpox in the Americas 1492 to 1815: Contagion and Controversy* (John Carter Brown Library Exhibition, Brown University, December, 2002): http://www.brown.edu/Administration /News_Bureau/2002-03/02-017t.html (accessed February 4, 2015).

CHAPTER 7: ONESIMUS

1. *Diary of Cotton Mather*, vol. 2: 619–620.

2. Ibid., 623.

3. Ibid.

4. Ibid., 620.

5. Ibid., 623.

6. Ibid., 620 (May 26, 1721).

7. Edmund Clarence Stedman and Ellen Mackay Hutchinson, eds., *A Library of American Literature from the Earliest Settlement to the Present Time*, vol. 2 (New York: Charles L. Webster and Company, 1888), 165; Silverman, *Life and Times*, 336.

8. *Diary of Cotton Mather*, vol. 2: 621 (May 28, 1721).

9. Emanuel Timonius and John Woodward, "An Account, or History, of the Procuring the Small Pox by Incision, or Inoculation; as It Has for Some Time Been Practised at Constantinople," *Philosophical Transactions of the Royal Society*, vol. 29 (January, 1714), 72–82, also at: http://rstl.royalsocietypublishing.org/content/29 /338-350/72.full.pdf+html (accessed February 4, 2015).

10. George Lyman Kittredge, "Some Lost Works of Cotton Mather," in *Proceedings of the Massachusetts Historical Society,* vol. 45 (Cambridge: John Wilson & Son, 1912), 422.

11. Charles Creighton, *A History of Epidemics in Britain,* vol. 2, *From the Extinction of Plague to the Present Time* (Cambridge: Cambridge University Press, 1894), 461. (Creighton recorded that "smallpox cut off 3138 in London and 'Great numbers in Norwich'" that year.)

12. Kittredge, "Lost Works," 422.

13. *Diary of Cotton Mather,* vol. 2: 620–621 (May 28, 1721).

14. Alexander Hamilton, *Gentleman's Progress: The Itinerarium of Dr. Alexander Hamilton, 1744,* ed. Carl Bridenbaugh (Pittsburgh: University of Pittsburgh Press, 1948), 116. (Hamilton met Douglass during his visit to Boston two decades after the 1721 epidemic. But this observation sums up the general impression of Douglass—and the impression he put forth in his writing—during this earlier period.)

15. *Diary of Cotton Mather,* vol. 2: 623 (June 2, 1721).

16. Kittredge, "Lost Works," 438. (Mather used the phrase in a May 4, 1723, letter to Dr. James Jurin.)

17. *BNL,* June 5, 1721, no. 900.

18. Kittredge, "Lost Works," 431–432.

19. Ibid., 431.

20. Cotton Mather, *The Angel of Bethesda*, ed. Gordon W. Jones (Barre, MA: American Antiquarian Society and Barre Publishers, 1972), 108.

21. Ibid., 107.

22. Ibid., 108, 107.

23. Ibid., 110.

24. Kittredge, "Lost Works," 434–435.

CHAPTER 8: THE EXPERIMENT

1. William Douglass, *A Summary, Historical and Political, of the First Planting, Progressive Improvements, and Present State of the British Settlements in North-America,* vol. 2 (Boston: n.p., 1755), 396.

2. *Diary of Cotton Mather,* vol. 2: 627, 626.

3. *BNL,* June 19, 1721, no. 904.

4. *Diary of Cotton Mather,* vol. 2: 627.

5. Ibid. (June 22, 1721).

6. The woman in question was named Sarah Winslow. On December 5, 1720, her husband, Edward, published a testimonial to Boylston in the *Boston News-Letter*

(no. 873). Sarah Winslow "had been laboring under the dreadful distemper of a cancer in her left breast for several years." Several physicians had tried to cure her without success. "When life was almost despaired of by reason of its repeated bleedings, growth, and stench, and she seemed to be in danger of immediate death," Edward wrote, he sent for Boylston, "who on July 30, 1718 (in the presence of several ministers and others assembled on that occasion), cut her whole breast off and dressed it in the space of five minutes by the watch of one then present." The result, he testified, had been "a perfect cure."

7. Reginald H. Fitz, "Zabdiel Boylston, Inoculator, and the Epidemic of Smallpox in Boston in 1721," *Bulletin of the Johns Hopkins Hospital* 22, no. 247: 318.

8. Gerald Marvin Mager, *Zabdiel Boylston: Medical Pioneer of Colonial Boston* (Doctoral thesis, University of Illinois–Urbana-Champaign, 1975), 93.

9. For Carrell's speculation on Boylston's cleanliness, see *Speckled Monster,* 422.

10. *BNL,* July 24, 1721, no. 912.

11. Zabdiel Boylston, *An Historical Account of the Small-Pox Inoculated in New England,* 2nd ed. (Boston: S. Gerrish, 1730), 1; Zabdiel Boylston and [Cotton Mather], *Some Account of What is Said of Inoculating the Small Pox* (Boston: S. Gerrish, 1721), 9.

12. Boylston, *Some Account, 9.*

13. Boylston, *An Historical Account, 38.*

14. Richard Lord Braybrooke, ed., *Memoirs of Samuel Pepys, Esq. F.R.S.: Comprising His Diary From 1659 to 1669 and a Selection of His Private Correspondence,* vol. 4 (London: Henry Colburn, 1828), 82.

15. Boylston, *An Historical Account,* 1.

16. Tourtellot, *Benjamin Franklin,* 361.

17. Levin, *Cotton Mather,* 54; Tourtellot, *Benjamin Franklin,* 361.

18. *BNL,* June 26, 1721, no. 906.

19. Boylston, *An Historical Account,* 43.

20. Ibid., 2.

21. Margot Minardi, "The Boston Inoculation Controversy of 1721–1722: An Incident in the History of Race," *William and Mary Quarterly* 61, no. 1 (January 2004): 64.

22. Boylston, *Some Account,* 9. (Credited to Boylston, this pamphlet was almost certainly a collaboration with Mather. Given the minister's defensiveness about his dependence on the testimony of Africans, and his tendency to overstate his case, I feel confident that this particular turn of phrase was his.)

23. Carrell, *Speckled Monster,* 182.

24. Ibid., 423.

25. Joel. N. Shurkin, *The Invisible Fire: The Story of Mankind's Victory over the Ancient Scourge of Smallpox* (New York: Putnam, 1979), 157.

26. *Diary of Cotton Mather,* vol. 2: 628 (June 30, 1721).

27. Boylston, *An Historical Account*, 45.

28. Ibid., 2.

29. Ibid.

30. Ibid.

31. Ibid., 3.

32. *Journals of the House*, vol. 3: 70.

33. *BNL*, July 3, 1721, no. 908.

34. *BG*, July 17, 1721, no. 85.

35. Boylston, *An Historical Account*, 7.

CHAPTER 9: MALIGNANT FILTH

1. Jeremiah Dummer to the Speaker of the Massachusetts House, London [June 1719?], in *Calendar of State Papers*, vol. 31: 145.

2. Jeremiah Dummer to House of Representatives, London, April 23, 1721, in Hutchinson, *History*, 290n.

3. *Journals of the House*, vol. 3: 39.

4. Hutchinson, *History*, 260.

5. *Journals of the House*, vol. 3: 76, 81.

6. Carrell, *Speckled Monster*, 429.

7. Boylston, *An Historical Account*, 51.

8. Ibid., 51–52.

9. Silverman, *Life and Times*, 342.

10. Boylston, *An Historical Account*, 4–5.

11. Ibid., 4.

12. Ibid., 53.

13. Ibid.

14. *BNL*, July 24, 1721, no. 912.

15. Ibid.

16. Carrell, *Speckled Monster*, 429.

17. *BNL*, July 24, 1721, no. 912.

18. Isaac Greenwood, *A Friendly Debate, or, A Dialogue, Between Academicus, and Sawny & Mundungus, two Eminent Physicians, about some of their late performances* (Boston: 1722), "Advertisement."

19. William Douglass to Cadwallader Colden, Boston, February 20, 1721, in *The Letters and Papers of Cadwallader Colden,* vol. 1, 1711–1729, Collection of the New-York Historical Society for the Year 1917 (New York: The Society, 1918), 115.

20. Douglass, *A Summary*, p. 350; Douglass to Colden, Boston, November 20, 1727, in *Letters and Papers of Cadwallader Colden*, 238; Douglass to Colden, Boston, 20 February 1721, ibid., 114.

21. Douglass to Colden, Boston, February 20, 1721, in *Letters and Papers of Cadwallader Colden*, 114; Douglass, *A Summary*, 384.

22. Douglass to Colden, Boston, February 20, 1721, in *Letters and Papers of Cadwallader Colden*, 114.

23. Douglass to Colden, Boston, July 28, 1721. See "Letters from Dr. William Douglass to Cadwallader Colden of New York" in Collections of the Massachusetts Historical Society, 4th series, vol. 2 (Boston: Crosby, Nichols and Company, 1854), 166.

24. Douglass to Colden, ibid., 167.

25. Boylston, *An Historical Account*, 6.

26. *BNL*, July 31, 1721, no. 913.

27. Boylston, *An Historical Account*, 51.

28. *BG*, July 31, 1721, no. 88.

29. Ibid.

30. Boylston, *An Historical Account*, 7.

CHAPTER 10: AMERICA'S FIRST INDEPENDENT NEWSPAPER

1. Edmund F. Slafter, *John Checkley or the Evolution of Religious Tolerance in Massachusetts Bay*, vol. 1 (Boston: The Prince Society, 1897), 34.

2. Duniway, *Freedom of the Press in Massachusetts*, 85.

3. Slafter, *John Checkley*, 14.

4. Ibid., 15.

5. Thomas Walter, *A Choice Dialogue Between John Faustus, a Conjurer, and Jack Tory His Friend* (Boston: N. Boone, B. Gray, and J. Edwards, 1720), 7.

6. Douglass to Colden, Boston, March 18, 1728, in *Letters and Papers of Cadwallader Colden*, 252.

7. Tourtellot, *Benjamin Franklin*, 371.

8. John Checkley to Edmond Halley, Boston, August 22, 1720, in Slafter, *John Checkley*, vol. 2: 152–153.

9. Sloane and Williams, *The Early American Press*, 24.

10. Craig Nelson, *Thomas Paine: Enlightenment, Revolution, and the Birth of Modern Nations* (New York: Viking, 2006), 31.

11. J. A. Leo Lemay, *Benjamin Franklin: A Documentary History: Printer 1657–1730* (see August 7, 1721), https://web.archive.org/web/20120502102128/http://www.english.udel.edu/lemay/franklin/ (accessed February 4, 2015).

12. *Autobiography*, 20.

13. *Publick Occurrences*, September 25, 1690.

14. Clark, *The Public Prints*, 119.

15. *NEC,* August 7, 1721, no. 1.

16. Ibid.

17. Ibid.

18. Ibid.; Lemay, *Benjamin Franklin: A Documentary History* (see August 7, 1721).; *NEC*, August 7, 1721, no. 1.

19. *BNL*, August 14, 1721, no. 915.

20. *NEC*, August 14, 1721, no. 2.

21. Ibid.

22. Ibid.

23. Thomas Walter, *The Little-Compton Scourge: or, The Anti-Courant* (Boston: James Franklin, 1721).

24. Tourtellot, *Benjamin Franklin*, 254.

CHAPTER 11: THE CUP WHICH I FEAR

1. *Diary of Cotton Mather*, vol. 2: 628.

2. Ibid., 631–32.

3. Ibid., 630, 632.

4. Ibid., 633 (July 21, 1721).

5. Ibid., 634 (July 27, 1721).

6. *BNL*, July 31, 1721, no. 913.

7. *BNL:* August 7, 1721, no. 914.

8. *Diary of Cotton Mather*, vol. 2: 635 (August 1, 1721).

9. Ibid.

10. Ibid., 636 (August 4, 1721).

11. Ibid., 637 (August 9, 1721).

12. Ibid., 637–38 (August 15, 1721).

13. Ibid., 638 (August 17, 18, 1721).

14. Ibid., 639 (August 22, 1721).

15. Ibid.

CHAPTER 12: THE HELL-FIRE CLUB

1. *NEC*, August 21, 1721, no. 3.

2. Ibid.

3. Ibid.
4. Tourtellot, *Benjamin Franklin*, 252.
5. *NEC*, August 28, 1721, no. 4.
6. Ibid. (see "Newport Rhode-Island, August 17").
7. *NEC*, August 21, 1721, no. 3.
8. *Spectator*, London, March 12, 1711, no. 10.
9. Verner W. Crane, *Benjamin Franklin and a Rising People* (Boston: Little, Brown and Co., 1954), 10.
10. *NEC*, September 4, 1721, no. 5.
11. Ibid.
12. *BNL*, July 6, 1721, no. 909.
13. *BNL*, August 28, 1721, no. 917.
14. *BG*, September 4, 1721, no. 93.
15. Tourtellot, *Benjamin Franklin*, 278.
16. *NEC*, September 4, 1721, no. 5.
17. *BG*, September 4, 1721, no. 93.

CHAPTER 13: A MAN ON A CROSS

1. *BNL*, August 28, 1721, no. 917.
2. *Diary of Cotton Mather*, vol. 2: 639 (August 25, 1721); ibid. (August 24, 1721); ibid., 640 (August 25, 1721).
3. Boylston, *An Historical Account*, 8.
4. *Diary of Cotton Mather*, vol. 2: 640 (August 25, 1721). (Mather's day-long prayer sessions were conducted face down on the floor. One of the earliest recorded in his diaries was in January 1686. Mather wrote: "This Day, with Anguish of Soul, in the Sense of my own Sinfulness and Filthiness, I cast myself prostrate, on my *Study-floor* with my mouth in the Dust." See *Diary of Cotton Mather*, vol. 1, 1663–1728 (New York: Ungar, 1957), 109.)
5. *Diary of Cotton Mather*, vol. 2: 640 (August 25, 1721).
6. Ibid. (August 27, 1721).
7. Ibid., 641 (August 28, 1721)
8. Ibid., 643 (August 30, 1721).
9. Ibid., 643.
10. Ibid., 640 (August 26, 1721); ibid., 641 (August 30, 1721).
11. Silverman, *Life and Times*, 274.
12. *Diary of Cotton Mather*, vol. 2: 643 (August 31, 1721, and September 1, 1721).
13. *Diary of Cotton Mather*, vol. 2: 644 (September 3, 4, 1721), 645 (September 5, 1721).

14. Ibid., 647 (September 19, 1721).

15. Ibid., 648 (September 24, 1721); ibid., 649 (September 26, 1721).

16. Cotton Mather, *Silentarius. A Brief Essay on the Holy Silence* (Boston: printed by S. Kneeland, 1721), 23. (Sermon preached September 28, 1721.)

CHAPTER 14: THE DEADLIEST TIME

1. Boylston, *An Historical Account*, 9.

2. Ibid., 8.

3. Carrell, *Speckled Monster*, 421.

4. Boylston, *An Historical Account*, 8.

5. Ibid., 11.

6. Ibid., 12–13.

7. Douglass to Colden, Boston, May 1, 1722, in *Letters and Papers of Cadwallader Colden*, 142.

8. Lemay, *Benjamin Franklin: A Documentary History, Printer 1657–1730* (see "September 18, 1721").

9. *NEC*, October 9, 1721, no. 10.

10. Nathaniel Hawthorne, "Lady Eleanore's Mantel," in *Twice-Told Tales,* vol.1 (Boston: Ticknor & Fields, 1865), 316.

11. Douglass to Colden, Boston, May 1, 1722, in *Letters and Papers of Cadwallader Colden*, 142.

12. Ola Elizabeth Winslow, *A Destroying Angel: The Conquest of Smallpox in Colonial Boston* (Boston: Houghton-Mifflin, 1974), 54.

13. *Diary of Samuel Sewall*, 295.

14. Ibid., 294.

15. Winslow, *Destroying Angel*, 54.

16. Ibid.

17. *BG*, October 23, 1721, no. 100.

18. Ibid.

19. Carrell, *Speckled Monster*, 438.

20. Hutchinson, *History*, 273.

21. James Thacher, *American Medical Biography* (Boston: Richardson & Lord, 1828), 187.

22. *NEC*, October 23, 1721, no. 12.

23. *BG*, October 30, 1721, no. 101.

24. Ibid.

CHAPTER 15: HONEST WAGS

1. *NEC*, September 4, 1721, no. 5.
2. Albert Furtwangler, "Franklin's Apprenticeship and the *Spectator*," *New England Quarterly* 52, no. 3 (September 1979): 380.
3. C. H. Timperley, *A Dictionary of Printers and Printing: with the Progress of Literature, Ancient and Modern* (London: H. Johnson, 1839), 596.
4. Nelson, *Thomas Paine*, 32.
5. Timperley, *A Dictionary*, 601.
6. Nelson, *Thomas Paine*, 32.
7. Ibid., 31.
8. Joseph Fireoved, "Nathaniel Gardner and the *New-England Courant*," *Early American Literature* 20, no. 3 (1985): 228.
9. Bernard Bailyn, *The Ideological Origins of the American Revolution* (Cambridge: Belknap Press, 1967), 45.
10. Ibid., 47.
11. Clinton Rossiter, *Seedtime of the Republic: The Origin of the American Tradition of Political Liberty* (New York: Harcourt Brace, 1953), 299.
12. Bailyn, *Ideological Origins*, 43.
13. *NEC*, September 11, 1721, no. 6.
14. *NEC*, October 16, 1721, no. 11.
15. Gordon S. Wood, *The Radicalism of the American Revolution: How a Revolution Transformed a Monarchical Society into a Democratic One Unlike Any that Had Ever Existed* (New York: Knopf Doubleday, 1993), 95, 98.
16. *NEC*, October 30, 1721, no. 13.
17. Lemay, *Benjamin Franklin: A Documentary History, Printer* (see September 11, 1721).
18. *NEC*, September 25, 1721, no. 8.
19. Fireoved, *"Nathaniel Gardner,"* 227.
20. *NEC*, September 25, 1721, no. 8.
21. *NEC,* October 2, 1721, no. 9.
22. *NEC*, October 9, 1721, no. 10.
23. *NEC*, December 11, 1721, no. 19.
24. *NEC*, January 29, 1722, no. 26.
25. *NEC,* January 1, 1722, no. 22.
26. Tourtellot, *Benjamin Franklin,* 288.
27. *NEC*, March 5, 1722, no. 31.
28. *NEC*, January 29, 1722, no. 26.

29. *NEC*, April 9, 1722, no. 36.
30. *NEC*, December 11, 1721, no. 19.
31. *NEC*, January 29, 1722, no. 26.
32. Tourtellot, *Benjamin Franklin*, 306.

CHAPTER 16: THE ASSASSINATION ATTEMPT

1. *Diary of Cotton Mather*, vol. 2: 654 (October 26, 1721).
2. Ibid. (October 27, 1721).
3. Tourtellot, *Benjamin Franklin*, 262.
4. Boylston, *An Historical Account*, 18.
5. Increase Mather, *Heavens Alarm to the World. Or A Sermon Wherein Is Shewed, That fearful Sights and Signs in Heaven are the Presages of great Calamities at hand* (Boston: printed by John Foster, 1681).
6. *NEC*, November 6, 1721, no. 14.
7. *Diary of Cotton Mather*, vol. 2: 656 (November 9, 1721).
8. *Record Commissioners . . . Selectmen*, 91.
9. *NEC*, December 4, 1721, no. 18.
10. *BNL*, November 20, 1721, no. 929.
11. *Diary of Cotton Mather*, vol. 2: 659 (November 19, 1721).
12. Thacher, *American Medical Biography*, 187.
13. Benjamin Colman, *Some Observations on the New Method of Receiving the Small-Pox by Ingrafting or Inoculation* (Boston: Green for Gerrish, 1721), 2 (November 23, 1721).

CHAPTER 17: A DEATH IN THE HOUSE

1. Hutchinson, *History*, 267.
2. Shute to Council of Trade and Plantations, Boston, September 8, 1721, in *Calendar of State Papers*, vol. 32: 407.
3. Ibid.
4. *Journals of the House*, vol. 3: 136.
5. Ibid., 137 (November 7, 1721).
6. Ibid., 118 (September 5, 1721).
7. Ibid., 152 (November 16, 1721).
8. Ibid., 148 (November 14, 1721).
9. Ibid., 149 (November 15, 1721).
10. Ibid., 155 (November 16, 1721).
11. Hutchinson, *History*, 271.

CHAPTER 18: POINTED SATYR

1. *Diary of Samuel Sewall*, 296.
2. *NEC*, December 4, 1721, no. 18.
3. *Diary of Cotton Mather*, vol. 2: 662.
4. *NEC*, November 20, 1721, no. 16.
5. Increase Mather and Cotton Mather, *Several Reasons Proving that Inoculating or Transplanting the Small Pox, is a Lawful Practice, and that it has been Blessed by GOD for the Saving of many a Life, and Sentiments on the Small Pox Inoculated* (Boston: S. Kneeland for J. Edwards, 1721), reprinted with an introduction by George Lyman Kittredge (Cleveland, n.p., 1921), 74.
6. *NEC*, November 27, 1721, no. 17.
7. *Diary of Cotton Mather*, vol. 2: 528 (April 14, 1718).
8. *NEC*, December 4, 1721, no. 18.
9. Ibid.
10. Ibid.
11. Tourtellot, *Benjamin Franklin*, 300.
12. *NEC*, December 4, 1721, no. 18.
13. *Diary of Cotton Mather*, vol. 2: 216 (June 5, 1713).
14. Miller, *New England Mind*, 357.
15. William Douglass, *Inoculation of the Small-Pox as Practised in Boston, Consider'd in a letter to A—S——* (Boston: printed by J. Franklin, 1722), Introduction, 1–2.
16. John Williams, *An Answer to a late Pamphlet, intitled, A Letter to a Friend in the Country; attempting a Solution of the Scruples and Objections of a Consciencious or Religious Nature, commonly made against the new Way of receiving Small Pox; by a Minister of Boston. Together with a short History of the late Divisions among us In Affairs of State, and some Account of the first Cause of them* (Boston: Printed and Sold by J. Franklin, 1721), 19.
17. *NEC*, November 20, 1721, no. 16.
18. Ibid.
19. Ibid.
20. Tourtellot, *Benjamin Franklin*, 309.
21. *NEC*, December 4, 1721, no. 18.

CHAPTER 19: AN EPIDEMIC'S END

1. Boylston, *An Historical Account*, 20.
2. Ibid.

3. Ibid., 21.

4. Ibid.

5. Ibid.

6. Ibid.

7. Ibid., 26.

8. Ibid.

9. Ibid., 28.

10. Ibid., 29.

11. [William Douglass], *A Letter from one in the Country, to his Friend in the City: In Relation to their Distresses occasioned by the doubtful and prevailing Practice of the Inocculation of the Small-Pox* (Boston: Nicholas Boone & John Edwards, 1721), 3, 4.

12. Williams, *An Answer to a Late Pamphlet*, 12.

13. Ibid., 13.

14. Ibid., p. 2, dedication.

15. William Douglass, *Inoculation of the Small Pox As Practised in Boston, Consider'd in a Letter to A—S—M.D. & F.R.S. in London* (Boston: James Franklin, 1722), 14.

16. Isaac Greenwood, *A Friendly Debate, or, A Dialogue, Between Academicus, and Sawny & Mundungus, two Eminent Physicians, about some of their late performances* (Boston: 1722), advertisement.

17. Ibid., 2.

18. Ibid., 17.

19. William Douglass, *The Abuses and Scandals of Some Late Pamphlets in Favour of Inoculation of the Small Pox, Modestly Obviated and Inoculation Further Consider'd in a Letter to A——S——M.D. & F.R.S. in London*, and *POSTSCRIPT to Abuses, &c. obviated. Being a Short and Modest Answer to Matter of Fact maliciously misrepresented in a late Doggrel Dialogue* (Boston: J. Franklin, 1722), postscript, 1.

20. Ibid.

21. Greenwood, *A Friendly Debate*, dedication, i; *NEC*, March 12, 1722, no. 32.

22. *BG*, January 15, 1722, no. 112.

23. *NEC*, May 21, 1722, no. 42.

24. Boylston, *An Historical Account*, 32.

25. Tourtellot, *Benjamin Franklin*, 240.

26. Boylston, *An Historical Account*, preface, iii.

27. Ibid.

28. Douglass to Colden, Boston, May 1, 1722, in *Letters and Papers of Cadwallader Colden*, 143.

29. Boylston, *An Historical Account*, preface, v.

30. Ibid., preface, vi.

31. Ibid.

32. Ibid., 32–33.

33. John B. Blake, *Public Health in the Town of Boston, 1630–1822* (Boston: Harvard University Press, 1959), 52; Mager, *Zabdiel Boylston*, 163.

34. Otho T. Beall Jr. and Richard H. Shryock, *Cotton Mather: First Significant Figure in American Medicine* (Baltimore: Johns Hopkins University Press, 1954), 126.

35. Cotton Mather to James Jurin, Boston, December 15, 1724, in Andrea Rusnock, ed., *The Correspondence of James Jurin, 1684–1750* (Atlanta: Editions Rodopi B.V., 1996), 284.

CHAPTER 20: SONS OF CATO, SONS OF CALEF

1. *NEC*, November 20, 1721, no. 16.

2. *NEC*, November 27, 1721, no. 17.

3. Clark, *The Public Prints*, 24.

4. *NEC*, December 4, 1721, no. 18.

5. *NEC*, December 18, 1721, no. 20.

6. Ibid.

7. *NEC*, December 25, 1721, no. 21.

8. *NEC*, December 18, 1721, no. 20; *NEC*, December 25, 1721, no. 21.

9. *NEC*, December 25, 1721, no. 21.

10. *NEC*, January 22, 1722, no. 25.

11. *NEC*, January 29, 1722, no. 26.

12. Lemay, *Benjamin Franklin: A Documentary History* (see 1721 introduction: business).

13. *NEC*, March 19 [*sic*], 1722, no. 33.

14. *NEC*, February 5, 1722, no. 27.

15. *BG*, January 15, 1722, no. 112.

16. Ibid.

17. *NEC*, January 22, 1722, no. 25.

18. *NEC*, February 12, 1722, no. 28.

19. *BG*, January 29, 1722, no. 114.

20. *NEC*, February 5, 1722, no. 27.

21. *BG*, March 19, 1722, no. 121.

22. *NEC*, March 26, 1722, no. 34.

23. Ibid.

24. Ibid.

25. Levin, *Cotton Mather*, 287.

26. Ibid., 243.
27. *NEC*, February 12, 1722, no. 28.
28. *NEC*, March 5, 1722, no. 31.
29. *NEC*, February 5, 1722, no. 27.
30. *NEC*, February 26, 1722, no. 30.
31. *NEC*, February 12, 1722, no. 28.
32. Claude-Anne Lopez and Eugenia W. Herbert, *The Private Franklin: The Man and His Family* (New York, W. W. Norton, 1975), 11.
33. *NEC*, February 5, 1722, no. 27.
34. *BG*, January 29, 1722, no. 114.

CHAPTER 21: THE INVENTION OF SILENCE DOGOOD

1. *NEC*, March 26, 1722, no. 34.
2. *NEC*, April 2, 1722, no. 35.
3. Ibid.
4. Ibid.
5. Ibid.
6. Ibid.
7. Tourtellot, *Benjamin Franklin*, 355.
8. *Autobiography,* 21.
9. *NEC*, July 2, 1722, no. 48.
10. *Autobiography*, 15.
11. Ibid., 18.
12. Tourtellot, *Benjamin Franklin*, 228.
13. *Autobiography*, 17.
14. Ibid.
15. Lemay, *Life of Benjamin Franklin*, 28.
16. *Autobiography*, 16.
17. Ibid., 16–17.
18. Ibid., 20; Tourtellot, *Benjamin Franklin*, 276.
19. *Autobiography*, 20.
20. Ibid.
21. *NEC*, April 30, 1722, no. 39.
22. Tourtellot, *Benjamin Franklin*, 334.
23. Ibid., 346.
24. Miller, *New England Mind*, 362.
25. Tourtellot, *Benjamin Franklin*, 335.

26. Walter Isaacson, ed., *A Benjamin Franklin Reader* (New York: Simon & Schuster, 2003), 9.
27. *NEC*, April 16, 1722, no. 37.
28. Ibid.
29. *NEC*, May 14, 1722, no. 41 (erroneously printed as no. 42).
30. *NEC*, June 4, 1722, no. 44.
31. *NEC*, August 14, 1721, no. 2.

CHAPTER 22: THE ARREST OF JAMES FRANKLIN

1. *NEC*, April 9, 1722, no. 36.
2. *NEC*, May 14, 1722, no. 41 (erroneously printed as no. "42").
3. Ibid.
4. Ibid.
5. Ibid.
6. Tourtellot, *Benjamin Franklin*, 298.
7. Ibid.
8. *BG*, May 21, 1722, no. 130.
9. Ibid.
10. *Journals of the House of Representatives*, vol. 4, 1722–1723 (Boston: Massachusetts Historical Society, 1923), 10.
11. Ibid., 11.
12. *NEC*, June 11, 1722, no. 45.
13. Ibid.
14. Ibid.
15. *NEC*, June 4, 1722, no. 44.
16. Tourtellot, *Benjamin Franklin*, 395.
17. *Journals of the House*, vol. 4: 23.
18. *NEC*, December 4, 1721, no. 18.; Lemay, *Benjamin Franklin: A Documentary History* (see September 11, 1721).
19. *Autobiography*, 21.
20. Tourtellot, *Benjamin Franklin*, 399.
21. Ibid.
22. *Journals of the House*, vol. 4: 31.
23. Ibid., 35.
24. Duniway, *Freedom of the Press*, 99.

NOTES

CHAPTER 23: THE PRINTER AND HIS DEVIL

1. Tourtellot, *Benjamin Franklin*, 104.
2. *Autobiography*, 22.
3. Ibid.
4. *NEC*, June 25, 1722, no. 47.
5. Ibid.
6. *NEC*, July 2, 1722, no. 48.
7. Ibid.
8. Ibid.
9. *Journals of the House*, vol. 4: 72.
10. *NEC*, July 9, 1722, no. 49.
11. Ibid.
12. Ibid.
13. *NEC*, April 16, 1722, no. 37.
14. Ibid.
15. *Journals of the House*, vol. 4: 72.
16. *Autobiography*, 22.
17. *NEC*, July 16, 1722, no. 50.
18. Ibid.
19. Tourtellot, *Benjamin Franklin*, 407.
20. *NEC*, July 23, 1722, no. 51.
21. Ibid.
22. Ibid.
23. Governor Shute to Mr. Popple, Boston, June 18, 1722, in *Calendar of State Papers, Colonial Series, America and West Indies*, vol. 33, 1722–1723, ed. Cecil Headlam (London: His Majesty's Stationery Office, 1934), 89–90. Also at: http://www .british-history.ac.uk/cal-state-papers/colonial/america-west-indies/vol33/pp79 -99 (accessed February 7, 2015).
24. *BG*, July 23, 1722, 139.
25. Ibid.
26. *NEC*, July 30, 1722, no. 52.
27. Ibid.
28. *NEC*, September 17, 1722, no. 59.
29. *NEC*, October 29, 1722, no. 65.
30. Tourtellot, *Benjamin Franklin*, 417.
31. *NEC*, December 10, 1722, no. 71.
32. *NEC*, August 13, 1722, no. 54.

33. Ibid.

34. *NEC*, September 24, 1722, no. 60.

35. Ibid.

36. *NEC*, October 8, 1722, no. 62.

37. *NEC*, December 3, 1722, no. 70.

38. *Autobiography*, 21.

39. Ibid., 20–21.

40. Miller, *New England Mind*, 342.

41. *Autobiography*, 21.

42. Furtwangler, "Franklin's Apprenticeship," 392.

43. *Autobiography*, 21.

44. Ibid., 23.

CHAPTER 24: THREE EXITS

1. Hutchinson, *History*, 278.

2. Ibid.

3. *Journals of the House*, vol. 4: 79 (August 8, 1722).

4. Ibid., 95 (August 18, 1722).

5. Ibid., 105 (November 17, 1722).

6. Hutchinson, *History*, 278.

7. Worthington Chauncey Ford, ed., *Journals of the House*, vol. 4: introduction, xi.

8. *Journals of the House*, vol. 4: 129 (December 1, 1722).

9. Hutchinson, *History*, 284n.

10. *Diary of Samuel Sewall*, 315 (December 21, 1722).

11. Ibid., 316 (December 25, 1722).

12. Ibid. (December 28, 1722).

13. Ibid., 317.

14. H.M. permission for Governor Shute's leave of absence, London, July 4, 1720, in *Calendar of State Papers*, vol. 32: 61.

15. Hutchinson, *History*, 288.

16. Tourtellot, *Benjamin Franklin*, 422.

17. Palfrey, *A Compendious History*, 398.

18. Hutchinson, *History*, 287–88.

19. Ibid., 288.

20. George Chalmers, *Introduction to the History of the Revolt of the American Colonies*, vol. 2 (Boston: James Munroe and Co., 1845), 11.

21. *BNL*, December 31, 1722, no. 987.

22. *NEC*, December 31, 1722, no. 74.

23. *NEC*, January 14, 1723, no. 76.

24. Ibid.

25. *NEC*, December 10, 1722, no. 71.

26. *Journals of the House*, vol. 4: 205 (January 14, 1723).

27. Ibid., 208 (January 16, 1723).

28. *Diary of Samuel Sewall*, 319 (January 27, 1723, referring to incident on January 20).

29. Lemay, *Benjamin Franklin: A Documentary History* (see January 20, 1723). (Lemay wrote: "As the only adolescent among the Couranteers, it seems probable that BF wrote the libel.")

30. Ibid. (see January 21, 1723). (Lemay wrote: "JF and perhaps BF knew that the Rev. Ebenezer Pemberton, when angry with Sewall, had the same stanzas from Psalm 58 sung in church on 3 Dec 1710.")

31. *NEC*, January 21, 1723, no. 77.

32. Ibid.

33. *Diary of Samuel Sewall*, 319.

34. *NEC*, January 28, 1723, no. 78.

35. *NEC*, February 4, 1723, no. 79.

36. Ibid.

37. *Autobiography*, 22.

38. *NEC*, February 11, 1723, no. 80.

39. Carl Van Doren, *Benjamin Franklin* (New York: Viking Press, 1938), 32.

40. *NEC*, March 4, 1723, no. 83.

41. *American Weekly Mercury,* February 26, 1723, no. 167 (Philadelphia: Andrew Bradford).

42. Tourtellot, *Benjamin Franklin*, 433–434.

43. *Autobiography*, 22.

44. Ibid.

45. Ibid.

46. *NEC*, July 15, 1723, no.102.

47. *Autobiography*, 22.

48. Ibid., 23.

49. Ibid.

50. Ibid.; Walter Isaacson, *Benjamin Franklin, An American Life* (New York: Simon & Schuster, 2003), 35.

51. Tourtellot, *Benjamin Franklin*, 436.

52. *NEC*, September 30, 1723, no. 113.

53. James Franklin, *The Life and Death of Old Father Janus, the vile Author of the late Wicked Courant. A Satyr* (Boston: James Franklin, 1726), 2.
54. Ibid., 7.

EPILOGUE

1. Raymond Stearns and George Pasti, "Remarks upon the Introduction of Inoculation for Smallpox in England," *Bulletin of the History of Medicine* 24 (March–April 1950): 113.
2. Ibid, 116.
3. Boylston, *An Historical Account*, preface, i.
4. Mager, *Zabdiel Boylston*, 133.
5. Beall and Shryock, *Cotton Mather, First Significant Figure*, 88.
6. Boylston, *An Historical Account*, preface, v.; ibid., dedication, v.
7. Mager, *Zabdiel Boylston*, 189.
8. Boylston to Sir Hans Sloane, Boston, December 1737, in Mager, *Zabdiel Boylston*, 187.
9. Ibid.
10. Ibid.
11. Ibid.
12. Genevieve Miller, *The Adoption of Inoculation for Smallpox in England and France* (Philadelphia: University of Pennsylvania Press, 1957), 195.
13. Bollet, *Plagues & Poxes*, 83.
14. Fenn, *Pox Americana*, 275.
15. Ibid., 48.
16. John Adams to James Warren, Philadelphia, July 24, 1776, in *Warren-Adams Letters: Being Chiefly a Correspondence Among John Adams, Samuel Adams, and James Warren,* vol. 1, 1743–1777 (Boston: Massachusetts Historical Society, 1917), 263; Donald R. Hopkins, *The Greatest Killer: Smallpox in History* (Chicago: University of Chicago Press, 1983), 260.
17. Benedict Arnold, Quebeck, Canada, "General Orders before Quebeck, prohibiting Inoculation for the Small-Pox," March 15, 1776, as quoted in Fenn, *Pox Americana*, 67.
18. Horatio Gates to George Washington, Ticonderoga, August 28, 1776, as quoted in Ilza Veith, "Benjamin Rush and the Beginnings of American Medicine," *Western Journal of Medicine* 125 (July 1976): 20.
19. Joseph J. Ellis, *His Excellency: George Washington* (New York: Vintage Books, 2005), 87.

20. Bollet, *Plagues & Poxes*, 85.

21. Oldstone, *Viruses, Plagues and History*, 74.

22. Mather to Jurin, Boston, May 21, 1723, in Silverman, *Life and Times*, 357.

23. *Diary of Cotton Mather*, vol. 2: 713 (April 2, 1724).

24. Ibid., 749 (August 13, 1724).

25. Ibid., 744 (July 28, 1724).

26. Ibid., 755 (August 23, 1724).

27. Silverman, *Life and Times*, 428.

28. Ibid., 417.

29. Ibid.

30. Ibid.

31. Ibid., 419.

32. Ibid., 422.

33. Carrell, *Speckled Monster*, 399.

34. Nathaniel Hawthorne, *Grandfather's Chair: A History for Youth* (Carlisle, MA: Applewood Books, 2010) (facsimile of 1898 edition published by Henry Altemus, Philadelphia), 117.

35. Silverman, *Life and Times*, 423.

36. Benjamin Franklin to Samuel Mather, Passy, May 12, 1784, in the Papers of Benjamin Franklin, American Philosophical Society and Yale University, digital edition by the Packard Humanities Institute: http://franklinpapers.org/franklin// (accessed February 7, 2015).

37. Ibid.

38. Lemay, *Benjamin Franklin: A Documentary History* (see "Rising Citizen," October 30, 1731).

39. *Autobiography*, 33.

40. Ibid., 111.

41. Murray N. Rothbard, *Conceived in Liberty* (Auburn, AL: Ludwig von Mises Institute, 2011), 644.

42. Tourtellot, *Benjamin Franklin*, 438.

43. Letter from Benjamin Franklin to Jane Mecom, Philadelphia, 1743[?], in Jared Sparks, ed., *The Works of Benjamin Franklin*, vol. 7 (London: Benjamin Franklin Stevens, 1882), 14.

44. H. P. Smith, "The Printer and the Press," chap. 5, *State of Rhode Island and Providence Plantations at the End of the Century: A History*, vol. 2, ed. Edward Field (Boston: Mason Publishing Company, 1902), 565.

45. *Autobiography*, 21; ibid., 20.

46. Ibid., 14.

47. Ibid., 21.

48. Lopez and Herbert, *The Private Franklin*, 11.

49. Ibid.

50. Lemay, *Benjamin Franklin: A Documentary History* (see "Rising Citizen," June 10, 1731).

51. Clarence S. Brigham, "James Franklin and the Beginnings of Printing in Rhode Island," *Proceedings of the Massachusetts Historical Society*, vol. 65 (Boston: The Society, 1940), 540.

52. Ibid.

53. Lemay, *Benjamin Franklin: A Documentary History* (see September 11, 1721). (Lemay wrote: "Gardner concluded with a sententiae that Franklin later echoed: 'he is not the Happy man, who has abundance, but he who is contented in the Enjoyment of what he has.'" (Cf. Poor Richard for July 1735: "Who is rich? He that is content.")

54. Joyce E. Chaplin, *The First Scientific American: Benjamin Franklin and the Pursuit of Genius* (New York: Basic Books, 2006), 47.

55. Miller, *New England Mind*, 336.

56. Doug Linder, "The Trial of John Peter Zenger: An Account." *Famous Trials*, http://law2.umkc.edu/faculty/projects/ftrials/zenger/zengeraccount.html (accessed February 7, 2015).

57. Ibid.

58. Hutchinson, *History*, 320; *Memorial History of Boston*, 53.

59. *New-England Weekly Journal*, April 10, 1727, as noted in Warden, *Boston,* 95.

60. Letter from Jeremiah Dummer to Edmund Quincy, London, May 25, 1727, in Publications of the Colonial Society of Massachusetts, vol. 17, Transactions 1913–1914 (Boston: The Society, 1915), 70n.

61. Miller, *New England Mind*, 391.

62. Richard L. Bushman, *King and People in Provincial Massachusetts* (Chapel Hill: University of North Carolina Press, 1985), 94.

63. Jonathan Belcher to Richard Waldron, Boston, December 3, 1733, in "The Belcher Papers," Collections of the Massachusetts Historical Society, 6th series, vol. 6 (Boston: The Society, 1893), 438.

64. John C. Miller, *Sam Adams: Pioneer in Propaganda* (Stanford, CA: Stanford University Press, 1936), 9.

65. Hutchinson, *History*, 391.

66. Warden, *Boston*, 124.

67. Ibid.

68. Hutchinson, *History*, 392.

69. Ibid.

70. Michael C. Batinski, *Jonathan Belcher: Colonial Governor* (Lexington: University of Kentucky Press, 1996), 144.

71. John Stetson Barry, *The History of Massachusetts: The Provincial Period* (Boston: Phillips, Sampson and Co., 1856), 133.

72. Nash, *Urban Crucible*, 140.

73. Ibid.

74. Bushman, *King and People*, 267.

75. Kneeland had purchased the *Gazette* and merged it with the *New-England Weekly Journal* in October 1741.

76. Miller, *Sam Adams*, 105.

77. Warden, *Boston,* 225.

78. Ira Stoll, *Samuel Adams: A Life* (New York: Free Press, 2008), 75–76.

79. Bernard Bailyn, *The Ordeal of Thomas Hutchinson* (Cambridge: The Belknap Press, 1974), 196.

80. Ibid., 197.

81. Andrew Stephen Walmsley, *Thomas Hutchinson and the Origins of the American Revolution* (New York: New York University Press, 1999), 138.

82. Bailyn, *Ordeal of Thomas Hutchinson*, 273.

83. Francis Bernard to the Earl of Shelburne, January 24, 1767, in G. B. Warden, "The Caucus and Democracy in Colonial Boston," *New England Quarterly* 43, no. 1 (March 1970): 21n. (See also Bernard Letters, IV, Sparks Collection, Houghton Library, Harvard University.)

ILLUSTRATION CREDITS

1. J. Carwitham, engraver, *A south east view of the great town of Boston in New England in America*. Library of Congress.
2. Samuel Harris, *Portrait of Elisha Cooke, the Son*. Courtesy of the American Antiquarian Society.
3. *Andros a Prisoner in Boston* as depicted in *Pioneers in the Settlement of America*, vol. 1 (Boston: Samuel Walker & Company, 1876). Wikimedia Commons.
4. Peter Pelham, *Cotton Mather*. Courtesy of the American Antiquarian Society.
5. Joseph F. W. Des Barres, *Boston, as seen between Castle Williams and Governor's Island, distant 4 miles . . .* (Detail). Map image courtesy of the Norman B. Leventhal Map Center at the Boston Public Library.
6. William Burgis, engraver, *The prospect of the colledges in Cambridge in New England*. Library of Congress.
7. John Greenwood, *Samuel Mather*. Courtesy of the American Antiquarian Society.
8. Wellcome Library, London.
9. EC7.B6988.B730e, Houghton Library, Harvard University.
10. EC7.B6988.B730e, Houghton Library, Harvard University.
11. John Bonner, *The Town of Boston in New England* (1723) (Detail). Map image courtesy of the Norman B. Leventhal Map Center at the Boston Public Library.

12. Jean Leon Gerome Ferris, *Capture of the Pirate Blackbeard, 1718*. Wikimedia Commons.

13. Robert Feke, *Benjamin Franklin*. Harvard Art Museums/Fogg Museum, Harvard University Portrait Collection, Bequest of Dr. John Collins Warren, 1856, H47.

14. Michael Dahl, *Joseph Addison*. Library of Congress.

15. Collection of the Massachusetts Historical Society.

16. Nathaniel Emmons, *Samuel Sewall*. Collection of the Massachusetts Historical Society.

17. Newport Historical Society.

18. Edward Truman, *Thomas Hutchinson*. Wikimedia Commons.

19. John Singleton Copley, C. Goodman & R. Piggot, engravers, *Samuel Adams*. Library of Congress.

INDEX

INDEX

Sloan, William, 35
Sloane, Hans, 269, 270
smallpox, 55–57
  causes of, 70, 85, 95
  continental North America epidemic
    (1775), 273–75
  deaths in twentieth century from, 276
  as divine retribution, 140, 200
  inoculation for, *see* inoculation
  in London (1710), 76, 87
  in New York (1947), 276
  ravages of, 89, 193, 275
  shipboard cases of, 5–7, 62–63, 65,
    67–69
  symptoms of, 5, 6, 88–89
  use of term, 55–56
  worldwide eradication of, 276
smallpox epidemic (Boston 1721), ix, 56–57,
    164
  abatement of, 191–94, 200
  cover-up of seriousness, 6–7, 65, 66–69,
    82, 95, 134, 149, 151, 199
  deaths in, 109, 127, 148, 149, 150, 152,
    165, 188–90, 191–94, 200
  economic consequences of, 6, 134,
    149–50, 151, 204
  fears of, 7–8, 71, 82, 90, 248
  inoculation in, *see* inoculation
  medical community's skepticism in, 76,
    82–83, 85, 87, 111, 138
  medical science propelled forward in,
    xiii, 195
  political aspect of, 116–17, 178–79
  previous occurrence of, 7
  spread of, 70, 71, 72, 76, 81, 103, 128,
    131–32, 148–51, 165–66
Smibert, John, 113
Smith, Ann, 263, 265. *See also* Franklin, Ann
    Smith
Society of Physicians Anti-Inoculators,
    138
Sons of Liberty, 21, 295–96, 298
South Sea Bubble, 25, 82, 157–58
Southwick, Solomon, 285
Spectacle Island, pest house, 4–7, 63, 67, 69,
    166, 192–93
Spectator:
  Benjamin Franklin influenced by, 286

  as model for *Courant*, xi, 118, 119, 120,
    121, 135, 155–57, 160, 185, 214, 217
  "Mr. Spectator," 156
  and Spectator Club, 156
  stamp duty on, 156
Speedwell (sloop), 265
Stamp Act (1765), 295, 296
Stearns, Raymond, 268
Steele, Richard, xi, 120, 156, 157
Steward/Stewart, George, 80, 100, 115, 123,
    188–89
Stewart, Frances, 89
Swift, Jonathan, 120, 156
Sydenham, Thomas, 76, 107

Tailer, William, 17, 257
Tatler, 120, 156
Tay, Isaiah, 20, 100
Taylor, Christopher, 25, 220, 225
Tea Act, 297
Teach, Edward (Blackbeard), 32
Tenth Congregational Society, Boston,
    280
Thacher, James, 171
Thacher, Peter, 49, 279
Timoni, Emanuel, on inoculation, 75, 76,
    77, 79, 80, 86, 87, 91, 93, 96, 104
"Tindal, Zerubbabel," 136–37, 155, 157,
    230
"Touchstone, Zechariah," 124
Tourtellot, Arthur Bernon, 138, 182, 186,
    193, 221
Town House meeting (July 21), 100
Townsend, Penn, 257
"Treackle, Ben," 163, 230
Trenchard, John:
  and "Cato's Letters," 158, 159–60, 289
  essays on liberty, xi, 185, 203
  influence of, 120, 185, 203
"Trueman, Eisha," 220
Tryon, Thomas, 214
"Turnstone, Timothy," 137, 230

US Constitution, 186

vaccination, 275–76. *See also* inoculation
Valentine, John, 146
Valentine, Samuel, 146–47

ABOUT THE AUTHOR

STEPHEN COSS lives in Madison, Wisconsin. This is his first book.